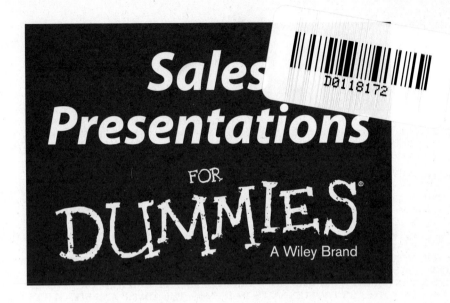

Sales Presentations

FOR DUMMIES
A Wiley Brand

by Julie Hansen

FOR DUMMIES
A Wiley Brand

Sales Presentations For Dummies®

Published by: **John Wiley & Sons, Inc.,** 111 River Street, Hoboken, NJ 07030-5774, www.wiley.com

Copyright © 2015 by John Wiley & Sons, Inc., Hoboken, New Jersey

Published simultaneously in Canada

For general information on our other products and services, please contact our Customer Care Department within the U.S. at 877-762-2974, outside the U.S. at 317-572-3993, or fax 317-572-4002. For technical support, please visit www.wiley.com/techsupport.

Wiley publishes in a variety of print and electronic formats and by print-on-demand. Some material included with standard print versions of this book may not be included in e-books or in print-on-demand. If this book refers to media such as a CD or DVD that is not included in the version you purchased, you may download this material at http://booksupport.wiley.com. For more information about Wiley products, visit www.wiley.com.

Library of Congress Control Number: 2015946683

ISBN: 978-1-119-10402-5

ISBN 978-1-119-10402-5 (pbk); ISBN 978-1-119-10415-5 (ebk); ISBN 978-1-119-10414-7 (ebk);

Manufactured in the United States of America

10 9 8 7 6 5 4 3 2 1

Contents at a Glance

Table of Contents

Introduction

● ●

A sales presentation isn't a motivational speech. You want your prospect to do more than feel good after your presentation. You want him to take action. Building and delivering a persuasive presentation requires a different strategy and approach than other types of presentations. You need more helpful advice than "Make good eye contact and don't read from your slides."

A sales presentation isn't a dull data dump either. Today's buyers are more informed than ever. Engaging today's busy decision makers — and keeping them engaged — is mission critical. Attention spans are low and distractions are high. Buying cycles have increased in length and complexity. Competition is fierce. Cookie-cutter presentations and long corporate overviews have gone the way of the fax machine. Yes, you can still use them, but your audience members will roll their eyes.

I wrote *Sales Presentations For Dummies* after training sales teams all over the world and recognizing that most are operating off beliefs and techniques from the 1970s, '80s, or '90s — well before prospects were able to escape to their smartphones or tablets the second they weren't engaged. With this book I hope to help you rise to the challenges of presenting in today's selling environment. Whether your presentation or demonstration is formal or informal, virtual or live, this book gives you the strategies and tactics you need to win more deals, more consistently.

About This Book

Regardless of industry, location, or company size, salespeople face three common challenges when giving a sale presentation today:

- ✔ How do you keep your prospect engaged long enough to hear your message?

- ✔ How can you differentiate your solution in a crowded marketplace?

- ✔ How do you present your product or service in a way that inspires your prospect to take action or is remembered when buying decisions are made?

In *Sales Presentations For Dummies,* you find the tools, techniques, and best practices for addressing those challenges and more. The techniques here are proven to shorten your sales cycle and have a dramatic impact on your win ratio. I organize this book around the sales presentation process, from planning your presentation to using discovery to closing with a strong, clear call to action, from developing a tailored message to delivering that message with confidence and skill. Along the way I explore a variety of contemporary presentation scenarios: virtual presentations, product demos, team presentations, and more. You also see examples drawn from real-world sales presentations and get step-by-step instruction on how to make your presentation more compelling, persuasive, and memorable.

Within this book, you may note that some web addresses break across two lines of text. If you're reading this book in print and want to visit one of these web pages, simply key in the web address exactly as it's noted in the text, pretending as though the line break doesn't exist. If you're reading this as an e-book, you've got it easy — just click the web address to be taken directly to the web page.

Foolish Assumptions

Just like you must do for a sales presentation, I have to make a few assumptions about you, my audience. You don't need to check all the boxes to qualify — all you need is one and this book is for you. Here are the assumptions that I make about you:

- ✔ You didn't arrive here by accident. You're in sales. Your title may be business development manager or sales engineer, but you have a role in persuading a prospect to purchase or lease a product or service.

- ✔ You give presentations or demonstrations. Formal or informal. Virtual or live. Long or short. No matter the kind, you engage in a purposeful sales conversation with the goal of closing or advancing the sale.

- ✔ You have sales experience but recognize you need new tools to engage and persuade today's busy decision makers in a highly competitive market.

- ✔ You're new to sales and you want to start off with best practices for today — not 1980.

- ✔ You have picked up a few good presentation basics. But because your competition has too, you need to up your game.

- ✔ You're not technically in sales, but you need to make a persuasive case that inspires someone — a manager, a committee, a partner — to take an action or change a behavior. Forget the fact that this is the definition of sales, and let me just say, Welcome. You are also in the right place.

Several of the preceding assumptions, a few, or just one may apply to you. No matter what, this book can help you elevate your sales presentation to start winning more deals right away.

Icons Used in This Book

I use the following icons in the book's margins. Use them as a roadmap for important information.

These are tricks, shortcuts, or best practices that separate you and your presentation from your competition.

These are points you need to become familiar with in order to build and deliver a persuasive case to today's busy prospects.

Watch out! This icon focuses on things that you can do to make your prospect question your credibility or cause you to lose valuable attention.

This icon directs you to free supplemental information at www.dummies.com/extras/salespresentations.com.

Beyond the Book

You can find some free articles online that expand on some of the concepts in the book, like the power of your opening to influence the sale, seven tips for storytelling success, and how to gamify your sales presentation. You can find links to the articles on the parts page and on the Extras page at www.dummies.com/extras/salespresentations.

In addition to the material in the print or e-book you're reading right now, this book also comes with some access-anywhere goodies on the web. Check out the free Cheat Sheet at www.dummies.com/cheatsheet/sales presentations for helpful tools like the performance tool checklist, props checklist, a list of opening hooks to get you started, and how to remember the difference between features, benefits, and value. Print them and keep them handy for when you're working on an opportunity.

Where to Go from Here

Ready to get started? Jump in! The great thing about *For Dummies* books is that you can begin at any point and not feel like you missed a day at school. This book isn't linear — so feel free to focus on a subject that you need some expertise on right away. If you have a new sales presentation opportunity, find out what you need to know to get started in Chapter 1. Tired of competing with your prospect's smartphone for attention? Find effective new ways to keep him engaged in Chapter 14. Need help coming up with a killer opening? Check out Chapter 5. If you have a product demonstration next week, check out Chapter 18. Have a web presentation coming up? Get right to it in Chapter 17. Want to leverage the power of storytelling in your presentation? Find innovative tips in Chapter 12.

This book is chockfull of techniques and ideas. I suggest you try a few at a time and add as you go. Keep this book handy so you can check out new ideas and continue to grow your presentation tool kit.

Part I

Getting Started with Sales Presentations

In this part . . .

- ✔ Understand what an effective presentation is and what you need to do to make sure your presentation is successful.

- ✔ Know all that goes into planning a persuasive presentation that makes a compelling case for your product or service.

- ✔ Identify the challenges of presenting today and turn them into opportunities.

- ✔ Uncover your prospect's business challenge and the impact it's having on his organization.

- ✔ Discover prospect insights and find out how to apply them for a competitive advantage.

- ✔ Build your presentation on a solid value proposition to differentiate your solution and build credibility.

- ✔ Tailor your message to resonate with different decision makers, stakeholders, and influencers.

Chapter 1

Embracing the Future of Sales Presentations

*W*ay back in the 1980s, salespeople didn't have to compete with smartphones and tablets for their prospect's attention. Rarely more than one or two decision makers were involved, and buyers had much less access to information on your product or service. You certainly didn't do virtual presentations or demonstrations. In the second decade of the 21st century, technology continues to change and so do your prospects. Yet when it comes to sales presentations, too many salespeople are still using tools and techniques from the '80s. At least they've dropped the leg warmers.

Today's selling environment requires a whole different approach to your presentation. To give a presentation that persuades today's busy prospects, stands out from your competition, and is remembered when buying decisions are made, you need to start carrying some tools from the present in your presentation kit.

This chapter serves as your jumping-off point into sales presentations of the 21st century. Here you discover the requirements for an effective presentation that resonates with today's decision makers. I introduce a persuasive structure that makes a compelling case for your product or service. You can see why paying attention to your voice, your body, and how you use your surroundings pays off. You also can discover what tools are winning the war for attention. And finally, I explain what adjustments you need to make in special presentations like team selling and web presentations.

Understanding What an Effective Presentation Can Do

An effective presentation in the past typically meant closing the sale. In today's more complex market, a successful presentation can be more like a play in football; it advances the sale. No matter how you spell success, all sales presentations today must meet the following requirements in order to be successful.

Tailoring to meet your prospect's needs

One size doesn't fit all. Today's prospects want to do business with salespeople who have a clear understanding of their needs, their challenges, and their goals. Tailoring your presentation to fit your prospect's unique needs and establishing a customized value proposition is the price of entry in today's competitive market.

It requires discovering how the problem is impacting your prospect's business and how he's currently addressing that problem. Tailoring for today's well-informed prospect often means delivering insights by recognizing areas of improvement or identifying gaps that can shed new light on your prospect's business and tie back to your solution. Tailoring forms the basis of a customer-focused presentation that allows you to show your prospect how you can meet his needs better than your competition. With the commoditization of many products and services, this kind of laser-sharp focus is what will separate you from the competition and turn you into a preferred solution.

Today's presentations must be structured around value, and answer one or both of the following two questions that are in every prospect's mind:

- **Why buy?** Many prospects are hesitant or afraid to change. Selling against the status quo is a much different strategy than the next question.
- **Why buy from you?** Making a case for you over your competition in your presentation requires clear and concise differentiation — not always easy when differences are slight.

In Chapter 2, you discover how to gain insights through a discovery process, and in Chapter 3 you find out how to apply those to tailor your presentation.

Gaining attention

Your prospect invites you to give your hard-fought presentation. You have all the decision makers together in one room at the same time. Quick reality check: Do you have their attention? Don't bet on it. Like you, prospects have other things on their minds. Perhaps they just got off a call with an unhappy customer or they're worrying about how to handle an unresolved issue.

Your first goal is to pull your listeners into the present and break through the mental clutter and physical distractions that plague today's business audiences. Understanding what drives attention and applying that knowledge to your presentation can give you a huge advantage over your competition:

- ✔ **Attention spans fall:** It's not just your imagination. Studies show that people's attention spans are falling faster than the Russian ruble — dropping an incredible 50 percent in the last decade — wait, is that a new LinkedIn request?

- ✔ **Attention bottoms out.** Attention isn't something you get once in a presentation and then you're done. Attention starts off high at the beginning of your presentation and drops to its lowest point in ten minutes, just when you were getting to your good stuff.

- ✔ **Multitasking is a myth.** Finally the truth is out. People can really only focus on one thing at a time. That has loads of implications for your presentation. For example, talking about one thing while an unrelated text-heavy slide is on the screen? Waste of your breath.

Knowing how to make adjustments in your presentation for these changes in behavior is critical. Read how in Chapter 4.

Planning a Killer Presentation

Hordes of data sandwiched between a company overview and an awkward "any questions?" closing neither engages nor persuades today's prospects. Although Ted Talks — short innovative speeches available at www.ted.com — have shed insight into what engages audiences today, you want your prospect to do more than feel good when you're done. You need a persuasive structure that leads to action, which I discuss in the following sections.

Hook them with the opening

Fair or not, during those critical first few seconds during your *opening,* your prospect is evaluating you, making decisions about how and whether they are going to listen to you. In fact, research has found that the majority of jurors decides on the verdict — and sticks with it — during the opening arguments. Although you're not on trial, you need to know what you need to accomplish with your opening:

- ✔ **Capture attention.** Use a relevant opening *hook* — something that makes your prospect put down his smartphone and pay attention, like a story, a quote, or an insight — to get off to a strong start.

✔ **Define the situation.** Quickly comparing how your prospect is dealing with the problem to what your prospect's situation looks like after the problem is resolved gives your prospect a reminder of why you're there and a vision of where you're headed.

✔ **Establish value.** Busy prospects hate to have their time wasted. Giving them a sense of value initially is critical to gain early buy-in.

✔ **Sell the next minute.** Like many movie previews, too many salespeople reveal the whole plot in their opening. Keep interest and attention high by holding something back to keep your prospect tuned.

Seem like a tall order for the top of your presentation? You bet it is. Don't leave your opening to chance. The sale could be riding on it. Find out more about creating a powerful opening in Chapter 5.

Create tension in the body

The *body* of most sales presentations is made up almost entirely of a long list of features that leave your prospect longing for a fire drill. In a persuasive presentation, use the body to build tension by exploring the gap between your prospect's current situation and where they want to be. Here's why:

✔ **Establish priority:** Prospects often have competing priorities. You need to make a case for why yours should take precedence.

✔ **Avoid pain:** Research proves that people are much more willing to take a risk to avoid pain than to embrace an opportunity.

✔ **Fight the status quo:** Getting prospects to move off an "If it ain't *too* broke, don't fix it" mentality requires cranking up the heat well before you get to the closing.

You can read more about ratcheting up the tension in Chapter 6.

Resolve with a solution

Every presentation ends, but very few close. A good *closing* resolves the tension and makes it easy for your prospect to take the next step. Afraid of being repetitive or sensing real or imagined impatience, salespeople often rush to wrap up things and skip or mumble through vague next steps.

As the final impression you make on your prospect, closings must shine as brightly as your opening, provide value, and give a clear and measurable call to action. Chapter 7 gives you more information about closings.

Devoting the Necessary Preparation

Too many great concepts fail to execute because of a lack of preparation. As a salesperson, you have to wear a lot of different hats — that of researcher, strategist, designer, and performer — which can cause you to feel stretched for time. But by applying some of these simple preparation strategies you can streamline your process and improve the impact and outcome of your presentation.

Creating dynamic presentation material

You probably have sat through your share of deadly PowerPoint presentations with their many bullet points, bouncing shapes, and dizzying animations. If slides are your medium of choice, get updated on contemporary design guidelines to keep your presentation from triggering nausea. Following are some key things to remember when planning your presentation material:

- **Start with a concept.** Most salespeople jump to create slides the minute they get the presentation on their calendar. Taking the time to stop and consider what you want to accomplish can save you from showing up with a PowerPoint collage of ideas and styles.

- **Focus on one idea.** The rule of "one slide — one idea" can keep your presentation clean, clear, and on point.

- **Set the tone.** Is it serious or light? Emotional or logical? The tone or feeling you want to create influences everything from your theme, your colors, your choice of pictures, and your fonts.

- **Say it with a picture.** A bold graphic can communicate an idea quicker than a slide full of text.

You can discover more helpful design tips in Chapter 9.

Using your performance tools

Like an actor, you're auditioning for a role in your prospect's business. To win the part, you need to do more than just memorize the lines. Most salespeople spend the vast majority of their time preparing the message and forget about the messenger. The following are your performance tools, and they're a ready resource for enhancing and reinforcing your message:

- **Your voice:** As the delivery vehicle for your message, your voice holds a lot of power, yet few people use it to its full potential. Variety in volume, pacing, pausing, and emphasis can draw attention to key messages and make your content come to life.

> ✔ **Your body:** How you use your body — gestures, movement, eye contact, stance — sends a steady stream of information to your prospect. That information can say "I'm credible and confident and you should listen to me," or "I wish I were anywhere but here!"
>
> ✔ **Your stage:** Your stage is your surroundings. How you move about your stage can renew flagging attention or be a source of distraction.

Refer to Chapter 11 for more about using your voice, body, and staging.

Leveraging the power of stories

Logic is great stuff and presentations are packed with it. But logic doesn't engage your prospect on an emotional level — and most purchases are decided with emotion and justified with logic. Stories are powerful vehicles for triggering emotions, changing opinions, and creating memories.

You may be hesitant to use a story in your presentation because you're concerned your prospect will get impatient. Of course, the real danger is if your story is too long, irrelevant, or trivial. In Chapter 12, you discover how to craft a purposeful story that addresses a specific need in your presentation and connects quickly and easily to your prospect's goals.

Dealing with Potential Problems

Texting during your presentation, prospects entering and exiting the room, technical difficulties, objections — can and will occur — when giving a presentation. How you deal with them determines whether your presentation gets back on track and running smoothly or ends up at the wrong destination.

These sections introduce you to a strategy for regaining your prospect's attention after you lose it and for handling objections when they arise.

Maintaining engagement and focus

Attention isn't constant. Planning to reengage your audience throughout your presentation is a necessity today. Luckily, certain things have the power to draw people's attention. Leveraging this fact by using a variety of these different techniques throughout your presentation can keep your presentation fresh and your audience engaged:

> ✔ **Introduce a prop.** A whiteboard, flipchart, a product sample, even an ordinary object like a phone, or a book, can serve as a visual cue to regain your prospect's attention and reinforce recall.

✔ **Interact with your audience.** Questions aren't the only form of interaction; try taking a poll, running a contest with a cool but inexpensive giveaway, or giving someone in your audience a role in your presentation to regain attention.

✔ **Use movement.** Getting out of the comfort zone behind your laptop is crucial in order to form a connection with your prospect. Look for opportunities to approach your audience, like when you're telling a story, posing a question, or discussing your prospect's challenges. If you're seated, use gestures to underscore your message and focus your prospect's attention.

Check out Chapter 14 for more fresh ideas on keeping your audience engaged.

Handling objections

Although most salespeople would prefer not to get any objections, *objections* are actually a sign of an engaged prospect. What makes it uncomfortable is not having a good process in place for handling an objection. Here are some quick tips for dealing with objections in a way that moves the sale forward:

✔ **Preempt an objection.** The best defense is a good offense! Brainstorm possible objections and come up with a response for each type — price, timing, features — and diffuse the objection by including it in your presentation before your prospect has a chance to bring it up.

✔ **Break up the objection.** Objections can trigger your fight-or-flight instinct, negatively affecting how you respond. Before you jump to answer the objection, take a deep breath, break it down by listening, pausing, and then clarifying to make sure you're answering the real objection.

✔ **Say "yes and . . . ."** This rule of improv is effective and easy for handling the toughest of objections. Simply acknowledge your prospect's objection (say yes), add your perspective (with "and"), and ask an open-ended question to collaborate on a solution with your prospect.

Head to Chapter 15 for more suggestions on how to prepare for objections and handle them during your presentation.

Preparing for Special Presentations

Although persuasive presentations share many common characteristics, certain types of sales presentations — team, virtual, demonstrations, and so forth — offer unique challenges. These sections give you a quick overview.

Presenting as a team

If you're involved in a strategic sale — high stakes, multiple steps — more than likely you're a member of a sales team. Your success rides on your team's ability to present a united front and a cohesive message. With unfamiliar team members often stretched for time, team presentations can start to resemble Frankenstein's monster: a mish mash of styles, an unsteady delivery, and unpredictable results. To make sure that everyone on your team is singing from the same songbook, remember these points:

- **Assign clear roles.** Having one person as the point person who collects all presentation materials and another who handles all the logistics can keep information from getting lost or balls from being dropped. Having a go-to person to handle certain types of questions can avoid missteps during your presentation.

- **Use good rehearsal practices.** Forget the dry run; team presentations require a full rehearsal — including those transitions and hand-offs where many teams lose valuable points.

- **Reading cues:** A *cue* is a predetermined body or eye movement, or sound that sends a signal to your teammate. Planning a few clear, memorized cues to use during your presentation can resolve much of the confusion and have you operating as a true ensemble.

See tips on how to present as a team in Chapter 16.

Delivering a web presentation

Fitting your content and your style to your medium is critical, as is improving your connection with your audience. Web presentations are typically live presentations crammed onto a small screen with understandably disappointing results. Remove the cloak of invisibility and increase the engagement in a web presentation through the following techniques:

- **Leverage the power of your voice.** Without your physical presence your voice plays even greater importance in getting your message across and engaging your audience.

- **Incorporate polls and other web tools.** Using your web tools can help break up some of the monotony of endless slides or screens.

- **Use a webcam.** Increase your visibility in a web presentation by using a webcam. People respond much more positively to faces than a disembodied voice. Because many salespeople still prefer to go unseen, you'll also have the advantage of standing out in your prospect's mind.

You can find out how to make your web presentation more engaging, interactive, and successful in Chapter 17.

Chapter 2

Discovering What You Need to Know Before You Begin

In This Chapter

▶ Figuring out the opportunity

▶ Developing a persuasive presentation

▶ Understanding where to find the information you need

▶ Having conversations that produce insights and build rapport

▶ Tracking your progress with a presentation plan checklist

*Y*ou have an opportunity to present your product or service to a qualified prospect, which is no easy feat in today's competitive landscape. After you finish high-fiving yourself, your team, or your dog, what's your first order of business?

✔ Pulling out the standard deck and you're ready to go.

✔ Diving in to PowerPoint to start cutting and pasting from previous presentations.

✔ Creating a presentation plan to gather all the information you need.

Whether you have 10 minutes to prepare or 10 days, the third option is the winning choice. In a competitive market, planning plays a more critical role than ever in the success of your presentation. Planning means gathering as much relevant information as possible about your prospect prior to your presentation so you can tailor your message to her specific needs in a way that motivates her to take action. Failing to gather the insights you need or ask the right questions with today's savvy buyers can damage your credibility and leave room for your competition to slip by and win the business. Because planning takes time, isn't fun or sexy, it's tempting to skip this step and jump right into picking out graphics and themes or loading up the standard deck — even though neither option may be a good fit for the current opportunity.

Planning a presentation is like building a house. You want to first make sure you have a design and a solid foundation that will produce the results you want. All of the cool videos and flashy graphics in the world can't make up for faulty structure or inconsistent messaging. Without a plan, you may find yourself dodging the following landmines when you're in front of your prospect:

- ✔ Disagreeing on value or goals
- ✔ Focusing on the wrong issue with the wrong person
- ✔ Being surprised by preferences or allegiances
- ✔ Fumbling through unanticipated objections
- ✔ Failing to make a logical and persuasive case

In this chapter, I show you how to create a solid foundation for your presentation. I help you determine what you must know before your presentation to successfully align your solution with your prospect's goals, establish value, and overcome potential objections. I help you uncover the prospect's challenge and define and quantify the impact on her and her organization. In addition, you discover how to prepare for a presentation that involves multiple decision makers by setting up and conducting discovery conversations and asking questions that produce valuable insights. You also find out how to keep everything on track — your team, your materials, and your technology — by creating a presentation planning checklist.

Evaluating the Presentation Opportunity

As a salesperson, you may have a knee jerk reaction to say yes to any opportunity to present your product or service to a potential customer. With the amount of time and energy that go into pursuing many business opportunities today, you need to make sure that the prospect is qualified and the opportunity is viable before you start to commit limited resources. Being a top sales performer requires being smart about where you spend your time and energy as well as having a clearly defined outcome.

Qualifying the prospect

A *prospect* is someone who has expressed an interest in your product or service and seems like a good fit for your business. Whether you've had an initial conversation or meeting with your prospect or just been handed a lead, before you begin planning, make sure that you have thoroughly qualified your prospect. That means your prospect should meet the following criteria:

1. **The prospect has a need or desire for the solution that you provide.**

2. **The prospect has the authority to influence or make the purchase.**

3. **The prospect (or the prospect's organization) is financially capable of making the purchase.**

4. **The prospect is likely to take action within a definite time period to resolve their problem.**

Qualifying the opportunity

Even if your prospect is qualified, you want to determine if the *opportunity* is worth all the time and effort you're going to put into it. It's always better to find out before you've spent two weeks preparing that your product or service isn't well-aligned with your prospect's needs. Here are two guideposts for determining if the opportunity is a viable one for you and your company.

✔ **You have a favorable chance.** Being the odds-on favorite from the start isn't always realistic, but it's best if the odds are at least even. Not every deal is in your wheelhouse. If your product or service isn't an ideal match, you can't compete on price, or if you don't offer deal-breaking features, you must decide whether to invest the time and energy into pursuing a long shot. Reserving your resources for those opportunities where your chances of winning are more favorable is better in many cases.

✔ **The outcome is worth it.** If you're going to invest a significant amount of time and resources in pursuing an opportunity — true in many complex sales — you need to know with some certainty that the payoff is worth the effort. Before you commit, factor in what it takes to win the deal and maintain the business as well as less measurable considerations, such as whether the partnership will be good, whether it can lead to additional business opportunities, or whether it will simply be more work that keeps you from pursuing more profitable business.

If you're unsure of your prospect's qualifications or the value of the opportunity, stop and get more clarity before moving on. Although there are exceptions, for example, you may have identified a problem or need but the prospect isn't fully convinced it's a problem yet, or the ultimate decision makers aren't involved at this stage, but your audience will have their ear, you may decide to move ahead with the presentation. But a little up-front effort can save you from wasting a lot of time and energy that you could put toward a more qualified prospect or viable opportunity.

Defining your actionable goal

Every presentation needs a clearly defined outcome. When defining that goal, the outcome must be measurable and specific. Otherwise, how will you know if you've achieved it? Actionable and measurable goals give your presentation focus, direction, and a clear call to action.

For example, a goal of "letting a prospect know what we offer" is neither measurable nor specific. In fact, it's not so much a sales presentation as it is public service announcement because no selling is actually taking place. A clearly defined goal would be, "to convince the prospect to recommend our solution to the financial decision makers within two weeks."

The ultimate call to action, of course, is to close the deal, but today's complex buying environment likely has some interim steps along the way to reaching the brass ring. For example, if you're a contractor, it may be to put together a fee proposal. If you're selling software as a solution (SAAS), you may need to secure a presentation to key stakeholders — people who also have an interest in the outcome or can influence the sale. In other cases, the action may be to schedule a deeper dive into a specific topic or secure a commitment to a product or service trial. The goal is to move the sale forward to the next logical action in the buying cycle. Use the following steps to help you determine your actionable goal:

1. **Determine what the next step is in the sales process after your presentation.**

   For example, scheduling a product demonstration.

2. **Identify the action your prospect needs to take at the end of your presentation.**

   For example, setting a date and inviting attendees to the demonstration.

3. **Create your call to action around this actionable goal.**

   For example, "For next steps we recommend setting up a demonstration to key parties within the next three weeks. Bill, if you agree, can you come up with a list of names of people who you think would benefit from attending?" Check out Chapter 7 for tips on how to build a strong call to action.

Determining the Nine Things You Need to Know

The success of your presentation is dependent on the quality of your information. Without relevant, insightful information, you can't make a persuasive case and build value for your prospect. You'll open yourself up to competition, negotiations on price, and longer buying cycles. If you're selling to the C-suite — an executive with the letter C in his title, for example CEO, CFO, or CTO — you won't win their attention or respect. That should make you want to spend more than a little time making sure you have the information you need.

In a world of information overload, more isn't always better. If you gather enough material to write a book on your prospect's problem but haven't uncovered what other options she's considering or the impact of the problem on her organization, you've wasted much of your time. Whether you have a month to prepare or you have to do a presentation on short notice — you're responding to a web lead or referral, or simply a prospect who has an urgent need that can't wait — you need the same type of information to create a new presentation or adapt a current one to fit your prospect's needs. In the following sections I introduce nine key areas of information that you need to tailor your presentation to your prospect and provide an example of how to apply them on short notice.

Identifying the challenge or opportunity

You may have a good idea of what your prospect's business challenge is but it's important not to make any assumptions at this early stage. Often times what the prospect thinks is her problem is really part of a larger problem. Be as specific as you can when defining the problem or opportunity. For example, "They're evaluating options to replace their current telecom system because their current system is unable to handle the volume and their contract is up for renewal" is a clearly defined scenario that can guide you as you start to build your presentation. "They're interested in hearing about our system," is vague and can lead to a generic overview presentation unlikely to resonate with your prospect.

Uncovering the trigger event

People don't typically wake up and say "Today I'm going to solve this problem." Usually some trigger event or catalyst has brought the problem to their attention and motivated them to address it. Knowing what that event is can help you evaluate and gauge the prospect's real desire to solve the problem. For example, "With the recent outbreak of security breaches in some well-known companies, they're concerned that their customer-sensitive data isn't as safe as it could be" indicates a real interest in a timely resolution of the problem and provides specific context to frame your message.

Recognizing the status quo

Unless the problem has just occurred or completely shut down your prospect's business, it's likely your prospect has developed some work-around solution. You need to find out how your prospect is currently dealing with the problem. Is your prospect whistling in the dark hoping the problem will go away? Or is she using a bandage when a tourniquet is clearly needed? Discovering how your prospect is coping with the problem can help you define the status quo, which may turn out to be your biggest competitor.

Defining the impact

Recognizing *impact* is key among today's decision makers. Knowing how the problem currently is affecting your prospect and her organization, and the potential impact of your solution can help you to develop important metrics around cost and value. Not having this information places you in a weak position against a competitor who has done their homework in this area. Here are two types of impact questions you want to be sure and explore with your prospect:

- ✔ **What's the impact of the problem?** How much does it hurt and can your prospect quantify the pain? In other words, is your prospect just a little bruised or is she spending a thousand dollars a week on physical therapy? Understanding the answer to this question can help you establish value in relation to cost and assess your prospect's motivation to change.

- ✔ **What's the impact of the solution?** Knowing the results of solving the problem or taking the opportunity can help you develop a sound *value proposition* — a clear statement of the results that your prospect can expect to receive from your product or service — for your prospect. Just like quantifying the impact of the problem, quantifying the value of the solution is just as important, especially if you're presenting to an executive. The prospect may be able to provide you with this information, for example, "Solving this problem would eliminate two redundant jobs" or "Gaining this advantage would increase our margin by two cents per unit." If you don't get the information from your prospect, look for similar clients, case studies, or industry statistics to give you direction and make your best educated guess. Find out more about value in Chapter 3.

Agreeing on clear goals

How does your prospect spell success? The goal may be obvious, for example, "to replace our equipment with a newer model as soon as possible," however many companies use some type of key performance indicator (KPI) to track and assess their business processes. It may be year-over-year growth in sales, return on investment (ROI), customer satisfaction, or retention rates. Whatever it is, define that measurement so that you can address performance in terms in which your audience can relate.

Identifying key players

Although smaller sales may involve only a single decision maker, most larger sales today involve multiple decision makers as well as key influencers and stakeholders — people who have an interest and/or influence in the product or service being purchased. Knowing who all these players are and what their role is in the decision-making process is important because you need to address each of their unique needs and interests to make sure your deal doesn't get stalled somewhere along the way. Most of the individuals involved in your presentation fall into one of the following three categories:

- ✔ **Problem owner:** These are the people affected by the problem and typically the ones who will be using your product or service or be directly impacted by it. For example, if you're selling medical equipment, it may be a nurse or medical specialist. If you're selling a CRM solution, it may be a salesperson. Although problem owners may not be directly responsible for making the decision or even be at the presentation, don't underestimate these key individuals' potential to make or break a sale. No organization wants to invest in a product or service that is a hard sell internally.

- ✔ **Problem solver:** This is the person who is seeking a solution to the problem and may be your point of contact at the organization. This individual may be the same as the problem owner, or she may be a manager, a consultant, or a buying committee who has been tasked with evaluating and vetting vendors. Like the manager of a sales team who needs a CRM system, the problem solver may be directly impacted

> by the problem; however, even if she isn't, she has a vested interest in the solution and your ability to do what you say you can do because her reputation is at stake.

> ✔ **Decision maker:** This is the person who is ultimately going to write the check to solve the problem. For larger purchases, this is typically a person from the C-suite whose interests are broad and usually take into account how the decision will affect the organization as a whole as well as how it fits in with other corporate objectives. The decision maker may not be at your presentation, but it's important to address her needs and expectations, especially providing financial validation and alignment of your solution to company goals to avoid your sale making it all the way up the ladder only to get vetoed at the top.

Getting a read on urgency

Having a prospect excited about moving forward only to be unable to meet her deadline is disappointing. Clarifying your prospect's expectations and timelines up-front can save you a lot of frustration later. Finding out about any time issues, deadlines, or objectives also gives you a good handle on your prospect's level of urgency. If she tells you there is no real timeline, take note. You may want to re-evaluate the opportunity, dig deeper into the impact of the current problem, or find out what would have to happen to make it a greater priority.

Understanding your competition

Even if you think you know what other vendors your prospect is talking to, asking the following questions is a smart practice because your prospect's answers may surprise you and affect your messaging dramatically.

> ✔ **What/who else is the prospect considering to solve the problem?** Knowing what or who your competition is going into your presentation is necessary to help you address key differentiators and competitive advantages; however, don't stop there.

> ✔ **Why is the prospect considering them?** Don't assume you know the answers. Let the prospect tell you in her own words. After all, you aren't competing against your competition as much as you are against your prospect's perception of your competition. Identifying current or prior allegiances or loyalties now can save you a load of heartache down the road. Refer to the later section on "Analyzing your competition" for more information.

✔ **What is their buying history?** Past behavior is the best indication of future behavior, so discovering how your prospect has made similar purchases in the past and what her experience was with them is certainly valuable. Were there any noncommitment or payment issues? Take these factors into consideration as you evaluate the opportunity and if you win the deal.

Gaining an edge with logistics

Who, what, where, and when are basic questions that every vendor will ask, but some finer points you can use to your advantage include the following:

✔ **Who can you contact?** Like most vendors, you want to find out who will be attending the presentation and what role each individual plays in the organization. Take it a step further and ask for each person's contact information as well. Your real competitive advantage will come from reaching out to additional influencers and problem owners within the prospect's organization prior to the presentation to gain insight and build rapport. Check out the section Speaking to decision makers and key influencers" later in this chapter.

✔ **What is the format?** Is this a high-level overview or a deep dive? Does your prospect expect you to follow a script or a particular agenda? How much time do you have? Although often the time is allotted to you as something like "90 minutes next Tuesday," you may be surprised to find that you can get additional time if you ask for it. Take a more assertive role in the planning stage and ask first what your prospect's expectations are and develop an agenda around it so you can recommend the time needed to address all concerns.

✔ **Where and when will it take place?** In addition to the basic information on location and timing that every vendor will receive, find out ahead of time how the room is laid out, if you can get in early to set up, and if other companies are presenting, what the order is.

If you're one of several presenting companies, always ask to go first. That way you get to set the bar, and the prospect will compare everyone else to you.

Applying the information on short notice

If you have to do a presentation without much time to plan — you're responding to a web lead or referral, or simply a prospect who has an urgent need that can't wait — you can still use this chapter's information to quickly get what you need to adapt your presentation on the fly. For example, assume that you're a real estate agent and you receive a phone call from a homeowner who wants to list her house. She is interviewing two agents that evening and only has a few moments to talk on the phone. Here's what you would quickly find out in your conversation using the preceding eight points:

Challenge/opportunity: The homeowner and her husband want to sell their condo.

Trigger event: The husband works at home and now the wife's office is closing so she'll be working at home as well.

Status quo: They live in a two-bedroom condo, with one room designated the husband's office. It's been recently updated and has great views of the city.

Impact: If they don't sell, the wife will be working out of the living room, they'll be cramped, and frustrations will grow.

Goals: She would like to get $400,000 for the condo. She recognizes this is above-market price, but they've added $50,000 in upgrades.

Decision makers: The wife is the problem owner, problem solver, and co-decision maker with her husband.

Urgency: Her office is shutting down in two months so she would like to be in new place by then so she can set up her office.

Competition: She is also meeting with her co-worker's cousin who just got his real estate license.

Logistics: Presentation scheduled for 7 p.m. today. You received the address and information necessary to research the property online and prepare a competitive market analysis. The homeowner also agreed to allow you to present first and come 30 minutes early to tour the property.

Now you have enough to adapt your listing presentation to meet your prospect's needs and gain a competitive advantage. Based on what you uncovered, you know to focus your presentation on the benefits of going with an agent who has a proven track record and the pain of delay that improper pricing and marketing can result in.

Getting the Information You Need

Gathering information is similar to the way you process leads in your sales funnel. Just like every lead doesn't result in a client, every piece of information you uncover doesn't necessarily end up in your presentation. Figure 2-1 shows you how a presentation funnel works. You fill your funnel with the information you gather in this section. After you have the information, you use it to develop your value proposition, which you can read about in Chapter 3, and help you build a persuasive case, as I cover in Chapter 4.

Fortunately, information is easier to come by than ever before. That also means your competitors can easily access it as well so dig a little deeper to stay in the lead. Here are some places to search and what to look for:

Searching the prospect's website

All sorts of information about your prospect and her organization is available to you on a company's website. The company history, key executives, products or services, and marketing messaging are some of the things you want to check out, but also look for the following:

- ✔ **Company goals and strategic initiatives:** Most companies have a vision or a corporate objective that it has set for the coming year. For example, "We want to increase market share by 10 percent this year."

- ✔ **Community involvement:** Look for pet projects or sponsorships. Perhaps the company sponsors a local sports team or runs an annual food drive for the homeless.

- ✔ **White papers or case studies**. Often organizations produce publications that address issues within their industry or show how they have helped solve problems for their customers. These can provide valuable insight into topical issues and industry trends.

Figure 2-1: A presentation funnel: how the information you gather helps you construct your presentation.

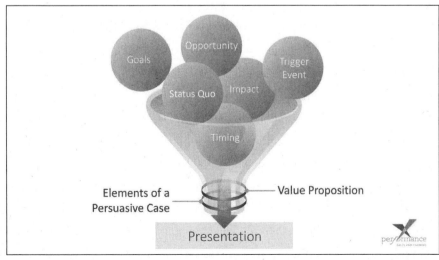

Illustration by 24Slides

Relying on other sources

A company's website isn't a full picture of your prospect. Finding out what others are saying about your prospect is equally important. Here are some places to look:

- **Reports by industry analysts:** Identify the trends or developments in your prospect's industry that affect how she views the problem. Most industries have recognized thought-leaders that provide research and whitepapers, for example, `Gartner.com` and `Techrepublic.com` for technology, and `Jdpower.com` for many other products and brands.

- **Business data sites.** Several companies provide competitive information and statistics. `Hoovers.com` and `Data.com` provide you access and reports for a fee, while `Owler.com` is a free crowd-sourced company sharing site for competitive information.

- **Google advanced search.** If you master a few tricks on Google, you can find all data published on other sites about your prospect's organization. For example:

  - **Allintext:** By entering "allintext: company name," you get a list of sites where your company is mentioned.

  - **Phrase search:** Enclosing the exact keywords you want to search in quotation marks results in only sites that have that specific information, for example, "ABC Organization U.S."

  - **Time and date search:** If you're looking for information from a specific time period, enter "daterange: company 2014-2015" to see results confined to that time period.

- **Social media:** A wealth of information on your prospects is available through sites like LinkedIn, Twitter, and Facebook. This information is helpful in getting to know the people you'll be presenting to. Furthermore, you can also use it to listen to what other customers, employees, competitors, or vendors who have experience working with your prospect are saying about the company through several free social monitoring sites, including:

  - **SocialMention:** Simply plug in the name of your prospect and `Socialmention.com` searches 100+ social media properties for mentions of the company.

  - **Hootsuite:** Monitor in real time what people are saying about your prospect on social networks, like Twitter, LinkedIn, Facebook, Google+, and Wordpress with `Hootsuite.com`.

Speaking to decision makers and key influencers

In a more complex B2B (business-to-business) sale, the stakes and the competition are high, and a consensus usually is required to make a decision. In this case a more thorough discovery process involving speaking to key individuals within the prospect's organization is necessary to help you develop a focused, tight case and differentiate yourself from your competitors.

The best source of information about a company is the one that is often skipped by most salespeople: the company's own employees, particularly problem owners, stakeholders, and other key influencers. Nothing sets you up for success more than having a conversation with these key people within your prospect's organization. These conversations should take place early in the planning process so that you can get on these individual's calendars and incorporate any valuable findings into your presentation. The following sections walk you through how to set up and conduct a discovery conversation.

Asking for a discovery conversation

A *discovery conversation* is a one-on-one meeting or phone call with someone in your prospect's organization who can provide insight or shed light on the challenge you're addressing in your presentation. Don't be shy about asking for input. It's a fair and reasonable request that benefits not only you, but also the prospect. Gaining a better understanding of your prospect's needs shortens your presentation and allows you to provide a more accurate and precise recommendation. The following steps help you secure a meeting with key individuals within your prospect's organization:

1. **Ask your primary contact for three or four names of key people to speak with.**

   These names may be people who will be attending the presentation, key influencers, or those who work behind the scenes and who are able to provide insight on the problem or challenge.

2. **Send a short, to-the-point email requesting a call or meeting with each individual.**

   Use one or two sentences to describe why you want to speak and how much time you're requesting, (for example 20 to 30 minutes.) See Figure 2-2 for an example. You can use the same template for each person, but be sure to personalize the names and contact information for greater response.

Figure 2-2:
An example email request for a discovery conversation.

3. **Offer two or three different options of times to speak.**

4. **Use a subject line that identifies your contact to increase your acceptance rate.**

5. **Follow up with a meeting invite to secure the time on the person's calendar.**

If prospects are hesitant to speak with you, they typically don't see the value. A quick statement like the following can make it easy for them to see the benefit in speaking with you: "I understand you're busy, which is why I don't want to waste any of your time (or your manager's time) during the presentation. Your input now will help me make sure I can get right to the point during the presentation and be sure to address your top concerns. Does that make sense?"

Conducting a discovery conversation

The key to a great discovery meeting is knowing what you want to find out and leaving room for your prospect to surprise you. For example, you may uncover additional challenges, competitive insights, or strategic goals that help you more closely align with your prospect's needs. Following are some key findings you want to look for when speaking with someone in your prospect's company:

✓ **Get everyone's point of view.** Don't assume that everyone within your prospect's organization has the same understanding of the problem or agree on the solution. Ask each person her perspective on the problem and expectations of a solution. You want as full a picture as possible. If the answers are conflicting, circle back with your primary contact and ask for help to ensure that you understand the issues so that you can properly address the best interests of the company.

✔ **Understand the decision-making process.** Figure out how the prospect makes decisions. Does the organization have a formal process? Do all decision makers have equal say or does one person's opinion have more weight? The more you know about the decision-making process, the more you can tailor your message. For example, if the CEO is the sole decision maker, you know to structure your presentation more around how your solution impacts the organization as a whole and less around the details of the process. See Chapter 3 for tailoring your message to decision makers.

✔ **Define the personal impact.** In addition to discovering how the current problem affects the organization, determine how it affects each prospect individually. The closer to home you can bring the problem and solution, the more powerful and memorable your presentation.

Comprehending additional benefits of discovery

In a competitive market more than likely you won't be the only one asking your prospect questions prior to the presentation. In fact, your competitor may be asking many of the same or very similar questions and use the answers to help build a case for its product or service. If you're the third or fourth vendor doing the questioning, your prospect's answers can sound quite perfunctory. Set yourself apart by recognizing the following underutilized benefits of the discovery conversation:

✔ **Revealing insights.** Each question is an opportunity to gain insight around a prospect's experience, expectations, and preferences. Don't just settle for a pat answer. Take a four-year-old's approach and ask why. Why do you do things that way? Why are you considering that option? Ask your prospect if there's anything you may have missed. You're looking for anything that can give you an insider's view, which may include information on how bad the problem is, what's at stake, and why the prospect needs to make a change. The answers you receive can help you to tailor your presentation to fit your prospect's needs and expectations. Read more about applying insights in Chapter 3.

✔ **Speaking your prospect's language.** Every company has its own buzzwords and acronyms. Instead of expecting the prospect to learn your language, make the effort to learn the prospect's and incorporate some of the terminology into your presentation to build your credibility. For example, does your prospect call its salespeople "account executives" or "business consultants"? Does it refer to "customers" or "clients"? You may want to ask pointed questions about how your prospect refers to specific things or just take note of her word choice when she speaks.

✔ **Planting seeds.** The discovery conversation isn't the time for a full-court sales press, but you do want the prospect to get off the phone with a sense of excitement and anticipation about your presentation if she's attending, or a motivation to pass on her support if she's not. Statements like, "It sounds like you could really use the extra time to focus on your new responsibilities if this were resolved quickly" can set expectations early. Aim for subtlety and be careful not to slip into a full-on selling mode.

✔ **Building rapport and interest.** Asking questions isn't just about getting answers. You have a prospect on the phone or in person, so use this valuable time to strengthen your relationship and create some early interest going into your presentation. Here are some effective ways to do so:

- **Really listen.** The discovery conversation is the time to listen. End users in particular may have never been asked their opinion before and therefore may be more than happy to share given the chance, so keep your pencil sharp and listen. This time isn't just about checking off a box. Don't make assumptions or finish your prospect's sentences. You'll have plenty of time to speak during your presentation.

- **Repeat back.** Make sure that you're clear on your prospect's meaning, especially on important points, by repeating back to her what you heard her say. If you don't understand something, ask questions until you do.

- **Respond with empathy.** Your conversation isn't a therapy session, but it also isn't a deposition. You're talking to real people about real problems. Taking a moment to express appropriate emotion can go a long way toward establishing rapport. For example, "Wow, that sounds really frustrating" or "I imagine that must create a lot of pressure for your department," will make your prospect feel validated and may get them to open up more.

Defusing potential objections

Not preparing for *objections* — reasons your prospect would have to not move forward with the sale — is like waterskiing without a life vest. You may glide along just fine for a while, but when you hit the water, you're going to be glad you planned ahead. Although most salespeople prepare to address objections in their presentation, you can begin to neutralize many of them early in the planning stage before positions have hardened by doing a thorough job of discovery with your prospect. Following are some common objections that may come up in your initial prospect calls or discovery conversations and how to nip them in the bud or lessen their impact during your presentation. Check out Chapter 15 for more tips on handling objections.

✔ **It's not that bad/we're in no hurry/other decisions are more pressing.** These objections all fall into the "lack of urgency" category. You can usually handle them early on by getting the prospect to acknowledge or share the full financial impact of not solving the problem. If the prospect still brings up her objections in the presentation, you'll be able to remind your prospect of the cost of delay.

✔ **It's too expensive.** When price is an issue, the prospect doesn't perceive enough value in your solution. Reaching agreement early on about the impact of resolving the problem or embracing the opportunity allows you to compare that cost objection to the value you're providing. If this objection still comes up in the presentation, reflect the agreement on the financial impact back to your prospect and ask him if anything has changed since you last spoke.

✔ **We prefer a competitor.** Consider this objection a gift if it comes up early in the planning stages of your presentation. Armed with a competitive analysis (see the next section), you can emphasize those attributes that differentiate you from your competitor throughout your presentation. Focusing on competitive strengths without necessarily mentioning your competition early on can diffuse this objection as can opening designed to address the objection.

Analyzing your competition

Some salespeople have a tendency to skip over this step. After all, you run up against the same cast of characters all the time. However, two important reasons not to underestimate your competition are

✔ **Familiarity breeds assumptions.** With so many new things to contend with each day, people often overlook that which they already know. That tendency to undervalue a competitor, "Oh, they're not a big threat," or operate off of old data "They've never been competitive in this niche" can lead to unpleasant surprises. Shifts in strategy, new product launches, or marketing campaigns can impact your prospect's perspective. Check your competitor's website and industry reports to get the most current messaging. Social media is a valuable resource for finding out what customers are saying about working with your competition. Approach each competitor with a fresh eye to maintain a competitive edge.

✔ **Bias blinds you.** Being critical of your competition is easy, but if you look at your competitors objectively, you can notice that they probably do some things well. In fact, they may even be able to solve your prospect's problem — maybe not as quickly, smoothly, or thoroughly as you — but they can probably do it. It's to your advantage to be as objective as possible about your competition in order to outsell them.

Rounding up the usual suspects: Who is your competition?

You probably already have a clear idea of who your direct competition is for this opportunity, but depending upon the scope of the problem, some additional players may have entered the field. Make sure that you prepare for each of them.

✔ **Direct competition:** *Direct competitors* are the companies you probably compete with on a regular basis. You typically share an industry, product, service, market, and/or niche.

✔ **Potential competition:** Although not direct competitors, these companies may overlap with you in a specific area, or they may be a less obvious choice. For example, if you're selling insurance, you'll certainly compete with other insurance carriers, but in certain cases you may also find yourself up against firms that outsource HR services as well.

✔ **Invisible competition:** Many salespeople often overlook this category and major player. Your invisible competition is all the other priorities that are competing for the time, attention, and budget of your prospect. For example, your prospect may be considering a big capital investment in equipment, opening a new office, or sponsoring a community project. Getting a clear picture of who or what is competing for the same piece of the pie gives you greater insight into the decision-making process and helps you position your product or service.

✔ **The status quo:** This may be your toughest competitor. Regardless of the business challenge that you're addressing, the status quo is almost always a major contender for two primary reasons:

- Many products that require a sizable investment, such as infrastructure, construction projects, or enterprise software, often lead to additional investments in other areas like training, staffing, or upgrading other systems. Change at this level can be overwhelming and lead to procrastination.

- The status quo is the path of least resistance. People get comfortable with the tried and true, no matter how flawed. In this case, the pain of *not* changing has to be greater than the pain of changing. Always treat the status quo as a favored competitor to avoid being blindsided.

Doing a competitive analysis

Knowing how you stack up against your competition is important as you start to develop your presentation. Getting an accurate handle on your competitors' strengths and weaknesses helps you position your product or service accordingly and highlight key differentiators. Here are some areas in which you'll want to look:

- **Product:** What are their primary capabilities and how do you rank against each? Are they a specialist in your prospect's niche or industry or do they lack experience in this area? How does that compare to you?

- **Service:** How do their service models, prices, and response times compare to yours?

- **Pricing:** How do you compare in terms of base price, add-ons, upgrades, and so forth?

- **Delivery:** Are they fast, reliable, and on time? Are their prices for these services clearly disclosed and competitive?

- **Resale:** How does their product hold its value?

- **Support:** What type of support staff do they have when problems arise? How does it compare to your support?

- **Marketing messages or themes:** What marketing promises are they making or expectations are they reinforcing in the market?

- **Unique selling proposition (USP):** What is their USP and how is it different from yours?

- **Company outlook:** Are they poised for growth or taking a loss? Consider mergers, acquisitions, and hiring activity.

- **Customer experience:** What are their customers saying about them in social media? Are they able to deliver on all promises?

Putting together a competitive analysis chart like the one in Figure 2-3 can help you quickly see where your strengths and weaknesses are in relation to your competition and help you focus your efforts.

Identify one or two competitors and write their name at the top of a column. Begin by ranking your product or service from 1–5 against the competitive factors on the left. Then, do the same for your competition. When you've completed the chart, note which company has the advantage in each area. Play up those areas where you have a distinct competitive advantage in your presentation and find ways to shore up or have a ready response for those areas where you aren't as strong.

Competitive factor	Your product	Competitor 1	Competitor 2	Advantage
Key marketing message				
USP				
Company outlook				
Customer experience				
Feature 1				
Feature 2				
Feature 3				
Feature 4				
Service				
Price				
Support				
Delivery				
Resale				
Other				

Figure 2-3:
An example
of a com-
petitive
analysis
chart.

Illustration by John Wiley & Sons, Inc.

Creating a Presentation Plan Checklist

As you prepare for your presentation, there are a lot of moving parts to keep track of, including logistics, research, audience members, message development, visual aids, rehearsal, technology, and so forth. Dropping the ball in one area can have major repercussions in others.

This type of checklist helps you keep track as you prepare your presentation. You can download a copy at www.dummies.com/cheatsheet/salespresentations. You also can download a copy of the checklist at www.performancesalesandtraining.com.

Use this checklist to uncover vital information as you begin planning your presentation. Check off each point as you get the data or perform the task and keep it up-to-date so that you don't miss anything.

Chapter 3

Tailoring Your Value Proposition to Fit Your Audience

....

In This Chapter

▶ Comprehending why value is critical

▶ Creating a strong value proposition

▶ Tailoring your message based on the decision-maker's role

▶ Weaving value throughout your presentation

....

*I*n an age where you can customize anything over the Internet or order any one of 87,000 varieties of drinks at your local coffee shop, to deliver your presentation in only one flavor is a recipe for disaster. Today's decision makers want to do business with salespeople who exhibit a clear under-standing of their issues, not a one-size-fits-all solution. Delivering a message focused on what is important to the prospect, as opposed to what you have to sell, allows you to create value and rise above the competitive noise to become a preferred vendor.

Value serves as the organizational principle around which your presentation is constructed. It helps you determine what out of the entire pool of informa-tion you've collected to keep and what you can leave on the editing room floor. Although simply throwing as many features and benefits into your pre-sentation as possible and hoping that some — or any — hit home is tempt-ing, this type of data dump presentation is a waste of time for both you and your prospect. After a prospect feels you aren't addressing his unique needs or challenges, you have few options to keep him engaged — 87,000 features notwithstanding.

This chapter helps you understand the often-confused differences between features, benefits, and value. You discover how to create a compelling value proposition and tailor it to address the varied needs and objectives of the decision makers and key influencers in your audience. I include several examples of value propositions and help you find out where to highlight value within your presentation to drive home your message.

Understanding Why Value Is King

Of course you didn't set out to sell a commodity, but if your prospects don't see a significant difference between you and your competitors other than price, you may as well be selling sugar, wheat, or pork bellies. Many salespeople put together beautiful, interesting presentations only to end up competing on price because they failed to establish value.

The competitive environment for most products has increased dramatically. Name a feature and your competitor either has it or soon will have it. Like designer handbags, a perpetual flow of look-alikes is poised to go after your customers. Even though these competitors may not offer the same quality, benefits, or service as you, you must acknowledge their existence and find a way to establish preference with your prospect. After all, if your competitor can offer the same value for less money, you won't win the business. In order to avoid the shifting loyalty and competitive price wars that are the unfortunate companions of selling a commodity, your presentation needs to deliver a strong, clear value message that resonates with your prospect and deliver it at strategic points throughout your presentation.

The meaning of value shifts over time so it's important to understand what makes value important in today's economy and how to make a clear distinction between value, features, and benefits.

Grasping what makes value important

Value, the importance, worth, or usefulness of something, isn't a new concept. However, in the past decade it has become front and center in the sales spotlight for the following reasons:

- ✔ **Multiple choices:** The days of having the only game in town are long gone for most companies and salespeople. Even new product innovations and service categories often only enjoy a brief honeymoon period before finding themselves facing renewed competition.

- ✔ **Similar features:** Although your product or service certainly has some unique qualities, often many variations of the same feature are available — or soon will be available — in the market that can also provide a solution to your prospect's challenge or help them achieve his goals.

- ✔ **Feature overload:** Especially with complex products, the sheer number of features to compare when evaluating a solution can overwhelm even the most hearty prospect and cause *decision fatigue,* a proven condition which can result in irrational or unpredictable buying behavior due to the depletion of willpower. Refer to the nearby sidebar, "Examining decision fatigue."

✔ **Similar messaging:** Maybe your product is completely unique, but the competition has done a good job of positioning its product in a way that makes it look or sound similar to yours, thus effectively blurring the lines of distinction in your prospect's eyes. Ultimately, value isn't about reality, but about your customer's perception of reality.

Understanding the difference between features, benefits, and value

You've managed to communicate some value in order to secure a presentation, but be assured your competitor has — and will — be tightening its focus on value as well. You now need to step up your understanding of value in order to use it to your full advantage.

In considering value, salespeople can easily get lost focusing on the many features of their product or service, assuming the benefits are obvious to their prospect. Or, alternatively, they talk about benefits and assume that they've done a sufficient job of conveying value. These common mistakes end up being very costly as they leave the interpretation of the value of the solution completely in the prospect's hands. Having a clear understanding of how features, benefits, and value differ is important.

The Doubletree cookie: Rising above commodity status

I was booking a stay in New York through a travel agent. She quickly identified several properties within my price range, near my destination, and within my budget. Comparing the availability of rewards programs, Wi-Fi, shuttle service, gyms, and so on, I still couldn't define a clear winner. Finally the agent said, "Have you ever stayed at a Doubletree?" "No," I said, "why?" "They give you these fantastic warm chocolate chip cookies when you check in. It makes you feel like you're right at home." Sold. A $700 business decision influenced by an item that probably cost the Doubletree less than a nickel. Doubletree found an innovative way to break out of the commodity business by communicating their value proposition — a warm reception and the promise of a consistent, quality experience — in a simple and memorable way.

Examining decision fatigue

Whole wheat, rice flour, double crust, or gluten free for your pizza? Cow's milk, soy milk, almond milk, or chai for your tea? The sheer number of decisions that people face today would send their ancient ancestors right back to the cave. Decision making is an act of will and your willpower can get depleted. And depleted willpower means poor decision making and even a reluctance to make a decision. This condition is referred to as *decision fatigue*.

Researchers discovered it when judges were much more likely to approve requests for bail during the beginning of the day. But as the day and the number of cases and decisions wore on, judges were more likely to say no and deny bail. They simply got tired of making decisions and defaulted to the easier decision. Decision fatigue can be exacerbated and even turn into *decision avoidance* (ignoring, postponing, or shifting the responsibility for the decision) when decisions are more complicated, notably those that involve trade-offs with a number of positive and negative elements that must be weighed on each side.

Features

A *feature* is simply an attribute or fact about your product, service, or company. As with most facts, a feature has no intrinsic value. Although the benefit may be obvious to you, it may not be obvious to your prospect, and, in fact, he may have an entirely different interpretation of what the benefit of a particular feature is. For example if I state, "Our company has 15,000 employees around the globe," that is a feature — a fact about my company. Now I may think the benefit is obvious: the prospect will have 24/7 access to personal service. But the prospect may think it means he is going to be a small fish in a big pond and miss that personal touch that is important to him.

An example of a feature: The car is fuel efficient and gets 50 mpg on the highway and 40 mpg in the city.

Never leave it up to your prospect to decide what the benefit of a feature is. Always associate a benefit with a feature.

Benefits

A benefit is not what you sell (your product or service) or how it works (features). A *benefit* is how that feature helps your prospect. Benefits are usually expressed in terms of loss or gain (for example, increasing sales, revenue, or profits or reducing time, cost, or effort), and are best when they're quantifiable. Benefits are typically stated after a feature and answer the question on your prospect's mind: What's in it for me – or WIFM?

An example of a benefit: The car is fuel efficient (WIFM?), which means that you'll save up to $20 per visit to the gas station.

Value

Value extends beyond what your product or service can do for your prospect and aligns your benefits with the prospect's larger goals and objectives.

An example of value: The fuel-efficient car allows you to reduce overall travel expenses by 20 percent and aligns with your goal of reducing your carbon footprint by 5 percent year-over-year.

 You may have similar features and benefits in each of your presentations; however, the value will likely be different for each individual prospect because it's specific to each prospect's objectives. Discover more about features and benefits in Chapter 6.

Developing a Value Proposition

A *value proposition* is a clear statement of the results that the prospect can expect to receive from your product or service. Because your presentation will be organized around this value proposition, spend the time necessary to get it right. A weak value proposition leads to a weak presentation with very little persuasive power, whereas a faulty value proposition can lead your prospect right into the waiting hands of your competition. In the following sections you discover what goes into a strong value proposition, how to customize it for your audience, and how to avoid falling into the typical value proposition trap.

Eyeing the qualities of a compelling value proposition

A value proposition needs to resonate instantly with a prospect in order to be successful. It does this by connecting the benefits of your solution to your prospect's unique goals and objectives using the following qualities:

- **Relevancy:** A good value proposition is always seen from the prospect's eyes and is relevant to his goals and objectives, not a simple rehashing of your marketing positioning statement or a list of your strongest benefits. For example, if your prospect's goal is to increase sales, the fact that your company provides tools for greater sales productivity isn't relevant as it stands. If you reposition it to say that "We can help you increase sales by giving your reps tools that allow them to respond to leads 25 percent faster," then you have shifted the focus away from your company and to your prospect's interests, making your value proposition much more relevant and compelling.

✔ **Specificity:** Vague statements of improvement aren't sufficient today. Your value proposition should include a specific claim in order to get your prospect to sit up and take notice. Sophisticated decision makers roll their eyes at general claims like, "We can save you money" or "We help improve your bottom line." Questions leap to mind: How much can you save me? In what time period? Where does that savings come from? Chapter 6 addresses in greater depth the detailed answers of how you achieve your claims during the body of your presentation.

✔ **Uniqueness:** Because most presentations answer not only the question "Why should I buy?" but "Why should I buy from *you*?" your value proposition needs to point out why you're superior to your competition in areas that are important to your prospect. It's true unless you're the exclusive vendor in your industry (and even then keep in mind, you're often competing with the status quo). Chapter 4 explores these two questions in greater detail.

✔ **Believability:** A strong value statement provides proof. In other words, your prospect wants to know, "How do I know what you're saying is true?" You need evidence which can come in several forms:

- **Testimonials:** Independent third parties, customer stories, or business case results can all help substantiate your claims.

- **Proof of concept:** Although often expensive to implement, the ability to test drive your product or service in the prospect's own environment can be the best way to prove value for skeptical prospects.

- **Tangible results:** External or internal research that shows actual data or ranking around the area of value can help prospects feel confident that you can do what you say you can.

Tailoring your value proposition

A much more robust value proposition that delivers on all of the qualities that I discuss in the previous section is tailored for your specific prospect and aligns your benefits with the prospect's goals to arrive at value. Here are the areas you want to customize to reflect the true value of what your product or service can do for your prospect's business:

✔ **The prospect's goal or objective:** During your discovery process you'll have defined what your prospect's goal — or goals — are. If your prospect has several goals, rank them according to their importance for your prospect and your ability to impact them. Check out Chapter 2 for information you need to gather before you plan your presentation.

✔ **An action verb:** This is what effect you have on the prospect's goal: Increase, reduce, drive, eliminate.

✔ **Outcome:** For your value proposition include the outcome of the area(s) that can have the most impact helping the client reach his objective(s). For example, employee retention, speed to market, sales revenue.

✔ **Figures or statistics:** Prospects want to see concrete results, not vague promises. Quantify what outcome they can expect to see from your solution. When you uncovered your prospect's goal, it was likely expressed in some type of key performance indicator (KPI), such as revenue, year-over-year growth, cost-per-unit, and so forth. Be sure to speak in the same terms that your prospect uses.

✔ **Competitive advantage:** Where do you outperform your competition? In almost every case your prospect has other choices when it comes to achieving his goal or solving his problem. Therefore a strong value proposition also states your key competitive differentiator, answering the question "Why should I buy from you?"

✔ **Proof:** Saying that you can solve the problem isn't always enough. High ranking executives demand proof. Claiming "we can increase your ROI by 10 percent" can raise healthy skepticism, but following it with "as recently achieved by one of our customers" provides assurance that you didn't just pull it out of the air. Letting your prospect know early on that you can justify your claims is a strong differentiator.

Refer to Figure 3-1 for an example of a slide illustrating a tailored value proposition

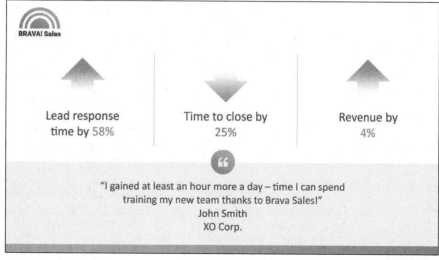

Figure 3-1:
A tailored
value
proposition.

Illustration by 24Slides

Comparing a tailored value proposition with the typical formula for value

Many feature and product statements masquerade as value propositions. These typical value propositions often follow the fill-in-the-blank formula:

"We do X for Y so that they can Z."

I compare two examples of typical value propositions to a tailored value propositions:

Example 1:

Typical value proposition: "We keep your data safe in the cloud so that you can provide increased security for your customers.

Tailored value proposition: "We keep your data safe in the cloud, which allows you to increase security for your client's data by as much as 90 percent (added figures) as our audited report will show you (added proof)."

Example 2:

Typical value proposition: "We help financial institutions reduce manual reporting, which allows you to reduce costly errors and cut administrative time spent creating reports."

Tailored value proposition: "We help financial institutions reduce manual reporting, which allows you to reduce costly errors and cut administrative time spent creating reports by 20 percent (added figures) based on the results our current customers are achieving (added proof)."

When you compare these two you can see that the typical value proposition isn't as relevant, unique, specific, or believable as the tailored version. In other words, it lacks the qualities of a compelling value proposition.

Applying Insights to Determine Value

Your presentation needs to build a persuasive case for the value of your product or service that resonates with your prospect. How do you determine what value to build your presentation around? Chapter 2 explains the planning process where you uncover a lot of valuable information that you can now start to apply, including:

✔ **Impact:** *Impact* answers how the problem is currently affecting your prospect or his organization and how your solution can resolve it. The ability of your solution to solve your prospect's business problem is the keystone of your value proposition. For example, a hospital is experiencing a rise in administrative costs because many of its processes are still done manually. It would like to cut its administrative costs by 10 percent. The impact is the rise in administrative costs.

✔ **Facts and figures:** In order to quantify the value of your solution, you need to find out some costs associated with the problem. For example, assume that you were able to find out that the hospital has 300 employees involved in administrative jobs at an average of $20/hour. You estimate that your solution can save each employee three hours a week. During 50 employee weeks that is the equivalent of $900,000 in savings.

If you're unable to get specific figures from your prospect, you can look for similar clients, case studies, or industry statistics to give you direction and make your best educated guess.

✔ **Goals:** Most companies use some type of KPI to track and assess their business processes. To ensure that you're in synch with your prospect, express their value in the terms that they use. For example, the hospital expressed its goal in terms of a percentage; therefore, you would convert $900,000 to a percentage of the known administrative costs, which equals 10 percent per year.

✔ **Competitive advantage:** Where do you outperform your competition? Assume you also discovered that your prospect is considering a competitor who positions itself as a full solution, but in fact it doesn't offer mobile access. This fact is a point of differentiation you want to include in your value proposition. Check out Chapter 2 for how to analyze your competition.

For this example, here is your value proposition: "Based on the data you provided us, we can help you reduce administrative costs by 10 percent by eliminating many redundant manual processes and providing all-time mobile access to your employees."

Prioritizing Benefits to Structure Your Presentation

More than likely you have multiple benefits that can help your prospect achieve his goals. In order to deliver the strongest value proposition possible, you need to prioritize your benefits to align with what's most important to your prospect as well as showcase your competitive advantages. Follow these steps to determine which benefits best deliver value for your prospect

1. **List your prospect's goals and objectives in order of priority.**

   In your planning process you probably identified several goals or objectives that your product or service can address and some that you can't. List the goals that you can impact by importance to your prospect. Make the top one or two the focal point of your value proposition.

2. **List all of the benefits you offer for each goal.**

   Brainstorm all the ways that your product or service can help your prospect reach the top one or two goals.

3. **Rank your benefit in terms of competitive advantage.**

   Compare how you stack up to your competition by ranking your benefits from 1–5 (one for a distinct competitive advantage, five for no competitive advantage.) See Chapter 2 for doing a competitive analysis ranking.

4. **Select the highest-ranking benefit(s) for your value proposition.**

   Select at least one benefit that you rank first and work it into your value proposition. Doing so makes sure that your value proposition highlights at least one of your competitive advantages. Figure 3-2 shows a ranking of benefits and competitive advantages by value.

The top line is a formula for aligning goals with benefits for your value proposition. The bottom gives you an example of goals and benefits by rank for a specific solution.

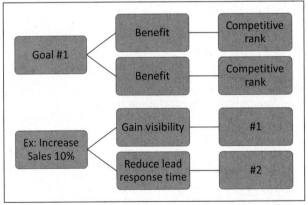

Figure 3-2:
Ranking benefits and competitive advantage by value.

Illustration by 24Slides

Recognizing Value and Benefits by Decision-Maker Type

In sales to larger organizations or those involving higher ticket products or services, multiple decision makers may be involved in the buying process. In fact, a recent study showed an average of five decision makers are involved in the purchase of a major business-to-business solution. Each decision maker's role within the organization influences his perception of value; therefore, knowing who the decision makers are in your audience is critical so that you can tailor your value proposition accordingly. These sections help you do so.

Catering value to meet the decision makers' needs

If you're like most people, you adjust your conversation to your listener's needs and interests all the time. For example, if you were talking to your mother about a wedding you attended, you may focus on the flowers, if you were talking with your catering friend, you'd probably talk about the cake, and with your girlfriend, the bride's dress. Same event but a personalized focus makes it easier for your listener to connect to your topic.

In a similar way you want to match up value to the needs and interests of your prospect. For example, although you would certainly want to talk to members of the administrative team about how fast a feature can help them accomplish a task, this message won't wow the executive members of your audience. You need to further tailor your value proposition to the people who will be in your audience, including:

- ✔ **Problem owners:** These are typically end users — the people within the prospect's company who are living with the problem and likely will be using your product or service. Although they have some interest in larger organizational goals like increasing profit, expanding globally and so forth, they're typically concerned about more direct and immediate goals that impact how they do their jobs. For example, problem owners are looking for your presentation to answer the following questions:

    "How does your product or service solve my problem?"

    "Will it make my life easier or more difficult?"

    "Will it help me do my job better (faster, more accurately, with less supervision, and so on)?"

- ✔ **Problem solvers:** These people typically are affected by the problem secondhand but tasked with the challenge of seeking out a solution. They're likely your point of contact within the organization. Although not directly affected by the problem, they must find a solution that works for both the end users and the decision makers. Therefore their concerns usually center around validating their recommendations, avoiding mistakes, and implementing easily. For example, problem solvers will want to know things like:

    "Can your product do what you say it can?

    "Will the end users adopt it?"

✔ **Decision makers:** In a significant sized deal, the person writing the check is often a high-ranking manager or C-level executive. With multiple responsibilities and interests, she is less concerned with the specifics of how you're going to achieve something and more interested in the financial viability of the solution and how it impacts the organization as a whole. For example the decision maker's concerns include:

"How does this solution compare to other priorities within our organization?"

"How does this help me increase market share by 10 percent this year?"

Consider the following example of how you can tailor value for these three types of decision makers using a product that as a salesperson you're probably only all too familiar with: a contact relationship management (CRM) system.

An insurance company went from 200 agents in three states to 1,500 agents across the country in the past year due to recent acquisitions. About half of the agents have their own CRM system, but there is no consistency across the group or easy way for managers to track progress.

Although the company has more agents, the revenue per agent has been steadily declining at the rate of 8 percent year to date, and the length of the average sales cycle has grown from three months to nearly four. Management attributes this decline in sales to the adjustments taking place from the acquisition, but also acknowledges that the inability to track deals and monitor close rates is probably responsible for half of that loss.

Even though you're still selling the same solution (a CRM system), you must tailor value to fit the interests of each decision maker to make sure your message hits home.

✔ **The problem owner:** These are the salespeople who are experiencing declining sales. If you talk exclusively about how your system can give manager's greater visibility into every deal in the organization's pipeline, you're not going to win over the sales team. The team members probably aren't going to be wildly excited about being more accountable to their managers either. What will excite them is how your product can help them close more deals. Some of them don't even have a CRM system and will be understandably concerned about things like, "How much work is this going to take for me to get up to speed? Is this going to make my life easier or harder?"

Problem owner value proposition example: "Within an hour we can get you set up with complete mobile access to all of your information so that you can start closing deals at least 12 percent faster, based on what the sales team at XYZ experienced."

✔ **Problem solvers:** These are the managers who are concerned with making numbers as well as spending their time wisely. They have a lot of new salespeople to keep track of and new territories to cover with this acquisition; therefore, they're spending much more time on the road, which means less time for going over long reports or troubleshooting.

Problem solver value proposition example: "We help you increase revenue by 4 percent by reducing closing time from four to three months as we were able to do with XYZ. This gives you 10 percent more time to lead and train your new team and full visibility so you can spend your time on areas that you can best impact."

✔ **Decision makers:** This group is interested in the bigger picture: turning around sales, fast. Having just invested in other companies, they have a great deal of pressure to make this work and getting all team members on the same page is a key goal.

Decision-maker value proposition example: "We can help you reach your goal of aligning your teams quickly and increasing sales revenue by 4 percent within six months based on the numbers you provided us and what we were able to achieve with XYZ."

As you can see, value is in the eye of the beholder. Although the product or solution is the same in all three cases, the value proposition is different when you take into account what is important to each type of decision maker. And nowhere have you mentioned any of the cool features you have available. But don't worry. Chapter 6 discusses features when I focus on the body of your presentation.

Weaving value into your presentation

You have a compelling value proposition designed specifically to fit the needs of your prospect. Where you use it in your presentation is important also. Value needs special attention in several sections of your presentation, including:

✔ **Opening:** As much as you need to engage and connect with prospects during your opening, remember why you were invited to the dance in the first place: — to provide value. Within the first 90 seconds to two minutes of your presentation, you need to let your prospect know what value you're going to add to his organization, especially critical with C-level executives. Rather than listing all of your benefits and setting out to prove them immediately, give your prospect a high-level view of what value you're going to prove. For example, "Today we're going to show you how through our group buying power we can help you lower labor costs and improve your ability to attract and retain high-quality employees with enhanced benefits. A recent client was able to save

$750,000 last year and reduce employee turnover by 20 percent." Refer to Chapter 5 for more discussion on the opening.

✔ **Body:** Each agenda item you discuss within the body of your presentation contributes in some way toward substantiating your value proposition. Your presentation's body is where you get into more nuts and bolts about how each feature contributes to value. Chapter 6 explores the body of your presentation.

✔ **Closing:** By the time you get to your closing you'll have delivered a compelling case for the value you can bring to your prospect's organization. You have proven it, and now it isn't just theory. In your closing, connect all the dots and restate your value proposition as a statement of fact for your audience, backing it up with relevant evidence to support your claims. Check out Chapter 7 for more information about your closing.

Relying on pro tips for killer value props

Often value propositions that sound good on paper fail to connect with your prospect. Here are some additional tips for delivering a killer value proposition:

✔ **Be clear.** Vague or unclear terminology only serves to confuse prospects and muddy your value proposition. Avoid using terminology that is unnecessarily complex or acronyms that have not been clearly defined.

✔ **Get specific.** Real figures or percentages give your value proposition more weight (for example, 40 percent ROI versus high ROI).

✔ **Avoid exaggeration.** Prospects are sensitive to hype and superlatives. Remember, your value proposition isn't a marketing message but a custom business proposal so avoid terms like "the best" or "most amazing."

✔ **Make it short.** A good value proposition should be instantly understandable and ultimately memorable; therefore, you need to keep it short and succinct. If you have multiple points of value, pick the highest level value or the one that has the greatest relevancy to your audience. Don't throw out the others, but weave them into your presentation where they makes sense.

Part II
Building a Blockbuster Presentation

Illustration by 24Slides

Prospects may not make a buying decision until days or weeks after your sales presentation. How do you ensure that your message is remembered? Check out six ways to make your presentation stick at www.dummies.com/extras/salespresentations.

In this part . . .

- ✔ Understand the science behind what drives attention and how to use it to improve prospect engagement and presentation recall.

- ✔ Use a persuasive structure that answers one of two key prospect questions: "Why buy?" or "Why buy you?"

- ✔ Comprehend the power of your opening and how it affects the success of your entire presentation.

- ✔ Build a logical and emotional case for your solution by ratcheting up tension in your presentation body.

- ✔ Organize your topics from your prospect's perspective so she can better relate to your presentation.

- ✔ Create urgency to act with a strong closing that reinforces value and provides evidence.

- ✔ Establish credibility with your introduction, differentiate with your overview, and provide direction with your agenda.

- ✔ Leverage the power of visual aids and choose the most effective presentation program and design for your presentation.

Chapter 4

Structuring a Persuasive Presentation

*L*ike a well-crafted movie, a sales presentation must grab your prospect's attention and continue to keep her engaged for the entire journey. Yet most sales presentations fail on one or both accounts because they aren't designed to take into account the plummeting attention spans of today's audiences and the changing ways that they consume information. Salespeople are operating off a dated structure put in place well before "smart" and "phone" became a noun.

Although the rest of the world has sped up in response to today's faster pace and increased responsibilites, sales presentations seem to be the one place a prospect can count on to catch up on her email or update her social media status. Using a modern structure that takes into account what draws your prospect's attention and how they assimilate information is critical if you want your message to be heard and to stick. If you make your audience work too hard to follow along, you'll lose them and all your efforts will be wasted.

This chapter gives you a peek into your prospect's mind and helps you to understand how and what drives attention and how to apply that to your presentation. I help you prioritize and organize your presentation for maximum attention. Furthermore, I introduce you to a structure that marries the best of contemporary presentations with a proven persuasive formula. Finally, you can see how and when to use a theme to provide a unifying thread for your presentation.

Understanding How Your Audience Thinks

Think about how people communicate today: Texts are 160 characters. Twitter? 140. The majority of people don't watch a video longer than three minutes. Your prospect is in that majority. Startling changes have occurred in the way people take in and process information, yet most sales presentations are based on principles from a bygone era when people had more time, fewer options, and less distractions.

If you want your presentation to have the best possible chance for success, you need to understand the mind-set of your prospect, what grabs her attention, what are the limits of that attention, and how can you package and deliver your message in a format that makes it easy for your prospect to pay attention and remember your presentation. The following sections can help.

Reaching your audience with neuroscience

Your audience fidgets, checks email, or sends texts during your presentation for a reason. Attention is a limited resource. You live in a time where the availability of information is at an all-time high while attention is at an all-time low. In order for your prospect to hear and remember your presentation, you must have her attention. To do so, you must understand what influences attention and apply that knowledge to the structure of your presentation. Neuroscience is discovering more and more every day about how people pay attention and what they pay attention to.

Here is what you need to keep in mind as you develop your presentation:

- **Attention spans are on the decline.** If a web page doesn't load within eight seconds, most people abandon ship. Sitting through commercials during a show? No thank you, say the millions who prefer to record or pay for services to avoid them all together. Studies indicate that attention spans have declined as much as 50 percent in the last decade. Blame it on increased responsibilities, the amount of information available, and the 24/7 news cycle, but whatever the cause, the outcome for your presentation is the same: You need a structure that makes it easy for you to gain and regain your prospect's attention — because after you've lost her attention, you'll struggle the remainder of the presentation to get it back.

✔ **Sustained attention is between 5 and 20 minutes.** *Sustained attention* is the ability to focus on one thing. Of course, you can pay attention for longer periods of time, either by the application of willpower (I am going to finish my taxes today if it kills me!) or by having your attention renewed, a technique used frequently in events that last longer than a few minutes, like movies, sporting events, or political speeches.

✔ **Big data is everyone's problem.** *Big data,* the overwhelming volume of information available today, isn't just a problem for organizations. Individuals too have to deal with their own big data on a daily basis — processing, analyzing, storing, and often acting on thousands of pieces of information each day. Earlier pre-cellphone generations didn't have to contend with it. Yet most sales presentations continue to use a presentation structure invented well before the cellphone — much less smartphone — existed.

✔ **Multitasking is commonplace.** Up until recent years, *multitasking* — doing several activities at once — was a term reserved for computers; now it's not unusual for people to talk on the phone while checking email or even driving while texting. Even though experts have proven that humans' brains aren't designed for multitasking, in fact, multitasking actually causes you to be less effective and increases stress levels in your brain, many people — your prospect included — persist in the delusion that it makes them more productive.

✔ **Attention isn't a constant.** Attention isn't something that you win once and then forget. Research shows that your audience's attention is at its peak during the first few seconds of your presentation and goes downhill from there, reaching its lowest point within 10 minutes. Yet 10 minutes into a presentation, many salespeople are talking about their company, introducing data, or discussing features — none of which is capable of reeling attention back in or keeping your prospect's mind from further wandering. You can avoid this by using a structure that takes into account what grabs and maintains an audience's attention and includes consideration for renewing waning attention. I discuss specific how-to tips in the following section.

✔ **Difficulty decreases attention.** Your capacity to pay attention decreases the more difficult the information or the greater the amount of learning required. That's because your brain is a muscle, and trying to master new information or pay close attention to complex ideas and concepts gives it a workout. The harder the workout, the faster the brain tires and the less effective it becomes at absorbing new information. When presenting a complex idea, you must take into account the reduced ability of your audience to pay attention for longer periods of time and work in breaks or transition to a lighter topic.

✔ **Brains take shortcuts.** In order to try and quickly make sense of all the information coming at you, your brain quickly scans the information and decides what to do with it. If you're familiar with the topic, your brain decides that you're safe and doesn't need to pay full attention to it. Without this filtering device, your brain would soon be so full of irrelevant information that you'd be unable to focus on a single task. This filtering device works against you if you do what everyone else does in a presentation. For example, if you open your presentation with the same old "we're so happy to be here, let me tell you about my company," you can count on lower attention levels as your audience member's brains conserve energy for more novel subjects.

Salespeople who account for the realities of how their prospect pays attention today and structure their presentation for maximizing that attention and increasing recall have a distinct advantage over the competition and give their proposal a much greater chance for a successful outcome. The following section shows you how to apply that knowledge to your presentation.

Embracing the seven-minute stretch

Based on what you know about declining attention spans, the smart strategy is to have a structure that renews your audience's attention every seven minutes. You don't want to wait 10 minutes, when your audience is at their lowest attention point, and you don't want to do it too often or you'll make your audience jumpy. Planning on a seven-minute renewal point means you have a good chance of always having an adequate level of attention from your audience. In fact, one presentation style called Pecha Kucha embraces this new reality by requiring presenters to deliver their presentation in less than seven minutes using only 20 slides (check out the nearby sidebar for specifics).

You need to renew your audience's attention every seven minutes to avoid it hitting the point of no return. In a 30-minute presentation, that means you need to renew your audience's attention four to five times. In a one-hour presentation, you need to renew it eight to nine times. The more times you need to renew attention, the more techniques you need at your disposal in order to avoid being repetitive. Here are a few tips on how to renew attention throughout your presentation:

- **Shift focus.** A simple way to regain attention is to shift the focus to a new topic. The seven-minute mark is a good transition point to move from one agenda item to the next or from the body to the closing.

- **Plan interaction.** The strongest way to regain your prospect's attention is to involve her in your presentation, either by asking her a question, conducting a poll, or asking her to write down questions from the audience on the whiteboard. You can find more tips on audience interaction in Chapter 14.

Pecha Kucha: The ultimate high attention presentation

Pecha Kucha is a concise presentation style that makes TED Talks seem positively rambling. Originated in Tokyo, Pecha Kucha has developed a worldwide following. Speakers gather in more than 800 cities to deliver a presentation lasting six minutes and forty seconds (yes, it's that precise!) by following the required format of presenting 20 slides that display for 20 seconds each. To make it even more interesting, the slides automatically advance, so presenters can't spend five minutes on one and one minute and forty seconds on the other 19. Interested in Pecha Kucha? Sounds like your cup of tea? Check for a group in your area at www.pechakucha.org/.

✔ **Limit distractions.** Whether it's ambient noise from the room next door or flickering overhead lights, distractions can reduce your prospect's ability to focus on your message. Do what you can to limit outside distractions to keep her attentive through the entire seven-minute chunk.

✔ **Keep it moving, but don't rush.** Many salespeople worry that they won't be able to get a point across in seven minutes; however, if you've ever tried to sit quietly for seven minutes, you know that it's actually a decent amount of time. Although seven minutes is certainly a guideline, the discipline of trying to convey a point in seven minutes or less is quite valuable. If you find it impossible to break up a topic into seven minutes or less, consider shifting your prospect's attention using something less abrupt, like moving from one side of the room to the other, writing on the whiteboard or flipchart, or asking your audience to weigh in on a topic.

Building a Persuasive Structure: The Key Parts to Your Presentation

A good structure is one that makes your job of both engaging and persuading your prospect easier. In the following sections, I look at why a structure is important and introduce a proven persuasive structure for you to follow.

Understanding the importance of a good framework

If you've ever sat through a presentation that went around the block a few times before finally arriving unsteadily — and late — at its destination, you understand firsthand the need for a good, clear framework for your message. Not only does the right structure help you efficiently get from point A to point B, but it also serves some other very important functions:

✔ **Organizing your message:** You've gathered a lot of insights and information prior to your presentation. You may well feel a bit overwhelmed by the sheer volume of it. Attempting to include all of it makes for a bloated presentation that doesn't necessarily hit the mark. You can easily get lost in the weeds by overexplaining or discussing topics that aren't relevant when you don't have a solid structure to follow. A good structure helps you get your arms around all that information, prioritize, and organize it in a way that has the greatest impact on your audience.

✔ **Simplifying your message:** Without a clear, easy-to-follow, and consistent structure, a presentation can make your product seem even more complex than it is. If your solution has any complexity to it at all (which of course applies to nearly everyone), you need a structure that makes your product or service appear, if not easy, at least not daunting for the prospect to adopt and put into use.

✔ **Moving your audience:** A good structure takes your audience on a journey that leads to a natural and obvious conclusion. Because buying decisions are rarely based on logic alone, your structure should allow room for making a strong emotional case as well.

The more complex your solution, the more critical you follow a clear structure.

Increasing the power of a three-part structure

The three part structure — an opening, a body, and a conclusion — is the basis of most presentations, speeches, film, television, and theater. Invented by Aristotle, it's a structure your audience is familiar with and can easily follow. This structure has many variations: chronological, vendor qualification/problem/solution, and situation, complication, and resolution, to name three. The structure you choose depends upon your goal.

Some types of three-part structures are better for educating, entertaining, or motivating audiences. In sales, you want to be sure to use a structure that persuades and drives home your message in a way that encourages your prospect to take action at the end of your presentation. The situation, complication, resolution structure is proven to be most effective at accomplishing that goal.

This persuasive structure places the focus on your prospect's challenge or objective — not on your product, service, or company. The way the situation, complication, resolution structure organizes your content has the ability to change your prospect's perception, open her mind to new ideas, and motivate her to take action. This structure also addresses many of the problems associated with the typical sales presentation structure and helps to increase your prospect's attention, keep her engaged throughout your presentation, and increase recall of your message.

The next sections take a closer look at these three parts of a persuasive presentation — called situation, complication, and resolution — to help you understand what to include in your presentation as well as the two organizational questions you must keep in mind.

Establishing the situation (the opening)

Your presentation's opening is your first impression with your prospect, so quickly set the stage for her by defining her current situation, for example, addressing the problem, opportunity, or challenge that you're there to solve and the impact it's having on her organization. By clearly defining the situation you are laying the groundwork for why your prospect needs to change as well as letting her know that you have a clear understanding of her situation.

After you've set up the current situation for the prospect, you want to tell her where your product or service can take her; in other words, you're painting a picture of a better future with your solution. This starts to create an uncomfortable but necessary disparity between where your prospect is and where she wants to be. Establishing the situation in your opening is a critical component for a presentation that needs to persuade. This by no means leaves out the need to entertain, engage, and interact; in fact, gaining your audience's attention during your opening is key to your success. Head to Chapter 5 for some pointers.

Building in complication (the body)

In the body you continue to widen that gap between pain and relief to increase your prospect's urgency to resolve the problem. You do this by introducing complications that create tension and make sticking with the status quo or putting off a decision less desirable options. Because most people are uncomfortable with indecision, tension taps into that human desire to solve the problem.

By exploring each challenge and the impact of not making a change, you're building a case for answering the questions "Why should the prospect buy the product or service?" and/or "Why should the prospect buy it from you?" Refer to the later section, "Eyeing two organizing questions central to structure" for more on those two questions.

Some controversy surrounds whether or how to address your prospect's *pain points* — a problem (real or perceived) that your product or service can address. Although pain has certainly been handled with a heavy hand in the past, bringing up and exploring pain with your prospect is important in a persuasive argument. Pain is an emotional reaction and a persuasive case needs to trigger that emotion. Logic alone isn't enough, as you discover in Chapter 6.

Pain trumps gain. Research shows that avoiding loss or pain is almost twice as strong a motivator as gaining something positive. Pain is a mighty motivator. Calling out the pain points in a way that is appropriate for your audience is necessary to promote action. If there weren't any pain, you wouldn't be there.

Finishing with your resolution (the closing)

Your closing is the time to relieve that tension by providing a clear resolution to the problem that's easy for your prospect to act upon. You've made a case for value now, and you can restate it as a statement of fact and substantiate your claims with evidence, facts, figures, research studies, industry statistics, and so forth. Your closing also needs to include a specific *call to action* — in other words, a statement of what you want your prospect to do at the end of your presentation — as well as some elements that make it easier for your prospect to remember your presentation. Chapter 7 gives you the lowdown on creating a memorable closing.

To help you organize the information you've collected into your opening, body, and closing, you need to know what question your presentation answers. The following sections give you some direction.

Eyeing two organizing questions central to structure

Whether your presentation is 20 minutes or two days, virtual or live, it must answer one or both of two central questions in your prospect's mind. Which question you address can help you decide what information to include in your opening, body, and closing and how to position your message in response. The two questions are

- ✔ **Why should I buy this product or service?** In this situation your prospect isn't yet convinced that your solution is the answer to her problem. She may have other alternatives or priorities, or she may not feel the problem is sufficient enough to warrant solving. In other words, the status quo is acceptable. Your presentation in this situation will center on convincing her that your solution is the best way to address her problem.

- ✔ **Why should I buy it from you?** In this scenario, your prospect agrees that the solution will solve her problem or address her need, but she isn't convinced that your product or service is the best choice. You can easily fall into a price war if you aren't deliberate about establishing value and communicating your competitive advantage. In this situation your structure will center on convincing the prospect that you're the preferred vendor.

Your presentation may have to answer both questions, in which case, you should thoroughly address the first question before addressing the second.

Modeling your presentation's structure after TED Talks

Unfair or not, Ted Talks have raised the bar on what the general population expects from a presentation. Because the people you're presenting to likely watch these talks and resonate with the format, it's important to be aware of how they work and what elements make sense to apply in your presentation.

If you had 18 minutes to deliver your presentation, could you do it *and* make it interesting, engaging, and inspiring? That's what thousands of TED speakers attempt to do each year — many with fantastic levels of success. What began as a conference for spreading ideas about technology, education, and design, TED as it's affectionately called, has since grown into a cultural phenomenon of short, engaging presentations on a variety of topics, from poverty to addiction to sales.

Even though your presentation is likely to last longer than 18 minutes and needs to do more

(continued)

(continued)

than educate or entertain, TED Talks include some important principles that are highly engaging and effective for reaching today's audiences.

✔ **Stick to one big idea.** TED Talks take on some pretty complex topics, all of which must be addressed in 18 minutes or less. Although this timeframe sounds like the recipe for a hailstorm of information, good TED speakers maintain focus by organizing their content around one main idea that ties it all together and makes it easier for the audience to remember.

✔ **Hook them with the opening.** TED presenters know they have to grab their audience with a powerful opening, and a hook is the way to do that. A *hook* is an attention-grabbing device that relates to or introduces the topic. Whether it's a story, a quote, an insight, statistic, or question, the hook starts the presentation off on a strong and relevant note. Chapter 5 includes some examples of opening hooks.

✔ **Use a catchphrase.** Successful TED Talks often repeat a phrase or soundbite that quickly summarizes their idea to help the audience remember it. Go to Chapter 5 for more on catchphrases.

✔ **Tell a story.** The most popular TED Talks open with a personal story. *Storytelling* is an extremely effective technique for increasing the emotional engagement of your audience. Relatively underused (or poorly used) in sales presentations, storytelling scores high on the attention meter because of the novelty factor as well. See tips on how to use storytelling in Chapter 12.

✔ **Rely on the situation-complication-resolution structure.** One of the most effective structures for persuasive speeches and presentations, this persuasive three-part structure is very popular among presenters, including Daniel Pink at TED Talks. Refer to the section, "Building a Persuasive Structure: The Key Parts to Most Presentations" in this chapter for more information.

You can find TED Talks on a wide variety of topics, but a few in particular are right on the money when it comes to addressing issues relevant to salespeople. Check out Ted Talks by Simon Sinek, Amy Cuddy, and Ernesto Sirolli at www.ted.com.

Knowing the requirements of a persuasive structure

In addition to serving as a frame for your presentation, your structure has other duties as well: Gaining attention, engaging your audience, and assimilating information. These sections examine some key requirements of a persuasive structure and how they help you move your prospect forward in the sale.

Gaining — and regaining — audience attention

If you're still talking about your company and haven't introduced value or a benefit within the first ten minutes, then your prospect is likely barely hanging on, despite the continued caffeine consumption. A good structure takes into account when prospect's attention wanes and builds in opportunities to renew her attention at these critical junctures. Here are some proven ways to grab attention that you can build into your presentation's structure:

- **Introducing novelty:** In order to survive, humans had to quickly decide whether new information was dangerous or critical to their survival. The result: People's attention is drawn to new and unusual things. A structure that introduces something new at key points within your presentation, whether it's introducing a new topic, telling a story, or interacting with your prospect, keeps your audience's limited attention on you and off their mobile devices.

- **Engaging the senses:** A police siren. A rain shower. The smell of fresh bread. Anything that engages one of the five (and for some of you six) senses naturally grabs your audience's attention. Although using smell and taste in your presentation is difficult (and perhaps risky), adding visual support whether it's a picture, a whiteboard, or a prop can improve audience engagement and message retention. Chapter 14 offers some insight on using props.

- **Triggering emotions:** Emotions are powerful magnets for drawing attention that the entertainment industry knows how to play for full advantage. In business, emotions are, shall I say, a bit more restrained? Yet when you incorporate them in an appropriate and relevant way — with a story or an insight or a challenge — at strategic points within your structure (like the opening), you can engage a prospect on an emotional level. Doing so is a sure way to draw valuable attention to your message or make a memorable point.

- **Responding to movement:** You could be in a room with Tony Robbins, Jimmy Fallon, and Tina Fey yet if someone else entered the room, you would likely turn to look. Humans are wired to respond to movement — a holdover from days spent running from predators. Although predators are less likely to pounce, movement is still a strong and sure attention-grabber that you can build into your presentation. Walking to the other side of the room, writing on a flipchart or whiteboard, and incorporating simple movements when you know your audiences' attention is on the decline are simple ways to keep your audience engaged while you focus on delivering your message.

For more strategies on gaining attention, see Chapter 5.

Conveying information in an easy to assimilate way

Organizing your message in a way that your prospect has the best chance of understanding and remembering it is important. Most sales presentations are structured around how their product or service works or the areas of strength for the presenter's company. Nothing about this organization is of great interest to your prospect or easy for them to remember.

A good structure is customer-focused and organizes information around your prospect's challenges and needs or use patterns as opposed to what you do or how you do it. Here are some ways to get your message across in a way that your audience will more readily understand and remember:

- ✔ **Chunking:** Breaking information into small bite-size pieces (called *chunking*) makes the presentation easier to understand and remember. For many years the magic number that people were thought to be able to easily remember (without repetition and practice) was seven (plus or minus 2). Researchers have since disproven that theory and found that the actual number of items that people can remember is closer to three or four. As a result, most sales presentations have no chance of being remembered by prospects today. A good structure breaks information into manageable chunks that your audience can easily digest and remember. Figure 4-1 shows breaking information in to chunks.

  In Figure 4-1a, your prospect is presented with a list of 10 items — much too many for her to remember. In Figure 4-1b, those same 10 items are chunked into four groups that make it easier for her to understand and retain.

- ✔ **Spacing repetition:** Not surprisingly, throwing a steady stream of new information at your prospect isn't conducive to developing a clear understanding or memory of it. Research has found that you can increase learning by up to 50 percent by using what's called *spaced learning,* or repeating information at various intervals. Use this concept in your presentation by breaking up information and then referring back to it at later points to reinforce those ideas and messages you most want to stick. See Chapter 7 for an example of bookending your opening hook and value proposition.

Highlighting value

You want your prospect to remember the benefits and value that she'll receive from your solution. Yet if repetition and engagement influence memory, then most sales presentations aren't effective at reinforcing benefits or value. A persuasive structure allows you to call attention to benefits and place a spotlight on value so that your prospect remembers what's important when she is prepared to make a decision.

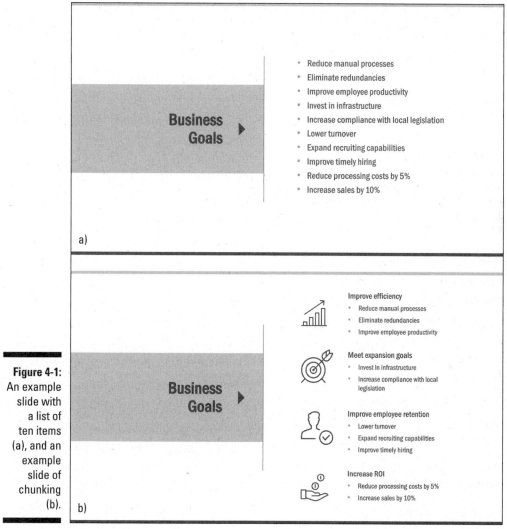

Figure 4-1:
An example
slide with
a list of
ten items
(a), and an
example
slide of
chunking
(b).

Illustration by 24Slides

Allowing for interaction

Most sales presentations are one long monologue. Very few circumstances today require people to sit and listen to someone talk without interruption for longer than a few minutes at a time (unless it's a lecture, a political speech, or a religious service), yet most sales presentations are structured that way. Having a presentation structure that encourages and plans for audience interaction at strategic points helps to renew your prospect's attention, because it involves more of her senses and improves her ability to remember your message.

Persuading to take action

You can structure a presentation many different ways, but in sales, your sales presentation first and foremost needs to be designed to persuade your prospect to take action at the end. Refer to the earlier section, "Building a Persuasive Structure: The Key Parts to Most Presentations" for ways to incorporate a call to action.

Analyzing the "average" sales presentation structure

The structure of the average sales presentation typically looks something like the following. Take a closer look and see if this list holds up to the requirements of a persuasive presentation:

- **Introductions and small talk:** Your audience's attention is at its peak, and you're wasting that opportunity to talk about the weather, how happy you are to be there, or how long you've worked at your company.

- **Corporate overview:** Certainly nothing novel about this opening. Predictable information in a predicable spot makes your audience ripe for distractions.

- **Agenda:** Attention is nearing that low point and you still haven't piqued your prospect's interest, delivered any value, or talked about your prospect's needs.

- **Description of problem:** Your audience's attention is gone and you're telling them something they already know. Where is that smartphone?

- **Present solution:** Fifteen to 20 minutes in and you're finally talking about benefits

and building value. Is anyone still paying attention?

- **Supporting evidence:** If this is the first time you're introducing evidence, you're too late. Your prospect formed her opinion early and used the rest of your presentation to justify her position.

- **Summary:** A long summary of what you've already covered is another predictable area and an opportunity for your audience to start thinking about what they have to do after your presentation.

- **Any questions?** This typical closing ends your presentation on a weak note and leaves next steps completely unaddressed.

As you can see from the preceding list, the average sales presentation structure isn't so much persuasive as it is informative. An informative presentation wastes your time and your prospects. It's time to bring your sales presentation into the present with a more contemporary structure.

Framing Your Presentation through Theme

You can give your presentation an even more polished look by adding a theme. A *theme* is a unifying idea or motif that embodies your prospect's objectives, your value proposition, or your competitive advantage. It's typically very short — one to four words — and lends itself to a clear visual image. Although used prominently in your opening and closing, a theme runs like a thread throughout the rest of your presentation, even influencing your slide design and messaging.

In order to strike a good balance between no theme and theme park, you need to have a solid understanding of when to use a theme and how to choose one that's right for your presentation and your audience.

Knowing when to use a theme

Themes aren't a necessary component of a presentation; however, a theme can be valuable in the following situations to help prospects remember your presentation and your value proposition.

✔ **Long presentations:** If you have a presentation that runs two to three hours or more, you're starting to cover a lot of ground. A theme is helpful in tying ideas together and making it easier for your prospect to see the relationship between different sections by providing a common thread. Check out Chapter 19 for more information about long presentations.

✔ **Multiple presenters:** The differing styles inherent with team presentations can make a message seem less cohesive than if delivered by the same person. Using a theme can give a sense of consistency and uniformity lacking in many team presentations. Chapter 16 addresses team presentations in greater detail.

Determining theme

When deciding on a theme, you need to consider these three questions:

✔ **What do you need to accomplish?** To inspire your prospects? To excite them? To motivate them? To challenge them? Different themes convey different emotions.

✔ **What is the tone?** Serious? Light-hearted? Humorous? The tone you strike must coincide with your message and will influence your choice of a theme. For example, if your message is about turning a company around from the brink of disaster, a theme about badminton may be a little lightweight to support such a substantial subject.

✔ **What are the visual possibilities?** A good theme lends itself to a clear visual. The more instantly recognizable the better. For example, two clasped hands may easily identify a theme of "togetherness," while a theme of "maximizing value" may be more difficult to quickly convey.

Finding your theme

Coming up with a theme is a creative endeavor, and you can approach it in a number of ways. Here are some suggestions to help you find the right theme:

Brainstorm

If you're working as a team, plan a brainstorming session with one rule: There are no bad ideas! If you can't all get together in one place, have everyone list off ten ideas and submit them via email by a certain date. You can then run a poll and pick the top one.

Know your core message

This is the 10,000-foot view of what you're trying to say to your prospect or how you're trying to make her feel. Your presentation itself can be a good source for this core message. Try looking in these sections:

✔ **The desired outcome:** In discovery you identify what the *desired outcome* was for your prospect. Can you describe it in a word or two? Is it freedom, innovation, visibility? Refer to Chapter 2 for more discussion on defining desired customer outcomes and goals. Figure 4-2 displays an example of using a desired outcome as a theme, in this case momentum.

• Background: Prospect is an apartment management company that has recently expanded from 10,000 to 20,000 managed units. The company has also doubled the amount of time it's spending marketing properties, processing applicants, and maximizing occupancy rates, which is keeping the company from achieving its goal of continued growth.

• Your value proposition: "Our solution allows you to cut the time spent marketing properties and processing applicants by 75 percent as well as maximize occupancy and rental rates across your portfolio so that you can continue to meet your growth objectives."

Illustration by 24Slides

Figure 4-2:
An example slide of a theme based on achieving a desired outcome.

✔ **Your competitive advantage:** If your presentation is focused on "why buy us," you may want to use a competitive advantage (as long as it's important to the prospect) and create a theme around that. A *competitive advantage* is an area where you outperform your competition. Check out Chapter 3 for more on competitive advantage. For example, "24/7 access" is a competitive advantage if you offer mobile features and your competitor doesn't, or "Global service" if you're the only vendor to provide full global support. If not, it's just a feature. In Figure 4-3 you can see an example of using a competitive advantage as a theme. Here's how that theme — The Power of Why — was developed:

- Background: The prospect is a healthcare provider currently experiencing a rise in call handling times and customer churn although the provider isn't sure why. It's considering replacing the outdated system in its call centers, although it isn't convinced that the impact of additional visibility warrants the investment or that your company is the best choice. Your competitive advantage is your ability to provide key information into why the company is losing customers.

- Your value proposition: "We can provide you with visibility into why call handling times are on the rise and customer loyalty is on the decline. The ability to act on this insight will increase agent efficiency and reduce customer churn, which will in turn increase revenue."

Illustration by 24Slides

Figure 4-3: An example slide of a theme based on competitive advantage.

- ✔ **Crowdsource it.** *Crowdsourcing* is gathering ideas and opinions from a group of people — typically on the Internet. If you're not sure about what theme to use, you can get input from others by crowdsourcing it in the following ways:

  - Do a poll or run a contest on Facebook.

  - Ask current customers what word, phrase, or image comes to mind when describing the results they achieved with your product or service.

  - Search your prospect's website for core values or causes they support.

- ✔ **Use a thesaurus.** After you narrow it down to a few words, check a thesaurus for synonyms or use `www.synonym-finder.com` to make sure you have the perfect word to convey your theme.

Noting some theme do's and don'ts

Themes can be a great unifying tool for providing a framework for your presentation and increasing recall. They can also be a hodgepodge of unrelated ideas awkwardly forced into a structure. Here are some ways to make sure your theme works to support your message — not detract from it.

- ✔ **Do keep it short.** A theme is different than a catchphrase or quote. It should be a powerful one or two words that provides the opportunity for great visual expression and interpretation.

- ✔ **Do incorporate your theme in your design.** Use your theme to provide direction for what template you use, colors, photos, and fonts, as well as any supporting materials.

- ✔ **Do consider takeaways.** Many themes lend themselves to interesting takeaways, whether it's a mousepad, power stick, or customized pen with your theme on it. Just be sure they're reflective of the quality of your product or service.

- ✔ **Don't do what's popular in your industry.** If you've seen a theme done in your industry, chances are your prospect has as well. Don't risk going in to a presentation and being the second golf-related theme she has seen that day.

- ✔ **Don't use your prospect's business.** One salesperson was working on a presentation for Disney and came up with the idea to use "It's a small world" as a theme. I suggested that out of the thousands of vendors that sell to Disney, they have probably heard their own themes reflected back to them numerous times. Don't go for the obvious because odds are someone else has thought of it as well.

- ✔ **Don't do a canned theme.** That includes anything from PowerPoint or a stock slide design that you've found on the web. Your theme should be custom to the prospect and her situation.

- ✔ **Don't use stock photos.** Like a canned design, stock photos can make your prospect feel like your presentation is generic and could be addressed to anyone. Use real photos with real people if possible. Check out Chapter 9 for tips on how to use photos in your presentation.

- ✔ **Don't go full theme park.** Remember, a theme is there to provide a memorable framework to hold your message together. Don't let it over-come your message by going too far overboard. One sales team who used a theme of "Take flight" dressed up like flight attendants and pilots, served mini-peanuts and drinks, and used an intercom to introduce team members. Although you have to give them an "A+" for creativity and execution, a debriefing with the executives in the room revealed that they found it a bit cheesy.

Putting Together a Persuasive Presentation in Ten Steps

This section presents the steps you can follow to create a persuasive presentation using the situation, complication, resolution structure. The ten steps are as follows:

1. **Plan your introduction.**

   A succinct preplanned introduction that establishes credibility and jump-starts your presentation is much different than the rambling streams of self-consciousness your prospect may be accustomed to hearing from salespeople. See how to create your own in Chapter 8.

2. **Start with a hook.**

   Just because your prospect is looking at you is no guarantee you have her full attention. You need to have a hook — a device, such as a quote, a story, or an insight — to engage your audience and create interest in your presentation. For example, "Every two days we create as much information as we have since the dawn of time. In your business that means . . ."

3. **Define the situation.**

   Quickly summarize where your prospect is at in regards to her problem or challenge and where you can take her. For example, "You're currently experiencing a high turnover that's affecting your bottom line and limiting your ability to expand and reach your goals . . ."

4. **Introduce value.**

   Value should make an appearance early on in your presentation, especially if you have executives in the room. For example, "We're going to talk about how to reduce turnover by as much as 50 percent based on what we were able to achieve with a similar customer . . ." Revisit the concept of value in Chapter 3.

5. **Provide an agenda.**

   Now that you've told your prospect what your destination is, lay out for them how you're going to get there with three to five agenda items focused on challenges and areas you can address. For example, "Today we're going to look at these three areas within your organization . . ." For tips on planning an agenda see Chapter 8.

6. **Identify each challenge, impact, and benefit.**

   As you go through the body of your presentation, explore each challenge, the impact of not resolving the challenge (or, if it's a "why buy us?" question, the impact of choosing another vendor), and the benefit you provide by solving each challenge. Chapter 6 discusses building your presentation's body.

7. Summarize your journey.

If it's been more than 45 minutes, you've covered a lot of material. As you move into your closing, take a moment to quickly recap the journey and highlight the benefits to reinforce them. For example, "We set out today to show you how we can help you lower your response times and increase your closing ratios in order to stay on track for hitting your goal of 25 million in global sales this year." Chapter 7 explains how to build an effective summary.

8. Bookend back to opening.

Call back to your opening hook by reminding your prospect of the story, quote, or insight you used earlier. For example, "We talked about how the invention of instrument flying opened up vast new opportunities for the airline industry by allowing planes to fly in all kinds of weather and circumstances, and how we can help you seize new opportunities by navigating the circumstances that are keeping you grounded today." Check out an example of bookending in Chapter 7.

9. Closing value statement and give your prospect one thing you want them to remember.

Reinforce your value proposition that you introduced in the opening and tell your prospect what one central idea you want him to take away from your presentation.

For example, "Based on what we've shown you, we're confident we can provide your sales team with the mobile responsiveness and the intuitive tools they need to respond to leads 50 percent faster and improve your closing ratio by 15 percent. I think you'll agree, faster is better." Find out how to develop the one thing you want your prospect to remember in Chapter 5.

10. Make a call to action.

You've delivered a compelling case, and your audience is smiling, so don't let the moment pass without asking for a clear, specific, and verifiable action. A *call to action* is a clear and specific statement of what you want your prospect to do after your presentation. For example, "I suggest we schedule a deep dive with our support team within the next 30 days. How does that sound?" Discover how to create and deliver an effective call to action in Chapter 7.

Chapter 5

Unleashing the Power of a Strong Opening

*I*magine you're sitting in front of your television deciding whether to watch a show. If you're like most people, if the show doesn't pique your interest in those first few seconds you change the channel or find something else to do. Your audience is no different than you. Although they probably won't physically leave the room if your opening fails to grab their interest (although don't bet on it), they can text, email, or simply mentally check out. Either way, you've lost them. And as any good performer knows, after you lose your audience, winning them back is an uphill battle.

All parts of your presentation aren't created equal. Your opening carries more than its fair share of weight when it comes to the overall success of your presentation. It affects not only whether your audience listens to you, but also how they listen to you. It creates a first impression, sets audience expectations, and influences buying decisions. That's a lot for a section that typically makes up less than 10 percent of your entire presentation! The opening is an area where the time you invest planning and practicing will pay big dividends throughout your entire presentation.

In this chapter you understand how a great opening can stack the odds in your favor when it comes to winning business. You discover precisely what you need to accomplish in that first minute and what ingredients go into the recipe for a successful opening. You find a variety of hooks to grab your audience's attention and find out how to combine them with value to drive home your key message. You see examples of several different types of openings that resonate with today's busy audiences. I also share some do's and don'ts for creating a strong opening that successfully grabs attention, creates interest, and sets the stage for you to deliver a winning presentation.

Understanding the Importance of the First Minute

Like an actor at curtain rise, your audience is going to be evaluating your performance from the very start. First impressions, although not always accurate, happen quickly and are often difficult to change. Your *opening* is your first impression with your audience and sets the tone and expectations for what is to come. Starting off with a long prologue, a weather report, or a thank you speech is a sure way to lose today's prospects. In order to make a favorable first impression and set you up for a successful presentation, your opening must accomplish certain key objectives that I explore in the following sections. I break down what goes into a good opening and look at the risk involved in winging your opening.

Recognizing opening objectives

A lot takes place during the opening, but if you boil it down, there are really three primary objectives, which are as follows:

Capture attention

Getting someone's attention isn't difficult. Wear a funny hat. Show photos of kittens. Give away a hundred dollar bill. But I'm assuming that isn't the kind of attention you want. Gratuitous attempts to capture a business audience backfire almost every time. You want to earn attention in a way that is relevant and appropriate for your audience and your purpose. Fortunately, some proven things naturally draw a human being's attention that you can leverage in your presentation, including:

- ✔ **Unpredictability:** Do something unlike any of the other presenters. Doing the same thing everybody else does is a sure way to be forgotten. Unfortunately, that's what you're doing every time you start a presentation with, "Thank you for having us. We're so happy to be here." Or "I want to start off by telling you a little bit about our company . . . " There are more ways to be unpredictable than predictable; for example, you could start off with a brief story, a quote, or a prop. Refer to the later section, "Eyeing the types of hooks for any audience."

✔ **Emotional:** People buy based on emotion and justify with logic. Emotions are a powerful thing, and if you can establish an emotional connection with your audience in the beginning, you can create greater connection throughout your presentation. Depending upon your goal, you may want to get a prospect to feel excitement, anticipation, or joy at the thought of a better way of doing what they're currently doing; conversely, it may be advantageous to have him feel frustrated or even a little angry about the way things are. Either way, if your prospect is emotionally invested in the beginning, he'll pay greater attention as you deliver your message.

✔ **Personal:** The opening should feel like it was created specifically for your prospect — not part of some standard deck. You can achieve this personal touch by including in your opening something of personal interest to your prospect. For example, if your prospect is an avid car collector and you start off with a story about a classic old Triumph you had and tie it to the reason you're there, you're sure to gain his interest. That's why the discovery process is so important — not only to uncover business insights, but personal insights as well that can help you connect with your audience.

✔ **Sensual:** In this context, I refer to pertaining to one's senses. Most sales presentations appeal to the audience's auditory and visual senses exclusively. Think about memorable experiences like Cirque du Soleil, Disneyland, or even the Apple store, where you can see, hear, feel, and taste (Okay, not at Apple) the product. The more senses you engage, the more attention you can claim. Although smell and taste don't usually lend themselves to sales presentations, using a prop is an effective way to get the audience involved. You also can think about using sensory descriptions beyond just visual and auditory when you're telling a story or describing an experience to your prospect. For example, consider the use of sensory language in the following opening:

"I love the idea of coffee. It smells rich and earthy with different flavors, like hazelnut, chocolate, and cinnamon. If only I were a coffee drinker. But the truth is, I don't like the taste of coffee. For me, the experience just doesn't live up to the promise. It reminds me of other solutions in the market who talk a lot about their ability to address the issue of government compliance, but in my experience, they just don't live up to the promise."

✔ **Movement:** When you're sitting in a meeting in progress and someone walks in late, without fail, everyone's head turns (except, perhaps the presenter.) Humans are wired to respond to movement. You can leverage this fact to increase attention during your opening. Most of the time presenters stand unnecessarily glued behind their laptop during a presentation. The opening is a great time to use your space, walk toward your audience, write on a flipchart, gesture, or pick up an object that supports what you're saying. Even a small effort to include movement greatly increases your audience's attention level. Find more tips on using movement in Chapter 11.

Define the situation

Your opening needs to address quickly both the problem and the solution in an engaging way that gets your prospect interested enough to take this journey with you. An effective way to do this is to show the disparity between the status quo and their desired outcome.

- ✔ **Status quo:** This is the reason you're giving the presentation — to address the problem or challenge that the prospect wants to or needs to overcome, or conversely, the opportunity that he is going to miss. *Status quo* is often where the prospect's *pain point resides.* Although your prospect certainly knows why you're there, it's valuable to set the stage as priorities or the level of pain may have shifted since you first set up the presentation. Your goal is to remind your prospect why the issue you're addressing should be his greatest priority.

- ✔ **Desired outcome:** After you establish where your prospect is, paint a picture of where he can go. Your prospect may have shared it with you in your prior discussions or you may have a few surprises up your sleeve. Although the opening isn't the place to go into great detail, you do want to give him an idea of what the payoff for staying tuned will be.

Sell the next minute

When I ask salespeople what their goal is in that first minute, many of them respond, "to make a sale." In a sense, they're correct. Even though you shouldn't be selling your product or service in your opening, you do need to sell your prospect on sticking around to hear the rest of your presentation, and the easiest way to do so is to make each minute count. If your current minute is compelling, your prospect will look forward to more of the same. You can also create some anticipation by dropping hints of interesting insights or value to come later in your presentation. Look for ways to make the next minute sound inviting without giving it all away up-front.

Thin slicing — the science behind first impressions

People's decisions aren't always rational. Numerous studies show that humans make many quick and important decisions based on a minimum of input. This process, called *thin slicing* is a type of unconscious judgment where people form a broad opinion of another person simply by observing a few seconds or a "thin slice" of their behavior. This is compounded by *confirmation bias,* which means after someone forms an opinion, he is usually on the lookout for other signs that support his initial assumption.

Eyeing the dangers of winging it

Many salespeople don't spend the necessary time to make sure their openings capture their audience members' attention. Rather they often wing it, saying whatever comes to mind. Unless you're a professional comedian, leaving your opening to chance is a big gamble. The sale may well be riding on it. Here's why:

✔ **Your audience is distracted.** The audience is seated, but the vice president is checking email, the department head is worrying about a mandatory budget cut, and a key influencer is tracking a storm that may affect her travel plans. Just because it's showtime doesn't mean your audience is paying attention. Your opening must break through the mental clutter and physical distractions that plague today's business audiences and pull them into the present.

Although you may have your own distractions prior to your presentation, as soon as you're on center stage, you have to push them aside. You have to be physically, mentally, and vocally engaged. Your audience has a less demanding role. They're seated, they're silent, and many seem to treat a presentation as an opportunity to catch up on email, texts, or the latest social media posts. You need to give them a compelling reason to put lingering thoughts or tempting distractions aside. After all, how exceptional the rest of your presentation is doesn't matter if your audience isn't listening!

✔ **First impressions are last impressions.** First impressions may not always be correct, but they do affect the way people listen to others and how people perceive others. According to research, many executives acknowledge that they decide to hire someone in the first few seconds of meeting them. The rare individual can overcome a negative first impression. Think back to singer Susan Boyle's audition on *The X Factor*. Everything about her first minute on stage screamed no. The audience snickered and the judges barely contained their skepticism until, of course, she hit those first superb notes. If, like me, you don't have a dramatic trick like that in your bag, you must make the most of your first impression to strengthen your last impression with your audience.

✔ **Decisions are made early.** If you've ever served on a jury, when did you decide whether the accused was guilty or not guilty? Did you remain completely impartial until all the evidence was laid out? Or did you arrive at your verdict during or immediately after the opening statement, as most jurors do according to a recent study? Trial lawyers spend a significant percentage of their time preparing their opening argument for this very reason: People start forming their decisions early. No, you're not on trial during your presentation, but you're making a case for your solution and the audience starts weighing the evidence right at the outset.

✔ **Memories are formed.** Buying decisions for some products and solutions, especially more complex or expensive ones, are rarely made on the spot. It may be days, weeks, or months before decision makers get together to discuss your proposal. Therefore, it's critical that your message is easy to remember. Research indicates that people start building memories when they're first introduced to a topic. Your opening can help ensure that your prospect has a strong, positive recall of your presentation.

Identifying the Qualities of an Effective Opening

There are more ways to open a presentation than Beyoncé has wardrobe changes, however successful openings share certain core qualities, including:

✔ **Cutting to the chase:** The *chase* is that point in your presentation that makes your audience sit up and pay attention. It eliminates unnecessary filler material that adds little in value and wastes precious time. What cutting to the chase *does* do is gain your audience's interest early on by zeroing in on a key issue, providing an insight, or introducing a benefit.

For example, think about where movies start. Does the director thank you for coming and braving the traffic, give you a backstory on why he made the movie, or describe where the characters went to school? No! Movies start with the car chase or the lovers meeting or some type of compelling action in order to grab the audience's attention. If this is your goal (and I assume it is), you must also cut to the chase.

✔ **Providing relevance:** Whatever you use to open your presentation, whether it's an insight, a quote, or a story, make sure that you quickly and clearly tie it to your topic. There's no quicker way to alienate your audience than to pull an opening bait and switch on them. Starting off with a cute story about your dog that has nothing to do with your presentation misses the mark entirely. Don't make your audience work too hard to make the connection.

✔ **Establishing value:** Busy prospects hate to have their time wasted and as much as you need to engage and connect, you have to remember why you were invited to the dance in the first place — to provide value. This is especially critical with *C-level executives* (high ranking members of a corporation whose titles often start with "C" — CEO, CIO, CFO). (Refer to Chapter 3 for specifics about C-level executives.) Fairly quickly in your opening, you need to let your prospect know what value you're going to add to his organization. Rather than listing all of your benefits, highlight a path to your prospect's overall objective. That way he can be confident that he's in good hands.

✔ **Setting expectations:** An interactive presentation needs to quickly introduce interaction. A challenging presentation needs to challenge. Your audience will take the lead from you on, not just the topic or tone, but things like, "What type of participation is required?" and "How closely do I need to pay attention?" Your opening should be congruent with the rest of your presentation or you may confuse your audience and damage your credibility.

✔ **Creating anticipation:** Think of your opening as a movie trailer where the goal is to give the audience just enough information to shell out money for a ticket. In the same way, the goal of the opening is to intrigue your audience so they will be motivated to see the rest of your presentation. You've probably seen a preview where they spell out the entire movie for you. Who needs to buy a ticket after that? Getting your audience excited about what's to come is great, but hold back a few plot twists to keep them in their seats.

✔ **Being succinct:** No matter how compelling your opening, your audience will lose patience and interest if it drags on too long. Shoot for two to three minutes — about the length of time you can expect to hold a prospect's attention before getting into the meat of the subject matter. That's also the length of time of commercial breaks, popular songs, and YouTube videos. That being said, if there's any chance your opening is even slightly less entertaining than the latest YouTube sensation you're probably safest to stay under three minutes.

✔ **Focusing on one thing:** Most experts agree on having one central idea as the core of your message in order to increase recall. For instance, imagine your prospect is telling his superior about your presentation the next day. What is the one thing you want to be sure he gets across? Of course, it's ideal if he remembers *everything*, but that's highly unlikely. Many presentations fail by trying to convey too much too soon so that nothing is particularly memorable.

The average American is exposed to 3,000 messages each day, so you need to focus your efforts on getting that one key message to stick rather than spreading it out over half a dozen that will get lost. Depending upon what your goals are, your one thing may be based on providing value, creating a sense of urgency, or reassuring your prospect that you're the right choice. Read more about creating your one thing in the next section.

You may be thinking, "That's a lot to accomplish for such a small percentage of my presentation," and you're right. Yet you must master the opening if you want to give your proposal the best possible chance for success.

Knowing the Building Blocks to Create a Strong Opening

An opening should have a natural, conversational flow to it; however, it still has some distinct parts. Here are the foundational blocks that put together, form a strong, memorable opening: (Figure 5-1 shows the building blocks to a strong opening.)

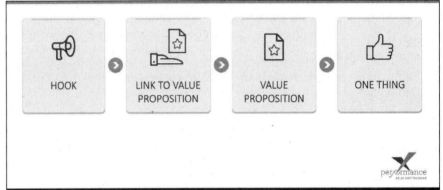

Figure 5-1:
Building
blocks to
a strong
opening.

Illustration by 24Slides

- ✔ **Hook:** A *hook* in your presentation draws the audience in and gets them interested or curious enough to give you their full attention. Check out the later section, "Eyeing the types of hooks for any audience" for different hook options.

- ✔ **Linking phrase:** Jumping right into your business reason immediately after your hook can be awkward. A *linking phrase* helps you transition conversationally as well as clarify what the connection is if it's not completely obvious to your audience. Here are some examples of linking phrases:

  - "In the same way . . . "

  - "In a similar fashion . . . "

  - "This reminded me of why we're here today . . . "

  - "How does this apply to your business?"

- ✔ **Status quo:** Quickly summarize where your prospect is at in regards to their problem or challenge. For example, "You're currently experiencing a high turnover that's affecting your bottom line and limiting your ability to expand." Refer to the earlier section, "Recognizing opening objectives" for more about the status quo and desired outcome.

✔ **Desired outcome:** Segue into where the prospect wants to end up or where you can take them, which will align with your value proposition. For example, "What we're going to show you today is how we can help you reduce turnover by as much as 50 percent and improve your ability to stay competitive and expand at a profitable rate."

✔ **One thing:** At the end of your opening tell your audience what that one thing you want them to take away from your presentation is. Doing so provides them with a point of reference so that every time you make a point that validates your one thing, your prospect will have a place to store that information in his brain. You can make it even easier for your prospect to remember by summarizing your one thing into a simple power-bite or catchphrase, thus making it sticky. That's not nearly as messy or difficult as it sounds. Look at the next section for ways to make your one thing memorable.

Making Your One Thing Sticky

Like a tag line for your theme, your one thing should have a similar universal quality to it. In other words, it's not simply another feature and benefit statement about your product or service, but something that rises above it to reveal a broader truth. Following are a couple of suggestions and sources for coming up with a memorable one thing:

✔ **The Advertisement Headline:** Advertisements typically have three parts: Headline, subhead, and body. The purpose of the headline is to summarize quickly the topic in a memorable way that makes you want to read the ad. It does this by creating curiosity, being pithy, or promising value. Here are some examples of headlines that could serve as an effective one thing for the right customer:

- "You can't afford to make this mistake."

- "What will you do with a 20 percent ROI?"

✔ **The Movie Pitch:** When writers pitch a script to movie studios, they often combine the ideas behind two successful movies to come up with an entirely new concept, for example: "It's like Die Hard on a bus" (*Speed*) or "Alien meets True Grit" (*Aliens vs. Cowboys*). This isn't limited to movies; by comparing what you do to something in popular culture you can create a quick, powerful visual for the audience. For example:

- "We are the Costco of drilling supplies."

- "You need the Jerry McGuire of real estate."

✔ **Ted Talks:** Ted (Technology, Education, and Design) Talks offer a great lesson in how powerful just a few well-chosen words are to summarize an idea. Many of the top-viewed Ted Talks use a short catchphrase or sound bite to encapsulate their message. Check out some of the best speakers and storytellers to get your creative juices flowing. For example:

- "Start with why." Simon Sinek

- "Lean in." Sheryl Sandberg (from her book inspired by her *Ted Talk*)

✔ **Twitter:** In the world of 140 characters or less, short and catchy phrases rule. Do a quick search or follow Twitter users who collect quotes, like these three:

- @TheBestQuotes

- @GreatestQuotes

- @QuotesGeek

✔ **Maxims, idioms, and proverbs:** Sayings that have been passed down through history can quickly and succinctly portray an idea. Sure, many of these have seen better days (The customer is always right), but some still hold up under the test of time (Fortune favors the bold). Try manipulating a common maxim or proverb, putting a fresh twist on it to suit your purposes. For example, "you can't judge a book by its cover," could be repurposed to: "You can't judge a company by its website."

Developing an Attention-Grabbing Hook

If you've ever picked up a book and been unable to put it down or turned on a television show and found yourself drawn in from the first few lines of dialogue, you've been hooked. You want to give your audience that same experience. Just as a book doesn't open with an autobiography of the author, your hook shouldn't open with an autobiography of your company. In the next sections I introduce a wide variety of hooks and explain why humor — on its own — isn't an effective hook.

Eyeing the types of hooks for any audience

In fishing, choosing the right hook can mean the difference between landing a big fish and throwing an undersized one back in the water. Selecting the right hook for your opening — one that gains attention and resonates with your audience to get them on board from the start. Here are types of hooks you can use in your opening — is just as critical.

Use alone or combine them, but don't overwhelm your audience by using more than three hooks in your opening. Save some hooks for other parts of your presentation, for instance, when you're transitioning from one section to another or need to reengage your audience after a lengthy session.

Use a quote

Opening your presentation with a memorable quote is a simple and effective way to grab your audience's attention. Look to your *theme,* the point you want to make or the challenge you're addressing, to help you come up with ideas for subject matter. A quick search on the Internet may yield a variety of choices. Here are a few general rules for using quotes:

- ✔ **Avoid overused quotes.** Give greater consideration to lesser-known quotes because many of the more familiar ones (think Steve Jobs, Bill Gates, Howard Schulz, Sam Walton, and Vince Lombardi) have been done to death in business and that familiarity can cause your audience's attention to wander. Worse, if they just heard that quote used in another vendor presentation, the quote is the sales equivalent of wearing the same dress to a party. To avoid possible redundancy, consider quotes from other countries or disciplines. For example:

  - "Vision without action is a daydream. Action without vision is a nightmare." Unknown author, Japan

  - "It is not the strongest of the species that survive, nor the most intelligent, but the one most responsive to change." Charles Darwin

- ✔ **Know your audience.** Quoting *Casablanca* to a millennial audience is sure to get you a bunch of blank stares just as quickly as quoting *Twilight* to a group of C-levels. Think about who is relevant to your audience, be it sports, entertainment, or business and avoid anything controversial by staying away from politics and religion.

Ask a question

Posing an intriguing question that leads into your topic is a quick and easy way to engage your audience. People are naturally curious and a good question can stimulate their thinking right away. Here are some things to think about when opening with a question:

Avoid the duh answer

Although generalizing what a good question is for your audience or topic is difficult, identifying a bad one is easy. They are questions that are complicated (such as more than one question or multiple questions). They are leading or they make the listener go, "duh." For example:

- ✔ "How many of you like to save money?" Duh.

- ✔ "If I could show you how this could improve your efficiency ten times, would that be something that would have value to your organization?" Duh.

- ✔ A better question might be: "When you have two equally qualified candidates for a position, how do you determine who to hire?"

Decide on the type of question

Different questions generate different responses. You dictate the type of response you receive by the type of question you ask. You can use three types of questions:

- ✔ **Rhetorical:** This type of question gets your audience pondering the answer without requiring a verbal response. It's a common way to start a presentation, and even though you don't expect an answer from your audience, make sure that you take a moment to pause and let your audience think about the answer before you move on.

- ✔ **Literal:** Asking your audience a question and expecting to receive an answer is a great way to set the rules of engagement early. To increase the probability of getting a response, keep the following in mind:

  - **Make sure it doesn't sound like a rhetorical question.** If your audience is confused as to whether or not you want an answer, they'll likely remain silent. Be very clear in your mind that you want an answer and that your tone and eye contact naturally convey your intention to your audience.

  - **Don't fill the silence.** I know that it's uncomfortable to have a room full of people staring back at you in silence, but you have to give them time to grapple with the answer. Remember, you're laying the ground rules for how your audience should participate. If you answer your own questions in the beginning, they will be even less likely to speak up later in your presentation.

  - **Be fairly certain of the answer.** Do some preliminary testing with your audience, either during your discovery conversations or prior to the start of your presentation so you know that the question is relevant and you have a sense of what the answer will be. Just in case, always have a back-up question ready in case the question you planned on using misfires.

- ✔ **Hypothetical.** Posing a what-if question allows your audience to envision what the future could look like, for worse or better, with or without your solution. Give them just enough detail to form a picture in their minds before you jump in and start to paint it for them.

Shock and awe

Opening with a startling statement or fascinating fact that shocks and awes can pull even the most technology-dependent people away from their smartphones. Be prepared to defend your facts or quote your source and always make sure that it's relevant to your topic. For example, "Every two days we create as much information as we have since the dawn of time," would be an effective kickoff for a presentation about improving data management. The same quote for a presentation on improving patient care? Probably not.

Consider this example:

> "In a survey of more than 500 business professionals in your industry from 71 countries, 75 percent admitted that they didn't have full visibility of their supply chain. Visibility is critical to any organization. Limited visibility is like driving with blinders on. Without a completely unobstructed view, not only are you in danger of running into other vehicles, but you are also at risk for missing the exit to your destination. Today, we're going to show you how we can help you increase visibility by as much as 50 percent so that you can make fully informed decisions that drive greater operational efficiency and innovation. Visibility creates opportunity."

Tell a personal story

Most business audiences are prepared for your presentation to open with a typical corporate overview or a rehashing of the issues to be addressed. Starting with a story provides an unexpected twist that quickly gains attention. It also provides the opportunity to create an early emotional connection with your audience and increases the likelihood of your message being remembered. In other words, why wouldn't you want to open with a story?!

You can use many types of stories: metaphors, analogies, personal stories, customer stories, and so on. Which type you use depends upon a number of factors, including your audience, the tone, your purpose, and so on. For example, you may use a personal story to create a stronger emotional connection with your prospect or help him to see an issue in a different light. Or, you may use a customer success story for a prospect that needs social proof. See more tips on how to use stories in Chapter 12.

Don't put your audience on notice that you're going to tell a story. "I'd like to start with a little story . . ." or "here's a story that made me think of you" are examples of trying to be thoughtful but actually shooting yourself in the foot by giving your audience a chance to put up resistance. Giving your story a preface like this defeats the purpose — to grab their attention. Consider this example of a personal story used in an opening:

> "I was skiing in Vail on a gorgeous spring day with my husband and ten-year-old son. As we approached the mountaintop on the lift, the white mountains against the blue sky were absolutely stunning, and

I said, "What a Kodak moment." My son looked at me and said, "Mom, what's a Kodak?" It struck me that there's now a whole generation that doesn't know that Kodak at one time owned 95 percent of the film and processing market. Unfortunately, they made one big mistake. They didn't prepare for the future. At its height Kodak stock was worth $95 a share. Does anyone know what Kodak stock is worth now? (Pause, take answers. Reveal the coin.) A nickel.

"I know that you have other priorities besides upgrading your system, but what I'm going to show you today is why you can't afford to put off having the best-in-class solution to give you a competitive edge. The future is now."

Rely on a prop

Using an object can add a touch of drama to your opening and intrigue your audience. If it's an object your audience is unfamiliar with, they will be eager to hear what it is. If it's something that they are familiar with (keys, a photo, or a book), they'll pay close attention to discover what its relevance is to your topic. Give special consideration to how and when you reveal your prop because if it's something that arouses a lot of curiosity, having it exposed earlier than necessary will split your prospect's attention between you and your prop. Check out Chapter 14 for more tips on using props effectively.

Share some insights

Because you likely interact with other businesses, particularly those within your prospect's industry or niche, you have the benefit of being able to offer a broader perspective that can be of great value to your prospective customer. For example, "We've found that 85 percent of our customers in your industry were experiencing higher sales volume, but actually losing market share" is an insight that serves dual purposes: It gives you credibility that you have experience and knowledge in your prospect's industry and reinforces the reason why they need your company. Of course, you don't want to reveal anything possibly confidential; after all, if they end up being a customer, they wouldn't want you spilling any top secrets to competitors.

The unfunny truth about humor

You may have noticed that I didn't include humor as a hook in the previous section. No, I didn't make a mistake. I love humor, but humor for humor's sake isn't a sufficient hook. Without appropriate relevance, humor by itself can appear both gratuitous and inappropriate. On the other hand, humor combined with one of the other hooks can be very effective: a funny story, an amusing quote, a funny prop. They all can work *if* they're relevant and appropriate, and you're comfortable using the humor.

The skinny on using humor

Even comedians need a few guidelines when using humor. If you're going to attempt to use humor with another type of hook, keep the following rules in mind:

✔ **Don't tell your audience something is funny.** Adding "This is funny" begs the response, "I'll be the judge of that." Humor stands on its own; you shouldn't have to promote it.

✔ **Keep canned humor in the can.** Stale old jokes, puns, or anything that causes your audience to collectively groan should be avoided.

✔ **Stay away from stereotypes.** This is especially true in a presentation where you don't want to risk offending anybody. When in doubt, don't.

✔ **Watch the extreme sarcasm.** Some people love sarcasm, whereas others find it negative or grating. Used sparingly and appropriately, it can be effective if it jives with your personality.

✔ **Humor is all in the . . . timing.** Practice your funny bit with an audience to see what the ideal timing is.

✔ **Don't mess up the punch line.** The number of jokes or stories that have been blown, botched, or forgotten must be astronomical. Don't make your audience or yourself suffer. Commit your punch line to memory.

✔ **Deliver it with confidence.** If you're going to tell a joke or a funny story, you can't be the least bit sheepish or embarrassed or your audience will pick up on it. Just jump in to the water and start swimming.

Just to be sure, ask someone who will tell you the truth about whether something is funny or not. Then test it out on several people who are representative of your audience. Nothing will suck the confidence out of you faster than starting off with a joke that bombs. You don't want to put yourself and your audience through the pain. If humor isn't your strength, don't sweat it. You have many other alternatives to choose from to engage your audience. If you want to include humor with one of the other hooks, check out the nearby sidebar for ways to do so.

Keeping Track of Some Key Do's and Don'ts for Openings

In addition to the suggestions that I outline in this chapter, there are some other things you want to do and some things you want to avoid doing in your opening.

✔ **Don't save the good stuff.** An award-winning comedy writer gave me this invaluable tip: Start with your best joke, end with your second best, and put everything else in the middle, because if you don't start strong, your audience isn't going to hear your good stuff.

✔ **Do know your first line.** Maybe you're someone who doesn't like to memorize what you're going to say. Even so, I strongly recommend committing your first line to memory. With nerves at their peak, getting your first line out without any hitches allows you to ride a wave of confidence as you move into the meat of your presentation.

✔ **Do test it.** Sometimes an idea that seems crystal clear in your head isn't obvious to your audience. It may just need a simple tweak to help your audience connect the dots. That's why running your opening by trusted friends or colleagues is a great practice to get into. Listen to the input. Check to see if your opening was clear and whether you need to add or cut anything. You can even give them the list from the earlier section "Identifying the qualities of an effective opening" and ask them to rate you on things like whether your opening was relevant, provided value, and cut to the chase.

✔ **Do rehearse it.** The opening is too critical to leave to chance. Rehearse it out loud. Then rehearse it again out loud. Work on content first, edit as you go, and then you can start to refine it and bring it to life by adding in vocal variation and movement. Find great tips on rehearsing your presentation in Chapter 11.

✔ **Do go for it.** Your opening sets the stage so don't be tentative. It's an area where you can and should show your personality. Half-hearted attempts to tell a story or anecdote fall flat. Fully commit to your opening for best results.

✔ **Don't look back.** So you didn't say a phrase the way you intended to or hit a punch line just right. Whatever you do, don't let your audience know that you're anything less than 100 percent satisfied with it. Whatever came out of your mouth (assuming it's not inappropriate or incorrect) own it. Apologizing only calls attention to something that your audience probably didn't notice anyway.

Always have two openings ready to go — one for C-level and one for end users. That way if an executive shows up late, you can still start on time and give another quick opening to get the key latecomers up to speed without boring the rest of your audience by repeating yourself. Check out more tips for managing your audience and the clock in Chapter 14.

Chapter 6

Ratcheting Up the Tension as You Build Your Case

. . . .

In This Chapter

▶ Exploring the parts of a persuasive case

▶ Creating urgency by building up tension

▶ Engaging emotions and driving attention

▶ Selecting topics with a customer perspective

▶ Structuring the body around your value proposition

. . . .

You have your prospect's attention with your opening. Now what? Eighty to 90 percent of your presentation is contained in the body. If your presentation's body doesn't deliver on the promise of your opening, your prospect may not be awake for the closing. The body is the meat and potatoes of your presentation, but meat and potatoes can be pretty bland without a little spice or gravy. Many sales presentations fall apart in this crucial middle section, devolving into one long monologue or product brochure. During your body, eyes can start to wander toward phones, exits, and fire escapes — anything to break up the monotony. The midsection of most presentations derail because they lose sight of the goal — building a persuasive case that advances the sale — and fail to take into account the new rules of engagement and attention.

What you include and how you structure your presentation's body determines whether your presentation moves the sale forward or has your prospect hitting the snooze button. Most sales presentations organize the body around their product, throwing in as many features and benefits as possible in the time allotted hoping to hit the winning number. Doing so isn't a strategy. It's a spin of the roulette wheel.

In this chapter I cover what needs to be included in order to build a persuasive case and the importance of triggering your prospect's emotions and maintaining her attention. I explore why you need to turn up the tension and create urgency and how to build in proof points and benefits into your topics. I examine how to organize the body of your presentation in a customer-focused way that supports your value proposition. Finally, I show you how to break your presentation's body down into persuasive, consumable chunks that give your presentation a natural rhythm and make it easier for you to close.

The body is the second part of a three-part structure of a persuasive case. Chapter 5 addresses your opening and Chapter 7 focuses on your closing.

Defining the Elements of a Persuasive Case

In the body of your presentation you set out to build a persuasive case for your product or service by introducing and exploring a list of topics. These topics eventually become your agenda, which I cover more in Chapter 8. After kicking off your presentation with an opening that grabs your prospect's attention and sets up a contrast between the way things currently are and the way that they could be with your product or service, your body needs to show your prospect just how you're going to make that happen.

In a "Why buy you?" situation, you show your prospect how you're going to take her from her status quo to her desired outcome better than your competition. In a "Why buy?" situation where you're competing with the status quo, you show her how you can get her from her existing conditions to a new reality — and why the new reality is better.

You spend the vast majority of your face — or virtual — time with your prospect in your presentation's body. As such, it can feel like a large, bottomless chasm to cross if you don't have a good solid structure underneath your feet. In order to build that structure, you need to know what materials go into it. Here are five elements that can help you build a strong body that sets you up for a successful close.

Creating a logical structure

Like any legal case, your presentation must be structured in a way that is logical and organized well and builds to an obvious conclusion. Trial lawyers spend weeks, often months, building a persuasive case for their clients. I'm assuming you don't have that long. Therefore, you need some help. As anyone who has taken on a home improvement project with the attitude of

"How hard can this be? I can do this myself!" knows, building from scratch is difficult and time-consuming, filled with lots of mismatched parts and trips back and forth to the neighborhood hardware store.

The next sections show you how to avoid wasting time and effort by applying a tried-and-true structure that helps you easily identify and define your topics; provides pre-built-areas for persuasive points, proof, and benefits; takes into account attention spans; and fits into the time constraints you must work with. Much easier than any do-it-yourself project!

Engaging emotion

Logic is never enough in sales. If it were, closing ratios would be through the roof. You must also present your case in a way that triggers your prospect's emotions. The most persuasive cases are a combination of logic and emotion. Although salespeople may give emotion some attention during the opening and closing of their presentations, they often forget about engaging their prospect on an emotional level during the middle of their presentation. This long, dry trek through the Sahara quickly loses your prospect's interest — and along with it any emotional connection you worked hard to establish in your opening.

As Chapter 4 explains, emotions are powerful aids in gaining your prospect's interest and increasing her ability to remember your message. Like attention, engagement isn't something you do once and then you're done. Especially in longer presentations, you need to continue to find opportunities to engage your prospect on an emotional level. Here are some ways to ensure your prospect stays engaged during the body of your presentation:

- ✔ **Tell a story.** Stories aren't just for openings and closings. The body of your presentation offers many opportunities to tell a quick story or anecdote about your features and benefits. Often you're tasked with talking about or showing processes or features that don't rank as blockbuster material, yet they're necessary to prove value or reassure your prospect that you're capable of performing them. Giving a quick story about a feature — how it's used, why it's important, and so on — gives it some much needed color and context that can help your prospect connect to it more easily. You can also use a personal story or an anecdote to illustrate your point and make an idea stand out in a sea of facts. Refer to Chapter 12 for specific ways to use storytelling in your presentation.

- ✔ **Show a day in the life.** When you introduce a feature or process, place your prospect — or someone within your prospect's organization — in the shoes of a product user and take her through the process of using your product or feature. For example, if you're presenting a medical device to a team of nurses and physicians, you can tell the story from a nurse's perspective. For example, "When a patient's chart indicates that he needs to be tested, you simply touch the display and enter your code."

✔ **Interpret statistics.** Talking about facts and figures is sometimes necessary, but if the middle section of your presentation is simply one graph or pie chart after another, even the most analytical members of your audience may beg for mercy. Connecting with cold, hard facts is difficult for most people. Make numbers more than an intellectual exercise by interpreting those stats for your prospect. Why are those stats important to your prospect? What do those numbers mean? For example, if I told you that we could save you 5 percent in IT costs per year, that may sound pretty good but have little emotional impact to you with nothing to compare it to. If I told you that a 5 percent savings in IT costs equated to 5,000 bottles of your favorite wine, I bet you would have a much clearer picture of the value — and you'd remember it a lot longer.

✔ **Use metaphors.** Metaphors or similes are especially useful when discussing features and processes that may be complex and difficult to grasp for your prospect. Comparing a lesser known item to something that is more familiar to your prospect makes it easier for her to understand and promotes memory.

For example, "Think of this feature as a Swiss army knife. Instead of having to collect all of these tools from multiple sources, you have everything you need right here in one spot."

Creating urgency

Watching salespeople deliver the body of a presentation would make one think it didn't matter one way or the other if the salesperson received her commission next month or next year. Each topic you cover must contribute to creating a sense of urgency within your prospect to get the problem resolved and get it resolved now. Not someday.

Although more traditional presentation structures place the emphasis on creating urgency in the closing, if you haven't primed the pump in the body, your closing can be like trying to get water out of a dry well. In order to move your prospect from where she is now to where you want her to go, you need to create tension by adding complications. Just like in the movies where a hero is at first reluctant to get involved — up until the situation has gotten so out of control and the tension so great that she is eventually compelled to take action, your prospect needs to have a compelling reason to take action as well.

Even though signing a contract may not be the heroic actions people have come to expect in the movies, it doesn't make your prospect's task any easier. If you're asking your prospect to change her perspective, risk her reputation, or change the way she's done something for 20 years, simply parading a bunch of evidence out and asking her to evaluate it isn't going to cut it.

People are prone to *homeostasis* — the desire to stay put, especially if the problem doesn't appear that bad to your prospect. Although it may appear bad to you, remember that your prospect has been living with the problem, adapted to it, and likely put a few bandages on it. Even a rut can be pretty comfortable if you decorate it nicely. You must give your prospect a strong nudge to get out of her comfort zone if you want her to take action at the end of your presentation.

The closing is too long to wait to start to close. Build a persuasive case and start to increase the tension in the body of your presentation to make your closing self-evident.

Amplifying the tension

In your presentation's body you must continue to increase the tension by exploring with the prospect the impact of either not addressing their challenge or using a competitor to address the prospect's challenge. Ratcheting up the tension creates urgency within your prospect to solve the problem, which is especially important when prospects have multiple priorities or challenges and limited time and resources, or if you're battling against the status quo.

By widening the gap between pain and relief and exploring the impact of not making a change — or of making the wrong change — you can increase your prospect's attention, keep her engaged, improve message recall, and speed up the sales cycle.

Building tension without getting tense

Many new sales philosophies embrace the idea of creating tension in order to move a prospect off of the tough to crack "no change" position. If you cringe at the thought of talking to your prospect about the impact of not making a change or the pitfalls of going with a competitor's product, remember that you don't have to deliver this news with ominous organ music playing in the background or while standing on a soapbox. In fact, I recommend that you don't.

Although increasing the tension can be uncomfortable, in reality you're simply exploring consequences. The consequences of no decision or a bad decision are real and sometimes quite painful. Just as in the legal world, ignorance of the law of consequences doesn't make a person immune from their effects. Supporting your prospect's denial ultimately doesn't serve either you or your prospect.

The fact is that more people are willing to take a risk to avoid pain than to seize an opportunity. In fact, recent research on the topic indicates that people have a three times stronger preference to avoid loss than to achieve gain. If you're still uncomfortable, ask yourself the following three questions to determine whether addressing the consequences makes sense for you:

✔ Are there negative consequences to indecision or a wrong decision?

✔ Can you help your prospect avoid potential negative consequences?

✔ Is your prospect able to take the steps necessary to avoid negative consequences?

If you can answer yes to all three of these questions, you owe it to your prospect — and yourself — to speak out.

Maintaining attention

Getting your prospect's attention is easy compared to keeping her attention. If you don't work to maintain your prospect's attention and keep it from lapsing throughout the body of your presentation, you're at risk of having your case thrown out and being charged with the crime of committing a boring presentation. Keeping your prospect engaged while you build a persuasive case for why she should buy your product or service and why she should buy it now is critical to the success of your presentation.

So here's a math question for you: If your prospect's attention falls to its lowest point after ten minutes on a topic, which research indicates, how do you keep them engaged during the 45 to 90 minutes stretch that makes up the body of your presentation? The answer is you must build in places to renew her attention — ideally, every seven to ten minutes. Some thoughtful advance planning can counteract those natural spots in your presentation where attention starts to wane.

Here are some proven ways to grab attention that can be built into your presentation's body:

✔ **Change the subject.** The easiest and most natural point to reengage your prospect is when you're changing topics — moving from one agenda item to the next. In a perfect world all topics take seven to ten minutes to cover, but that's not always the case, so you need to work in some other places and ways to regain your prospect's attention. See Chapter 8 on how to make your agenda interactive.

✔ **Introduce a prop.** If you've been talking about one subject for nearly ten minutes and are only halfway through, break it up with something new that relates to what you're discussing. To do so, tell a quick anecdote or story, show a video clip, or write on the flipchart or whiteboard. New stimulus creates renewed interest.

✔ **Interact with your audience.** One of the quickest ways to get your prospect's attention is to ask for it. Here are a few ideas on getting your prospect involved:

- **Check in.** Asking if anyone has any questions on what you've just covered is an effective way to engage your prospect as well as find out if your message is resonating or if you need to clarify a point.

- **Use names.** Nothing gets people's attention like hearing their own name. If your audience is reluctant to jump in after you've posed a question, choose an individual in your audience to direct your question to and ask her by name. Doing so usually gets the ball rolling.

- **Take a poll.** If your topic lends itself to it, you can do a quick poll or survey to get a consensus before you jump back into the topic or move to the next. Asking your audience to make a choice gets your prospect actively involved and interested in your presentation's next section. Find out more about polls and interacting with your audience in Chapter 14.

Interacting with your audience can eat up a lot of time, so be sure and watch the clock. Intersperse audience interaction with other less time-consuming techniques to help you stay on track. Chapter 14 has more on engaging and managing your audience.

Providing proof

In order to have your prospect believe you, she needs proof. Making fantastic claims at the end of your presentation without providing some small pieces of evidence along the way can evoke skepticism in your prospect. Build up to it. Save the big reveal for the closing but substantiate some smaller claims along the way to prime your prospect to accept your final results.

Producing evidence — in the form of facts and figures, testimony, or industry statistics — throughout your presentation as you build your case is like bringing witnesses to the stand. Each one adds to the overall impression of a strong, overwhelming case with a preponderance of evidence in your favor. It also makes your closing easier to deliver and self-evident. At the conclusion you want your prospect to say to herself, "That makes sense. I can see how they could get there." Not "What are they claiming they can do? Is that a typo?"

Supporting your case: New persuasion techniques for judge and jury

Lawyers are always looking for new techniques for persuading a judge or jury to take their side in a case. The most important factor they've found in the ability to persuade is, not surprisingly, making a strong argument for your case and being seen as a credible source. But recent research on the subject of persuasion reveals some surprising new ways everyone — not just lawyers — can improve their persuasive abilities, including:

✔ **Eliminating hesitant or vague language from your delivery.** The "ah's, umms, and errs" must go, and replace the "maybes, sort ofs, somes, and a lots" with clear specific language. Check out a local Toastmasters group if you need help in this area.

✔ **Asking your prospect to think of some reasons why your position makes sense.** This works because much of the persuasion process happens internally within that ongoing dialogue in your prospect's head. Giving her time to figure it out and come to a conclusion is a powerful persuasive tool and just one reason why stories work so well to change a person's mind.

✔ **Making your strongest case when people are worn down and more receptive to adopting new ideas.** Although it sounds like an unfair advantage, people are more easily persuaded when they're tired. Using this finding is okay as long as you aren't the reason your prospect is worn down.

✔ **Revealing to your prospect some of your competitor's weakest arguments.** This one is like "popping the balloon," but instead of taking on the big points in your competitor's case, you use the weaker ones. The theory is that it allows your prospect to build up some resistance to your competitor's larger attacks — sort of like a flu shot.

Developing Customer-Focused Topics: Focus on Value

The vast majority of sales presentations are organized around what your product or service can do, in other words, features. This may be logical from your perspective, but it makes little sense from where your prospect sits. You're not selling features. You're selling what your features can help your prospect do. In other words, you're selling value. Although some salespeople are starting to tailor their opening to address their prospect's unique challenge and introduce a custom value proposition, they usually lose their customer-focus during the body of the presentation, falling back into a company-centric approach that focuses almost exclusively on their own products, services, features, and capabilities. Selecting topics based on your products or features comes across as one long sales pitch. You want to present your message in a way that your prospect has the best chance of understanding and remembering.

Consider the following typical lead-in into the body of a presentation:

> "Our goal today is to help you become more efficient in your workplace so that you can continue to grow at your projected rate. Here are the topics we're going to address today: our analytics evaluator, our one-touch report-writer, our metrics converter, and our optimization tool."

All of these topics, from the analytics evaluator to the optimization tool, have at least one thing in common — they're all given from the salesperson's point of view. It's easy to slip into auto-pilot and start talking about your product or service in terms you frequently use. But that's not going to resonate with your prospect. They aren't in your business. Don't mistake the fact that they did some due diligence on you and are able to use some of your terminology for a thorough understanding of your industry or product. Nor should they have to. It's your job to understand theirs and make the connection between the two as clearly as possible.

In these sections you discover how to step into your prospect's shoes to gain a customer-focused perspective. You find out how to use value to determine your topics, how many topics you should have, and the elements that go into each topic.

Gaining an outsider's perspective

You may have a ready list of topics in mind, for example, "I want to show them our mobile app that allows customers to check the status of their order in real time!" But take a step back first. What sounds good to you may not be the best choice for your prospect. A good topic is customer focused and organizes information around a customer's challenges, needs, or use as opposed to what you do or how you do it.

In order to build a persuasive case for your solution, you must be able to see your product or service through your prospect's eyes. You must present your case in a way that speaks directly to your prospect, as if your product were made just for her. However doing it is easier said than done. The problem is that you know too much. But you must try and cast it aside and look at your product or service as an outsider if you really want to get a sense of how to connect your topics to your prospect's interests and needs.

Here are two ways to help you to adopt an outsider's point of view:

- ✔ **Forget what you know.** Set aside everything you know about your product, your features, and your marketing. Start with a blank slate when you want to get customer focused. Prospects are deluged with facts and figures from dozens, maybe hundreds, of vendors. They can't possibly remember or have the depth of knowledge you do. Let go of all your terminology and think in terms of what your product does, why someone needs it, and what would an outsider call your features or processes.

✔ **Step into your prospect's shoes.** Immerse yourself in your prospect's circumstances, the challenges, the opportunities, the competitive options, and answer these questions:

- What *if* you were in this situation?

- What would you want to know about this product?

- What are the five most important points about this product?

- What might convince you to move off your current product and adopt this one?

The answers you come up with can help you to get a much better handle on what is really relevant to your prospect.

✔ **Ask your prospect.** If you have an internal advocate within your prospect's organization, you can simply ask her what the four to five major issues are that the audience wants to see addressed or get some feedback on the topics you're considering covering. This verification can often save you from assumptions that may take you way off track.

Taking a look at your product or service from your prospect's perspective is an extremely valuable exercise. It can help you gain some needed insight and structure your presentation around your customer instead of your product or company. Use this information to test your topics and refer back to as you build your presentation's body. By applying these questions to the earlier example, you can come up with a very different list of topics:

"Our goal today is to help you become more efficient in your workplace so that you can continue to grow at your projected rate. Here's what we're going to cover over the next hour: The goldmine in your data, one-touch reports, actionable metrics, and workflow optimization.

As you can see, this example is not only more customer focused, but it's also more interesting.

Organizing your body around value

If you don't use your product or service or your features as topics, where do you get your topics? You need look no further than your *value proposition,* the results that the prospect can expect to receive from your product or service. The value proposition is an easy and natural place to start searching for topics to build your case. A presentation that is organized around value starts off on the right track and has a good chance of staying on track through the course of your presentation. Chapter 3 discusses how to develop a solid value proposition based on discovery and insight.

Gaining customer focus with the actor's Magic If

The Magic If is an acting tool developed by Constantin Stanislavski, a Russian actor and director living in the late 1800s and early 1900s who believed in the actor's truthful pursuit of a character. He proposed that actor's truly understand their character's motivations and actions by asking themselves a series of questions based on the Magic If, like "What if I were in the same situation as my character?" or "What would I do if I found myself in my character's circumstances?" By answering these questions, the actor could play roles that were even unlike himself with a surprising degree of honesty. The answer to these simple questions is the key to being able to not just understand another person's motivations, but to empathize as well.

Using your value proposition as your North Star keeps you in good position to deliver a customer-focused presentation. Each topic you discuss within the body of your presentation should contribute toward substantiating your value proposition. Within your value proposition are the topics, or the elements that make up your topics and are represented in your agenda (refer to Figure 6-1).

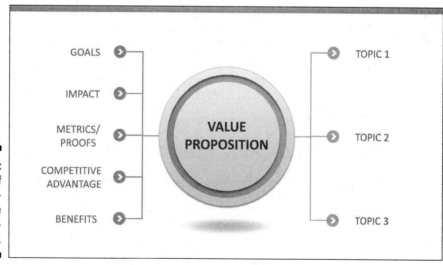

Figure 6-1: Diagram of deriving topics from the value proposition.

Illustration by 24Slides

Determining the ideal number of topics

In order to determine the number of topics in your presentation and the time you spend on each topic, you must take into consideration several factors, including:

- ✔ **Know how to address your prospect's expectations.** What topics do you need to cover to meet your prospect's expectations?

- ✔ **Keep recall in mind.** The number of items that people can easily remember is around three or four. If you have ten topics, your prospect has no chance of remembering them unless she is a national memory champion. This is where the concept of chunking comes into play that I discuss in Chapter 4. Grouping two or three like topics together to give you a fewer number of groups increases the odds of your prospect remembering your presentation.

- ✔ **Consider presentation length.** If you're presenting for three, four, or even seven hours, you obviously have more topics to cover than if you're presenting for 30 minutes. Aiming for three to five topics is a good goal for most presentations. You can find some guidelines for longer and multiday presentations in Chapter 19.

- ✔ **Work with attention spans.** People's sustained attention — the ability to focus on one thing — is anywhere from 5 to 20 minutes. Stay on one topic for longer than 30 minutes and you're going to lose your prospect — or at the very least, wear her down. If you want your prospect's full attention for each topic, keep your topics less than 20 minutes if possible.

- ✔ **Avoid choppiness.** Too many short topics — five minutes or less — makes your presentation sound abrupt and disjointed. Try combining shorter topics into a larger topic for a less rushed, more natural flow.

Arriving at the right number of topics

Taking into consideration all of the preceding factors to arrive at the ideal number of topics for your presentation may feel like arm wrestling an octopus. The following steps provide you with a guideline to help you balance presentation topics, avoid overshooting your time, all while managing the attention of your prospect:

1. **Determine the real time you have available to present the body of your presentation.**

   Calculate real time as total presentation time minus introductions, opening, closing, transitions, breaks, and questions. For example:

   60 minutes – 2 minutes introductions – 5 minutes open and agenda – 3 minutes transitions – 5 minutes close = 45 minutes

2. **Make a list of all of the topics you want to cover that can help support your value proposition.**

Brainstorm all possible topics; no idea is a bad idea. Revisit your discovery notes for ideas. See Chapter 2 for tips on finding information.

3. **Narrow your list down to five to seven to ten at most relevant.**

Cut down your list by asking yourself how closely each topic aligns with your value proposition. If it scores low, cut it.

4. **Estimate how much time you need to address each topic.**

Keep in mind that you aren't just presenting the topic, but need to provide some background on it, explore the impact, provide proof, and deliver a benefit, so budget time accordingly. I discuss doing so in the next section. For example:

6 topics at 15 minutes each = 90 minutes or 1.5 hours

5. **Prioritize your topics.**

If you're like most salespeople, you have more to cover than time to cover it. Make sure you put the must-cover topics at the top of your list. Go through the rest of the steps to further wean down your list.

6. **Consider consolidation.**

Determine whether any of your shorter topics are a sub-group of a larger topic. For example, two of your topics may be "one-touch reporting" and "actionable metrics." If both are fairly short, you can combine them to fall under the larger topic of "taking action on your data."

7. **Consider splitting up topics.**

If you only have two topics to address and you plan on spending 90 minutes covering them, find a way to break them up into more audience-friendly sections; otherwise you'll be pushing the limits of your prospect's attention span. For example, if one of your two topics is "increasing awareness," consider breaking it down into two separate topics "frequency of message" and "audience reach."

8. **Ask for more time.**

If after going through the previous steps and pruning your topic list to as succinct a number as possible, you find that you simply can't cover everything you need to in order to make a persuasive case in the time you're allotted, consider asking your prospect for more presentation time. Position it as a benefit to your prospect — providing her with more insights and value — and you may be able to get it.

Although no definitive rule specifies the number of topics to use, if you aim for three to five, you'll be in-line with people's ability to recall information and stay focused.

Here are two examples of topics derived from value propositions:

Value proposition: "Today we're going to show you how we can help you grow sales by increasing awareness of your brand among customers and reaching them more frequently through various touch points throughout the day."

Based on this example, three of your topics could be:

- ✔ Increase brand awareness
- ✔ Generate frequent engagement
- ✔ Create multiple touch points

Value proposition: "We can help you speed up the time it currently takes you to get a product to market by 70 percent, increase visibility into your customers' buying habits, and respond quickly to changes in the market.

Based on this example, the topics could be:

- ✔ Speed to market
- ✔ Customer visibility
- ✔ Response to change

Building out a topic

After you have your list of topics, you get to discuss your cool features — but not so fast. This is the heart of your case. You need to put some sound strategy around it. Introducing the topic and just jumping into features can undo all the planning you've done so far. You need to shed some light on why the topic is important, how it relates to your prospect's current challenge, and the impact it's having on the prospect's business, all before you start talking about features.

Because you may devote up to 20 minutes on a topic, you need to have a game plan about what goes in that time. The strategy involves introducing the challenge, as it relates to the topic, the impact that it's having on the prospect's business, how your product/service addresses it, back it up with proof, and cap it off with a benefit. In other words, you're providing much more than just a list of your features and all the cool things they can do.

As you go through the body of your presentation, explore each challenge, what the impact is of not resolving the problem (or, if it's a "why buy us?" focus, what the impact is of choosing another vendor) and what the benefit is from solving each challenge.

Here are the building blocks for covering a topic.

Topic 1: A key outcome from your value proposition.

- ✔ **Challenge of topic 1:** Identify what the challenge is related to the topic. Provide some context on the challenge to help your prospect to gain a deeper understanding of why it's important. Note why it is a challenge and when it's a challenge.

- ✔ **Impact:** Pinpoint the impact of this challenge. Determine what it means in terms of time, effort, and money. A good technique for doing so is called *raising the stakes,* which means increasing the tension to a peak by exploring the consequences of no decision or the wrong decision. You can read more about it in Chapter 12.

- ✔ **Resolution:** Outline for your prospect how your product or service solves the challenge. This is the point where you discuss or show how specific features or processes addressing this particular challenge.

   Your features probably do more than just address one individual challenge, but it's important to stay focused on the specific challenge you're discussing. Veering off into other functions, at the very least, confuses or waters down your message, and at its worst, brings up a problem you may not be prepared to address.

- ✔ **Proof:** Show your prospect why she should believe you. Here you introduce some evidence that your product or service can do what you say it can. It can be in the form of numbers, testimonials, case studies, or industry statistics.

- ✔ **Benefit:** Identify the overall benefit of solving this challenge. It may be obvious to you, but remember that you have the Curse of Knowledge, which happens when you know more about a subject than your listener and find it hard to imagine not knowing (refer to Chapter 4 for more information). Benefits need to be reinforced after you've covered a topic to seal them in your prospect's mind.

Repeat with Topic 2, Topic 3, and so on, until you cover all of your topics.

Here's a business example of building out a topic.

Topic 2: Increasing brand awareness.

- ✔ **Challenge:** The brand is relatively new, and sales are below forecast. The competition has much greater presence and dominates the market. The prospect needs to increase brand awareness to drive new business and retain current business.

- ✔ **Impact:** If the prospect does nothing (or uses a competitor that doesn't offer her the level of support you do), she is going to continue to see a lack of awareness among new entrants into the market as well as current customers. Without brand awareness, customers may confuse the prospect's messaging with that of their more active competitor, leading to a loss in revenue and a continuing decline in profits.

- ✔ **Resolution:** Using our combined media platform of television, print, and on-line media, the prospect's brand will be in front of new and current customers so that the prospect's brand is top of mind when customers are ready to buy.

- ✔ **Proof:** Brand X was in a similar situation to the prospects when we first started working with it. After a six-month schedule, that brand went from being the fourth most recognized brand in its category to number two among its target demographic.

- ✔ **Benefit:** The schedule we're proposing will create top-of-mind awareness for the prospect's brand when customers are ready to buy.

Deciding on features

With some of your topics, knowing which feature(s) or processes to include will be obvious. For others, you may have a choice of features and need to determine which ones are most relevant or make for a stronger case. Think about what each feature does and how it relates to the topic. If it doesn't relate to the topic, it doesn't belong in your plan.

Say your topic is "increasing awareness" as in the previous example. You can use three different products to do that: online, television, and print. You can cover each of them; however, if the prospect isn't a print advertiser and likely will never be a print advertiser, this diversion — no matter how short — can confuse the issue and cause your prospect to tune out during an otherwise stellar case. Sticking to a discussion of the television and online features presentation and leaving out print will make the strongest case for this prospect.

Pick your battles. Just because a feature is part of your package or offering doesn't mean you have to show it. If you're unsure, do some on-the-spot discovery to find out if there's interest before launching in to a topic that isn't relevant.

You want to make sure that every feature you present supports your case. The following tips can help you stay on course:

- ✔ **Hone in on a few features.** Keep in mind that more isn't always better. You want to present just enough features to intrigue your prospect and make your point, but not venture into feature overload.

- ✔ **Avoid irrelevance.** Put every feature through the relevancy test by asking yourself, "What does this mean to my prospect?" If your features aren't tied to your topic, they're just a distraction and weaken your case.

- ✔ **Get creative with features.** There's more than one way to talk about features. A long list of features told in the same way "This is feature A. This is what feature A does. These are the benefits of feature A" can get old very quickly. Try the following to liven things up:

  - **Tell a story about your feature and its use or application to make it more engaging.** Consider how your prospect can use this feature in her situation and bring that to life with a story to help your prospect envision using your solution. This is especially effective if you're near the seven-minute attention nose dive. Check out Chapter 12 for more advice about how to use storytelling.

  - **Using the whiteboard or flipchart to write the major points out.** Visual aids increase recall of your message by nearly two-thirds, so writing out what you want your prospect to remember about your features is both engaging and memorable.

- ✔ **Avoid training.** Remember that your prospect isn't a new employee. You aren't there to train her how to use your product or service. Stick to the high-level view — unless this is a deeper dive into the specific capabilities of your product — and eliminate the boring processes that don't do anything to further your prospect's understanding of how your product will help her achieve her goals.

- ✔ **Use simple language.** You can easily slip into buzzword nirvana when you're discussing features. "Our 3D rendering process offers nondestructive animation workflows . . . " Unless you're talking to a group of users who use those terms themselves, simplify what you're trying to say and use your prospect's terminology whenever possible.

Pulling it all together with transitions

Your topics will be your agenda items. Chapter 8 explains how to build an agenda in greater detail, but for now, you've covered a topic and it's time to go on to the next. As I mention in the "Maintaining attention" section earlier in this chapter, the introduction of a new topic is a great time to re-engage your prospect as well as orient her to where you are in the presentation.

Transitions are what often separate the pros from the amateurs. A smooth transition moves logically and seamlessly into the next point. An awkward or abrupt transition takes your prospect out of the flow and disrupts attention. To avoid an awkward transition and make your presentation logically flow from one point to the next, plan a transition statement and a method to move back and forth from your agenda.

Using a transition statement

Because your topics are all linked to your value proposition, there should be some common thread that you can use to connect each one that creates a logical flow. Using a transition statement helps you deliver it smoothly. Here are some examples of transition statements after finishing one topic and leading into a new topic:

> "Now that we've looked at how to create reports with the touch of a button, you're probably wondering how to take action on this data. In the next section we'll cover . . ."

> "We've seen how an on-air campaign can put your message in front of more than 150,000 potential customers each week. Now let's take a look at how we can create multiple touch points with your customers that will take them from awareness to action."

Transitioning to your agenda: The how-to

When you introduce the next topic, go back to your agenda to give your prospect a sense of where you are in the presentation. Here are several ways to do it with a slide deck:

- ✔ **Place an agenda slide after each topic.** The easiest way to remember to refer back to your agenda is to place an agenda slide at the end of your topic. So if you have four topics, you need five copies of your agenda slide: one at the beginning and one after each topic.

- ✔ **Toggle back to PowerPoint.** If you're in another program, you need to go back to PowerPoint to access your agenda slide. Make sure the program is open and hit ALT TAB to go back and forth between programs. See Chapter 21 for more PowerPoint tips.

- ✔ **Jump to an agenda slide.** If you know the slide number of your agenda, you can simply enter the number of the slide you want to go to while in Slide Show mode to go there. See Chapter 8 for more on using an agenda.

Chapter 7

Creating Closings That Make Your Prospect Take Action

*P*rofessional performers strategically plan their endings to leave their audience clamoring for more in order to sell CDs, T-shirts, and future tickets. Salespeople too need to put some planning into the closing of their presentation in order to leave prospects on a high note, ready to take those next steps.

A great closing has the power to drive home your point and move your prospect to take action, whereas a weak or unclear ending can derail even the most stellar presentation. The closing is your chance to make a lasting final impression on your prospect. However, closings typically receive an embarrassing lack of attention from salespeople. Much more time and effort go into the flashier parts of the presentation — the opening, slide design, features — before a quick closing. Unfortunately, this type of thinking can make your presentation an afterthought for your prospect.

Many sales presentations fail to inspire prospects to leap to their feet and ask, "Where do I sign?" Business is left on the table when a lackluster closing fails to give prospects a compelling reason to take the next step — or even tell them what the next step is. You worked hard to create an opening that grabbed your prospect's attention; now make sure you develop a closing that lives up to that.

In this chapter I explain why it's important not to leave your closing to chance by using proven techniques to drive home your message. I discuss four cliché closings to avoid and help you discover the key elements that go into creating and delivering a powerful finale for your presentation. You can find examples of encore-worthy closings and understand how to build your own closing. I also present tips on developing and asking for a clear call to action and leave-behinds that support your message and inspire your prospect to take action.

Prioritizing the Mighty Closing

A bad ending to your presentation can wipe out any positive feelings or interest you have created during your presentation and equal a lost opportunity. Although most presentations fall well short of bombing, mediocre closings are the rule rather than the exception in sales, leaving many prospects confused or ambivalent and ultimately slowing down or impeding the sale.

In the following sections I examine why it's critical that you have a powerful closing, what the consequences of a poor closing are, and the differences between closing and simply ending your presentation.

Why ending on a strong note is important

As the final impression you make on your prospect, your closing deserves the same amount of thought and practice you give to your opening. Consider the following:

- **Endings are memorable.** Good or bad, if you ask most people what they remember about a movie, chances are they would tell you the ending, followed by the opening and maybe a few key scenes. Researchers have found that the way an experience ends affects a person's memory of the entire experience. Whether it's the last bite of a meal, the last few notes of a song, or the closing of a presentation, lasting memories are shaped by those final moments.

- **Your audience is restless.** If your presentation is more than 20 minutes, you've officially reached the outer limits of your prospect's attention span. Of course, you will have reengaged them at planned points as I discuss in Chapter 14, but no matter how compelling your message, your slides, or your delivery, after your audience senses the end is near, they're going to be restless. Closings that go on too long or simply repeat what's already been said without adding an insight or a fresh twist are merely going to aggravate that sense of restlessness and tune out.

✔ **Listening is hard work.** If long lectures make you sleepy, you may not be at fault. Studies show that the act of listening is surprisingly taxing on the brain. Listening to your presentation fires millions of neurons in your prospect's brain, which can wear it out just like any overworked muscle. To engage a tired brain, you need to package and deliver what you want your prospect to remember in a way that his brain can absorb.

✔ **Recall is at stake.** The way you end your presentation plays a critical role in whether your prospect remembers your message when making decisions or whether your message falls off the radar entirely. By using techniques like repetition and re-engagement, you can ensure that all of your hard work is not forgotten as soon as your prospect walks out the door.

When closings are the weakest link

A chain is only as strong as its weakest link. A weak closing means a weak presentation. If you haven't spent much time thinking about how to close your presentation, you're in the majority. Most closings can be characterized by one word: "anticlimactic." Here are the four primary reasons that most closings fail to live up to their full potential:

✔ **Lacking planning.** You can easily put all your efforts into the earlier parts of your presentation (the opening, the slides, the demo, and so on) when your mind is fresh and ideas are flowing. Closing your presentation seems like something that should come naturally after you've made your case, but the fact is that a good closing doesn't just happen. It requires planning and preparation like any other part of your presentation.

✔ **Fearing repetitiveness.** Salespeople often fear repeating themselves too much, but in a 45-minute or more presentation you have likely covered a lot of material. Don't mistake your familiarity with the material with your prospect's level of familiarity. Repetition is important in order to encourage recall, and your prospect can often benefit from revisiting a few key points. Just be sure to repeat only those items that are truly important. Refer to the later section, "Defining the Key Elements of a Persuasive Closing" in this chapter for more information.

✔ **Assuming your point is obvious.** When you know the point you're trying to make or the benefit associated with a feature, it seems hard to imagine that it isn't also blatantly obvious to your prospect. Don't let this curse of knowledge trick you. Keep in mind that this is the first time your audience is being exposed to the information. (Check out the nearby sidebar.)

Beware of The Curse of Knowledge

The *Curse of Knowledge* is a term coined by economists to describe a phenomenon that makes it extremely difficult for people who have more information to see things from the perspective of a person who has less information. Charades are a good example. When you're the one acting out the clue — a movie, a song, or situation — it's difficult to believe that your partner can't immediately (or ever) figure it out. You can lessen this proven bias by being aware that your listener has a beginner's mind and by using concrete examples when explaining new information in terms that your listener can relate to.

✔ **Feeling pressured.** The real or perceived thought that you have gone on too long or that your audience is ready to go can make you want to start packing up your laptop and bolt for the door. Unfortunately when you rush, your audience senses it and becomes even more restless. Maintaining your composure and taking the time to end properly is better than speeding through your closing and wasting your time and your prospect's. See an example in the later section "Avoiding Cliché Closings."

Knowing the difference between closing and ending

How many presentations have you seen where the presenter finishes his final point and says, "Well, we've reached the end of our presentation. Thank you for having us and we'll open it up to questions." The presentation certainly came to an end, but it doesn't necessarily qualify as a closing.

Closing is a process that either completes a sale or moves you a step closer to it. If all you've accomplished is arriving to the end of your presentation without stating your case or asking for the next step, you haven't really closed.

Imagine being on trial for something you didn't do and after the final testimony, your lawyer simply rested her case, leaving it up to the jury to make sense of all the testimony to decide on a verdict. You probably would be irate. You'd want your lawyer to take advantage of that one final opportunity to summarize your case for the jury.

The same applies to when you're presenting and ready to end. Revisit the compelling points. Support them with evidence. Call back to what you set out to prove in your opening and leave your prospect with the strongest most compelling point to remember before adjourning. You've built the case, and now you have earned the right to ask for the verdict. Closing arguments are typically even more passionate than opening arguments for a reason. Both arguments are designed to persuade.

Defining the Key Elements of a Persuasive Closing

The power of a strong closing is undeniable. It has a satisfying ring to it. It revisits main points. It ties up loose ends. It inspires action. When you're on the receiving end of a great closing, it seems almost effortless, but don't be fooled into expecting the perfect words to appear at the right time.

In my experience, successful impromptu closings are as rare as a no-hitter in baseball. Ending on a strong note takes planning and practice, but it's well worth the time invested. These sections examine certain elements that go into a closing that make it both persuasive and memorable.

Bridging from your agenda

Your agenda serves as a natural transition point, moving from the body of your presentation into the closing. You've covered anywhere from three to five topics in the body, so you quickly want to recap the journey for your audience at the end.

Although doing so may seem redundant, remember that a significant amount of time may have passed since you discussed your first agenda item to your last. Here's how to bridge from your agenda:

> ✔ **Use one or two sentences to summarize each agenda item, including the topic and the overarching benefit.** Quickly recapping the highlights helps your prospect put those new ideas into context and increases the likelihood of him remembering them. For example, "We started out talking about quality assurance and how we can help you avoid delays and the expense of noncompliance. Then we looked at project management and saw how we can help your team stay on schedule, improving efficiency and allowing you to meet deadlines . . . "

Use your agenda slide or write on a flipchart to help your audience visualize what you've accomplished. Figure 7-1 shows an agenda slide that summarizes what you've covered.

Figure 7-1:
An example
agenda
slide that
shows
what topics
you've
covered.

Illustration by 24Slides

✔ **Time yourself and make sure that your bridge is less than 90 seconds.** Any longer and you risk a mass exodus of attention.

If your bridge is longer than 90 seconds, you're either introducing new material or going into too much detail. If it's the former, take that new information and either include it when you first speak about the topic or drop it all together.

Bookending your opening hook

You have a great opening *hook* — a story, a theme, or an interesting fact that grabs your audience's attention and draws them in. Don't just deliver it once and let it die. Revisit it during your closing. People love the symmetry of coming full circle. (Chapter 5 discusses how to develop a hook.) Here are some ways to bookend your hook:

✔ **Remind your prospect of the theme, story, or quote you used earlier with a quick reference.** Doing so seals your message in your prospect's mind. For example, "We talked earlier about how the flight industry improved dramatically after they moved to instrument flight, allowing planes to fly in all kinds of weather and circumstances and how our solution can give your company the ability to navigate circumstances that are keeping you grounded."

✔ **Use a slide or image from your opening to visually anchor your message in your prospect's mind.** If you used an image in your opening, such as an airplane in the story above, reintroduce it in your closing and include any new insights, proof, or value you've established in your presentation. Check out Figure 7-2 that shows you an example of a closing slide that uses a picture from the preceding opening story and benefits.

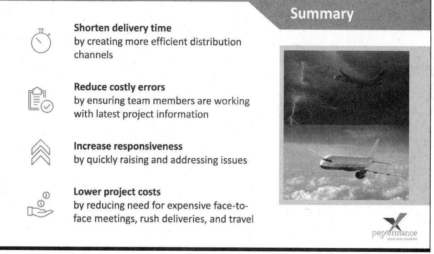

Figure 7-2: Example of an opening hook revisited in the closing.

Illustration by 24Slides

✔ **Rather than just repeat the hook, try revealing another side to it.** Expand on the analogy, add an addendum to your story, reveal a surprising finding about a fact you shared, or another use for the prop.

- For example, consider this scenario: You're selling a print management solution. The prospect has many choices and you are not the most inexpensive. The prospect is not sure why she should choose any but the lowest priced vendor.

- Your opening hook: You revealed a 3D printer and told a story about the ongoing changes in the printing industry and aligned that with changes that the prospect's industry is facing.

- The one thing that you want your prospect to remember: Plan for today. Prepare for tomorrow.

- Your closing: "You shared with us that your goal is to find a way to manage the incredible amounts of information flowing into your company and reduce your overall printing costs by $500,000 this year. We've shown you how we can help you do that by cutting your printing costs by 30 percent — or nearly $750,000 based on the figures you provided us. As we've seen, 3D printing is just the latest in technological advances in the printing industry. Like the printing industry, what you need to run your business today can change tomorrow. With the investments we're making you can be assured that we will continue to change with you and support you as you grow. Plan for today. Prepare for tomorrow.

- "I have wallets for all of you that we made on the 3D printer earlier that you'll need to keep all the money you're going to save in. Can we count on you sending a written recommendation to your president to approve our proposal?"

Recalling the objectives

Touch on the main message from your opening, in other words the disparity between the status quo (the problem, challenge, or pain point identified in your discovery) and your prospect's desired outcome (life with your solution).

For example, "We set out today to show you how we can help you address the issues you're facing: the rising response times and lower closing ratios that are keeping you from reaching your goal of hitting 25 million in global sales this year."

Restating your value proposition

You introduced your *value proposition* (a clear statement of the results your prospect can expect to receive with your product or service; refer to Chapter 3 for more information) during the opening of your presentation. It was only theoretical to your prospect at that point. Now that you've shown your prospect how you're going to achieve that value proposition, clearly and emphatically restate it as a fact.

For example, "Based on what we've shown you, we're confident that we can provide your sales team with the mobile responsiveness and the intuitive tools they need to respond to leads quicker, resulting in a 10 percent increase in sales and getting you to your goal of 25 million."

Validating with proof

In your presentation, you've shown prospects how and what you're going to deliver, but today's decision makers demand proof. In your closing, include a concise summary that, if possible, substantiates your claims by providing evidence. You can use several types of proof or evidence:

- ✔ **Facts and figures:** Quantifying proof using figures and data is the strongest form of proof for most prospects. For example, "Based on the listing price we discussed of $600,000 and the current market statistics for similar homes in your area, we believe we can have your home under contract within 90 days."

- ✔ **Case studies:** In instances where you don't have access to your prospect's data, you can use a case study from a customer with a similar challenge.

  For example, "Bluehole Drilling, a current customer of ours, found themselves in a situation much like yours. With our help, they were able to reduce downtime in the field by 18 percent, which resulted in a savings of $1.75 million last year."

  If you used a case study in your opening, focus on another relevant finding from that case study to avoid simply repeating the same story.

- ✔ **Industry research:** Every industry has its own recognized leader in research and statistics; for example, there's Gartner for technology, and J.D. Powers for many other products. Most prospects recognize relevant statistics that support your case from these trusted sources as impartial and credible.

  For example, "According to J.D. Powers, customers who have a higher customer satisfaction rate with their investment firm are 29 percent more likely to recommend their current firm to others. Based on that, we can assure you not only happy current customers, but a wealth of new customers as well."

- ✔ **Customer reference:** If you can't provide quantifiable results, use a favorable reference or testimonial from a current client.

  For example, "Bob Stevens of SVP Global Sales said, 'Albatross was able to provide the kind of one-on-one service we were looking for and it opened up new doors for us in the global market.'"

Make sure you're prepared to back up any claims you make with data and sources, and always get permission to use quotes and proprietary information.

Reinforcing your one thing

You want your audience to remember one central theme from your presentation, so make sure that you reinforce it at the end of your presentation. If you can condense your one thing into a short, memorable statement, you greatly increase the odds of your prospect remembering — not just your central idea — but more of your presentation.

For example, in the earlier section, "Bookending your Opening Hook," the one thing used in the example was, "Plan for today. Prepare for tomorrow." See Chapter 5 for tips on developing your one thing.

Making a call to action

You've delivered a compelling case; your audience is smiling and nodding as you approach the home stretch. Don't let this feel-good moment pass! Tell your audience what you want them to do. Don't be shy or assume it is obvious. Here are some qualities of a *call to action* — a request to take the sale to the next step — that gets heard:

- ✔ **Simplify.** Calls to action are often too complicated for an audience who has just sat through a long presentation. Don't overwhelm them at the final gate with too many steps. Make the call to action a single, simple action your prospect can take.

  For example, "To ensure you get the best rates, I recommend signing the paperwork today so we can move forward."

- ✔ **Specificity.** Vague requests produce vague results. Be very clear about what you want your prospect to do. Ask for specific actions that a prospect can take, like, "a recommendation to the board to move forward with our proposal," instead of "a positive recommendation."

- ✔ **Provability.** Come up with a call to action that can be validated after it's accomplished. For example, emailing you on a copy of a recommendation to stakeholders or partners, responding to a calendar invite, making a deposit, and so forth. If your call to action is vague, such as "take this under consideration" or "review it with your team," you can't prove that your prospect has actually done it.

- ✔ **Timing.** No matter how excited your prospect is about your solution, he may forget all about it tomorrow when the next pressing need arises. Use a defined timeframe to increase your prospect's commitment to take action and to give you a reason to follow up. For example, "I suggest we schedule a deep dive with your support team within the next 30 days."

- ✔ **Uniqueness.** Use your call to action to continue to set yourself apart from the competition by personalizing it in a way that fits your prospect or addresses his goals or concerns. You want your prospect to remember it, so make it unique and memorable. For example, "To make sure you feel completely confident as we move forward I think the best next step would be to do a value assessment to quantify the ROI."

Stay away from these types of closings: "We're asking for your business" and "We hope you'll consider us as your business partner." Besides not requiring any specific action or timing, using these perfectly forgettable statements make you sound like every other vendor.

✔ **Appealing.** If the call to action sounds like a dental appointment that your prospect must keep, he's not going to meet it with great enthusiasm. Keep in mind that you have just made a strong case to take your prospect from a state of pain to an island of relief. Any next step that gets him closer to that goal is a happy occasion. Deliver your call to action with that type of confidence and belief in the value of your solution, and your conviction will be contagious.

Taking the next steps

Not every presentation ends in a signed contract. In fact, in the case of most complex sales, a signed contract is rare. However, you must ask for some next step, otherwise you have just invested a lot of time and energy delivering an informative talk. Here are some examples of next steps:

✔ **Additional information provided:** If it's been more of a preliminary presentation, you may have uncovered additional needs or questions that you need to address. Take good notes and be timely in your response to move things along.

✔ **Product demonstration or deep-dive presentation:** If your presentation was more of a high-level overview, the next step may be to give a product demonstration or focus in on specific areas or capabilities for the prospect's technical team or product users.

✔ **Product trial:** Ask for a commitment from your prospect that if your product does perform according to predetermined goals, he is willing and capable to make a purchase. Be sure to establish clear guidelines around usage, timing, and liability, and get everything in writing.

✔ **Visit to corporate office or facility:** For large investments like capital equipment, a prospect may want to visit the facility or plant, or meet additional team members that he will work with. Make sure you have a good understanding of your prospect's expectations and arrange everything well in advance.

✔ **Recommendation to final decision maker or board:** Ask for the recommendation within a specific timeframe. Don't be afraid to ask how the decision-making process works and how you can help expedite it as well.

✔ **Conversation with current customer:** Sometimes prospects need assurance from a third party to help them over that last hurdle. Have your current customers prepared in advance to respond to a request for a reference to avoid delay.

✔ **Presentation to additional decision makers:** Perhaps you gave your presentation or demo to one or two people within your prospect's organization so that they could validate that your product is a good fit before bringing you in to present or demo for executives.

✔ **Verbal commitment:** For larger products or strategic sales you may need to accept a verbal commitment as your prospect's legal team produces a contract. Stay involved in the process and secure a deadline if possible.

✔ **Deposit or partial payment:** A deposit shows that your buyer is committed. Make sure your contract is explicit on how the deposit is applied, and under what circumstances it can be refunded to avoid problems.

✔ **Signed contract:** This is the ultimate goal and the logical next step for many smaller products or services. Don't forget to have contracts ready and supporting documents available so you're not scrounging around at the last minute.

Avoiding Cliché Closings

To win the attention of your audience, you make a compelling case and earn the right to ask for the business. The last thing you want to do then is to fall back on a cliché closing that puts your audience to sleep or makes them look for the nearest exit. Here are some common cliché closings to avoid:

The "Any Questions?" close

"So that's our presentation, now I'd like to open it up to questions."

This is the most common closing in the world, and seasoned pros and new salespeople alike do it. If you've crafted an interactive presentation, you'll have invited questions at specific points on topics throughout your presentation so the need for questions should be minimal. Chapter 14 discusses how to manage your audience with questions. Regardless, you need to have a hard closing and here's why:

✔ **Loss of control:** You never know where questions are going to lead. If a question ends up putting you on the defensive or you can't provide a satisfactory answer, instead of leaving your prospect with a strong message you want him to remember and an inspiring call to action, he's going to remember the negative question experience.

✔ **Restlessness:** Have you ever noticed that the last ten minutes of a flight, a car ride, or a race always seem to be the longest? When they know something is almost over, most people are more than ready to move on to the next thing. If parts of your audience feel compelled to stay because one person has a question, they may get annoyed. Unfortunately that annoyance can quickly become directed at you for not taking charge of the ending.

✔ **Weak closings:** If you do open your closing up to questions, they'll eventually trail off, leaving an awkward silence and then, "So, if that's all the questions, I guess we'll close." There goes your opportunity for a strong ending.

You don't want to discourage questions, but you definitely want to be proactive about how and when you handle them. Here are some tips:

✔ **Have planned spots for questions.** If you take questions at strategic points throughout your presentation, for example, at the end of each agenda item, it keeps the questions focused on a specific topic and allows you to assess any need for clarification as they arise.

✔ **Build in questions prior to your closing.** A great time to take questions is just before the final recap of your agenda. Saying "Let's take ten minutes for questions before we close," cues your audience that there is more ahead and helps you stick to your closing. Refer to the earlier section, "Bridging to your agenda" for more information.

✔ **Get rid of the question slide.** Don't use the slide with a giant question mark or a picture of a person with a puzzled expression on his face to indicate it's time for Q&A. Your prospect knows what to do when you ask him a question. Instead of the question slide, go to a black screen and ask for questions from the audience. That places the focus on you and your prospect. For PowerPoint tips on how to go to a black screen, head to Chapter 20.

✔ **Let people go.** If you've closed or you're at the end of your allotted time, and an audience member still wants to stick around and ask questions, you can acquiesce, but first offer to let those that need to go, leave. They will be forever grateful.

✔ **Schedule a follow-up.** If the questions are especially long or complex or your time is short, schedule a follow-up meeting or call with the interested parties to give it the proper attention it deserves.

The Whimper close

"Okay, so I think I've shown you some ways we can help you reduce costs and improve profitability. Hopefully you can see the value in our solution? So, unless there are any more questions, I guess we'll wrap up."

If you're not sure of your ending, your prospect certainly won't be either. Closing is no time to be timid about what you're going to say or how you say it.

To fix this type of cliché, do the following:

- **Keep up your energy.** Just because you're near the end don't let up on the gas pedal! That doesn't mean speed through it, but rather put every last bit of energy you have into communicating your message to your audience with your voice, body, and words. Check out Chapter 11 for tips on using your voice and body to support your message.

- **Steer clear of tentative language.** Use words like "We've shown you" or "You can see that" as opposed to words like "hopefully" or "I think" to project confidence.

- **Know your last lines.** If you don't know what your destination is, you won't know when you've arrived. Decide exactly what your final two or three lines are and practice them until you hear them in your sleep. Having those final lines down gives you a much greater sense of confidence as you head into your closing.

- **Focus on your intention.** Take a pause before you close and focus on what you're trying to accomplish and how you're trying to impact your audience. Do you want to re-energize them? Challenge them? Motivate them? Bring that intention into your closing, and your audience can't help but feel drawn in.

- **Use your stage.** Attention levels commonly wander toward the end of a presentation. Use your stage to reengage your prospect's attention and shift the focus in the room. If you're stuck behind your laptop, walk out and approach your audience. If you're standing on one side of the room, move to the center. When you arrive at your destination, stand firmly planted with weight equally balanced on both feet and deliver your close. If you're on a web presentation, turn on your webcam and/or use your voice to reengage your audience.

- **Put a period on it.** Avoid trailing off at the end of sentences or ending on a statement as a question. For more tips on vocal power, see Chapter 11.

The Surprise! close

"Oh! I guess that's the end of my deck. Any questions?"

Being surprised by your own ending usually comes either from too many last-minute changes in the deck or a lack of practice. Whatever the reason, being caught off guard during your own presentation makes you look unprofessional and robs you of the opportunity to deliver a strong close.

To fix this cliché, do the following:

- ✔ **Memorize your closing.** You never want to rely on your slides to serve as cue cards, and nowhere is that more important than during your opening and closing. You need to have these sections committed to memory so that you can put your focus where it belongs — on connecting with your prospect and delivering an impactful message.

- ✔ **Limit last-minute changes.** Establishing a firm cut-off date of at least two days before the presentation for any changes in the deck (unless you have new insights you need to act on) allows you to be familiar with the flow. Most last-minute changes are cosmetic anyway and combined with nerves, they can throw you off your game.

The Race-to-the-Finish-Line close

"Well that's it. Thanks very much."

Some salespeople start heading off stage before their final words are even out of their mouth. The real or perceived thought that you have gone on too long or that your audience is anxious to get going can send you rushing to the nearest exit. Unfortunately, from your prospect's viewpoint this closing looks like you can't wait to get out of there as well, which may be just how your prospect feels after your rushed closing!

To solve this cliché, use these tips:

- ✔ **Track your time.** Keep track of time during your presentation so that you don't run out of it at the end. If you notice that you're running behind earlier in your presentation, cut some lower priority parts as you go. Doing so is much better than trying to cram everything in at the end. Chapter 14 offers some time management tips.

- ✔ **Watch your pace.** There's a difference between quickening your pace and rushing. Although picking it up a bit at the end is natural, if you're rushing to finish quicker or are a fast talker anyway, be careful not to break into hyperspeed or you'll leave your audience in the dust.

- ✔ **Focus on connecting.** After you've arrived at the closing, stop worrying about the time, what everyone else is thinking, and whether you're going to make that flight. Stay in the moment and place your focus on connecting with your prospect and driving home your message.

Ultimately, presenting isn't about how you feel, but about how you make your audience feel.

✔ **Don't assume.** Every little movement from your prospect isn't a sign that they're tired of you. Your prospect's incessant leg tapping may well have nothing to do with you and simply be a nervous habit or an attempt to wake up a sleepy muscle.

✔ **Jump to value.** Your sponsor is motioning for you to wrap it up or the CEO is heading for the door. When there's no denying that you need to end quickly, skip the summary and jump right to the value statement. Again, don't rush and say it with confidence. Make it your goal to hold your prospect's attention to the end and finish strong.

✔ **Check your content.** If you find yourself consistently running out of time, you may be cramming too many points into your presentation, underestimating how long it takes to deliver, or forgetting to budget for questions. Practice running through your presentation at full performance level, taking the time to pause and hear your audience's questions, pass out handouts, or show videos. That way you can get a true read on how long your presentation is and determine whether you need to make some cuts.

Delivering an Encore Inspiring Closing:

How you deliver your closing has as much to do with what your prospect takes away from your presentation as *what* you deliver. Don't settle for an average closing. Strive for an encore performance by following these guidelines to make your closing shine:

✔ **Be conversational.** Closing seems to bring out the unnecessarily formal side of most salespeople. Be honest. Do you ever end a conversation with a friend or co-worker or even your manager with the following phrases?

> In conclusion . . .
>
> In summation . . .
>
> I'd like to summarize by saying . . .

Using these types of phrases are an abrupt departure if the rest of your presentation is delivered in a more casual style. Strike a more conversational tone when closing by using every day language. For example:

> As you've seen . . .
>
> Some final thoughts for you to take away . . .
>
> What does this mean for you?
>
> To wrap up . . .

✔ **Go easy on the gratitude.** Your presentation isn't an acceptance speech at the Academy Awards, and you've already thanked them in the opening. You want to be perceived as a trusted adviser or business partner, so going overboard on gratitude can make you seem less than an equal partner. By all means be polite, but a simple thank you will suffice.

Different cultures have different expectations of formalities and expressions of gratitude. Be sure to check what's appropriate for the audience you're presenting to or the country you're presenting in.

✔ **Keep it short.** Though your closing has several distinct parts, the whole section should seamlessly connect and not take more than three to four minutes. The end of your presentation is never the time for a long monologue when prospect's attention spans are at their shortest.

✔ **Use dramatic pauses.** You've reached the grand finale. Don't just toss off those last few lines like unimportant asides. Pause before you transition into your closing, after you deliver your value proposition, or before your one thing that you want your prospect to take away. This pause gives your audience a sense of anticipation and lends a greater importance to your message.

✔ **Connect with your audience.** Your closing is no time to be looking at your slides or standing behind your computer. Confidently approach your audience. Look directly at them. See them. Smile at them. Propose your call to action.

✔ **Be silent.** Treat your call to action like any question you ask where you expect an answer. Resist the temptation to fill the space and wait for your prospect to respond. He may surprise you with a simple yes or reveal some piece of information or obstacle that you otherwise wouldn't have discovered. Chapter 14 provides insight about handling questions.

✔ **Strike a power pose.** Many times the end of a sales presentation isn't clear because the salesperson is still walking and talking. Stand still when you're closing and maintain eye contact. Don't undo a strong impression by explaining what you just said or rushing off the stage. Hold the moment wherever you are before thanking your audience and exiting.

✔ **Make a smooth exit.** Be aware of what is going to happen for your prospect after your presentation to facilitate a clean exit and avoid awkward handoffs. Find out from your internal contact if your audience is going to remain in the room for additional meetings, if someone is waiting to set up, or if everyone is leaving. That way you can transition accordingly. For example, "Thank you. (Take a pause.) And now I understand you have further meetings so I'll let you all get to it!"

✔ **Be ready to improvise.** Your prospect has to take an urgent call. The building is being evacuated. You never know when you have to jump ahead to the closing. Be familiar enough with your closing (and where your closing is in your deck) that you can jump ahead and give your prospect the final value proposition and call to action before he runs out the door. See Chapter 19 on how to give an abbreviated presentation.

Providing the Right Leave-Behind

Research shows that providing your prospect with a *leave-behind* (something tangible to take away from your presentation) can help create stronger memories. Although anything that makes it easier for your prospect to remember your message seems like a win, you want to take into consideration some things when deciding on a leave-behind for your presentation. A good leave-behind should fit the following criteria:

- **Appropriate:** Giveaways like candy, gift cards, and gadgets may work with a group of end users; however, they may seem like a lame attempt to buy favor and back fire with C-level prospects. The more formal the presentation is, the more formal the leave behind should be. Know your audience before you buy those custom gummy bears.

- **Unique:** Standard gifts have another flaw. You can't be guaranteed that your prospect is going to remember if it was you or your competitor who gave that coffee gift card. Get credit where credit's due by giving your prospect something that is unique and tied to your topic or theme. For example, a smartphone or tablet cover with one of your key visuals and your one thing printed across it is a more certain path toward being remembered.

- **Relevant:** Samples of your product or a giveaway that pertains to the topic say "remember me." Tickets to a local sporting event beg "please, buy me." If you're going to provide a giveaway, make sure it has something to do with why you're there. For example, the wallet to keep all the money they're going to save from buying your solution as seen in the "Bookending your opening hook" section earlier in this chapter.

- **Useful:** Anything that you can get in front of your prospect's eyes on a daily — or even weekly — basis is worth consideration. For example, a custom flash drive with your message printed on it that contains copies of graphs and other key data from your presentation.

- **Professional:** Your leave behind should be a good reflection of the quality of your product and solution. As your final memory, you don't want to leave your prospect with something that's going to fall apart in three days. Printed leave-behinds should be in full color and printed on good stock. Opt for professional binding over those cheap plastic folders. If you can't afford to do a quality giveaway, then skip it.

These sections examine more tidbits you may need to know about leave-behinds.

Eyeing important tips for leave-behinds

As the final thing your audience will take away from your presentation, be sure to put some thought into how and when you're going to get it into your prospect's hands. Keep these tips in mind:

- ✔ **Ease their minds.** If you're going to hand out a summary at the end, let your prospect focus on listening by telling him up-front so he doesn't have to take a bunch of notes.

- ✔ **Get creative.** Instead of just handing him a copy of paper that can easily get lost in a pile on his desk, give your prospect a professionally printed binder, a flash drive, or miniDVD with the needed files pre-loaded on it.

- ✔ **Save it until the end.** Don't hand out your leave-behind until the end of your presentation. Giving it out any time prior to the end eliminates one of your most powerful engagement techniques: the element of surprise. If you put something to read in front of your audience members, it's human nature that they will indeed try to read it — and you'll spend much of your time during the presentation staring at the top of their heads. Wait until you have done your closing and then hand it out as a takeaway.

- ✔ **Create an interactive piece.** Many times prospects want to capture important facts and figures during your presentation that can help them in their decision-making process. You can make this easier for them as well as make it a more interactive activity by creating a piece that they can fill in as they go.

- ✔ **Recap with a custom follow-up piece.** Instead of preparing a handout in advance of your presentation, consider preparing a custom follow-up piece afterwards to capture the dialogue that occurred during the course of the presentation. Doing so serves several purposes: it provides a more accurate reflection of what occurred in the presentation and is therefore more likely to be read, and it can serve as a good reminder in a few days when memories are starting to fade.

Leaving behind slide decks or not

Giving your prospect a copy of your presentation is rarely a good idea and here's why: A slide presentation isn't meant to be read; it's meant to serve as support to you, the person delivering the message. Besides, if you've followed best practices in creating your slides (refer to Chapter 9), your presentation won't make sense to your prospect or provide the information he wants, ultimately confusing or disappointing him.

But sometimes prospects insist on getting a copy. Some executives even request them in advance to sort through for relevance. And sometimes handouts are nice to have for your prospects to jot down notes. Here are a couple things you can do when asked to share your presentation.

Clarifying why your prospect wants a copy

If your prospect does ask for a copy of your deck, asking what he wants to see can prove very enlightening and save you a lot of time and headaches. Often the prospect really just wants the details of your proposal — the what, when, and how much — so that he can compare it to others. He may want access to specific data, graphs, or research that you used in order to do his own internal evaluation. If so, consider any of the following methods for getting him what he needs.

Handing out your slide deck: Some alternatives

Even if your prospect hasn't requested it, it's a good practice to prepare one of the following as a leave-behind for your presentation to serve as a memory device as well as to make a preemptive strike against a request to send him your whole deck.

- ✔ **Print key slides.** Bring along copies of slides that summarize key points. For example, provide copies of the agenda with a full list of benefits, the value proposition, or any evidence that you included in your presentation.

- ✔ **Make available online.** To keep it environmentally friendly, you can provide your prospect with a link to Google docs or Dropbox to access key slides or PDF notes from your presentation.

- ✔ **Offer to recap.** Sending your prospect a recap of all the relevant points from your presentation is additional work, but it can serve as a great support piece and reminder in a format that is easy for your prospect to read and quickly digest.

- ✔ **Print your PowerPoint notes.** For a more informal presentation, consider printing selected some PowerPoint notes if you've used them in your presentation. Remember to edit them so they're more than just a cue for you. Here are the steps to printing your notes in PowerPoint:

    1. **In PowerPoint open the View tab.**

    2. **Click on Notes Master.**

    3. **Click on the slide to edit the style, including changing fonts, colors, themes, and so on.**

    4. **Click Insert if you want to add a chart, graph, or picture.**

    5. **Go back to View and Click on Notes Page to preview how your notes will look.**

    6. **Click on Print.**

    7. **Select Settings and select Note Page to print your notes.**

Chapter 8

Crafting Your Agenda, Intro, and Company Overview

. . . .

In This Chapter

▶ Keeping your audience's attention during your agenda, intro, and overview

▶ Developing and following an interactive agenda

▶ Establishing credibility with your introduction

▶ Creating a customer-focused overview

. . . .

Since the beginning of time, or at least PowerPoint, salespeople have begun their presentations with an introduction, an agenda, and a slide, handout, or a hieroglyphic showing:

✔ A picture of the company's headquarters

✔ Customer logos

✔ A timeline of product launches, acquisitions, and company growth

✔ Industry awards, achievements, or accreditations

✔ Bios of the executive team

Here I refer to the corporate or company overview. Like the introduction, salespeople and customers alike dread it. Why? Because it's as boring to give as it is to receive. Not to worry. It's not your fault. Even Samuel L. Jackson couldn't make the typical company overview sound interesting! Here you can find out about transforming transitional sections like your agenda, the introduction, and the overview into engaging, valuable sections of your presentation.

In this chapter, you can discover how to develop and follow an agenda that not only guides your audience but provides interaction as well. I also discuss how you can leverage an introduction for a boost of credibility right at the beginning of your presentation — where you need it most. Finally, I introduce you to a new way of delivering a company overview by applying the WIFM (What's-in-it-for-me) Test and placing it where it can provide the greatest impact on your audience.

Maintaining Attention during Transitional Sections

The opening has drama, the body has sizzle, and the closing has action. Those parts that string it together are the introduction, agenda, and company overviews. Unfortunately many salespeople lose their audience in these sections because they are typically generic (company overviews), not well-thought out (introductions), or just plain boring (agendas). And they all violate Rule No. 1 of audience engagement: Be customer focused.

Transitions are what separate the pros from the amateurs. Each of these sections (the introduction, agenda, and company overview) in your presentation serves a key, but often an unrealized purpose. Agendas reveal the topics to be covered and they can also give your audience a needed sense of progression, and provide an opportunity for interaction. Introductions let your audience know who you are, and they also create a lasting first impression and affect your credibility. Company overviews deliver facts, and when used strategically, they can also help you align with your customers and build a case for purchasing your product or service.

Smooth transitions that keep an audience engaged and go beyond taking your audience from Point A to Point B are subtle but powerful. Your prospect may not walk out saying, "Wow, that was an awesome company overview," but she may say, "I didn't realize how much the fact that they have a location in Japan is actually going to benefit us."

Letting Your Audience Know Where You're Going: Your Agenda

Remember driving around with your parents and asking "Are we there yet?" That thought can take hold of your prospect when your presentation doesn't appear to follow a clear structure. In a day and age where at any point in time you can locate your exact GPS position on the map or determine how long it takes to get from Akron to Antarctica, it's unnatural to be kept entirely in the dark about where you're headed and how long it's going to take to get there.

Most of the day your prospect is in charge of her agenda. Yes, she has handed over the controls to you for the next 30 minutes, hour, or two hours, but letting go of the wheel can be difficult for some people, especially executives. By giving audience members an agenda, sticking to it, and referring back to it at regular intervals, you're letting them know that they're in good hands, you're heading toward the destination, and you're not going to veer off track.

But the agenda is capable of so much more. As an early section in your presentation, to use the agenda exclusively as a place-marker is a waste of valuable real estate. In the following sections you discover how to create and navigate an agenda that not only informs, but also engages and allows for flexibility to move between sections, and how to use your agenda to interact with your audience.

Defining your agenda

A *basic agenda* lets your audience know what topics you plan to address and is often displayed at the start of your presentation. The following steps help you to make your agenda more engaging and memorable for your prospect:

1. **Define your agenda items.**

   They're the main topics or sections that make up the body of your presentation. Aim for three to five topics for any given presentation. For longer presentations, you may have a few more, or you may simply have higher-level agenda items and more subtopics within them. See Chapter 6 for more on developing agenda items.

2. **Choose a simple word or short description of one to three words for each agenda item in your prospect's language.**

   The topic should describe your prospect's issue or business process, not your product. For example, instead of "Hybrid customer retention module," use "Keeping good employees." This isn't the place to teach your prospect product names or fancy new terminology.

3. **Determine the relationship between agenda items.**

   For example, decipher whether they're steps in a process, departments within an organization, challenges, or opportunities. How they're related can help you determine the best design format.

4. **Visually define your agenda items.**

   Mine your theme and message for ideas that you want to reinforce visually. For example, if your theme is "Innovate to win," you may use a different innovative product – lightbulb, computer, smartphone – for each agenda item to give them their own identity. Chapter 9 offers some tips on designing your agenda.

Using an agenda to promote interaction: The secret agenda of an agenda

To make your agenda more interactive while you keep your audience informed, always refer back to it before covering each new agenda item. As you refer back to it you can reinforce the main takeaway from the agenda item – how your solution can benefit them – and invite interaction. There are two ways to do this, the first is for a linear type of presentation, and the second is for a non-linear presentation where the topics can be discussed in any order based on audience input.

Linear agenda

If discussing your topics in a specific order is important, use the following steps for a *linear agenda* to refer back to your agenda and interact with your audience:

1. **After you finish talking about your first topic, refer back to your agenda slide.**

   Insert a copy of your agenda slide after the final slide for each agenda item, or create a hyperlink within the final slide of each agenda item that takes you back to the agenda slide. In the next section, you can find out how to create hyperlinks. Figure 8-1a is an example of an agenda slide indicating you have covered the first item with a checkmark. You can add a checkmark in PowerPoint through animation or annotation. Check out Chapter 21 for ten PowerPoint tips.

2. **Summarize the agenda item you've just covered.**

   In a brief sentence or two, recap the high-level points of what you've discussed. For example, if your agenda item is "Getting customer-focused," you can say, "We've seen how important it is to structure a presentation from the perspective of your prospect . . . "

3. **Invite interaction.**

   If you've spent more than ten minutes on your agenda item, your audience's attention is at a low point. The agenda is an excellent place to do something to reengage your audience. Ask a question about the topic you just covered or are about to cover, take a poll, or show a quick video clip. Keep your activity relevant to the topic and use it to reinforce how your solution provides value for your prospect.

   For example, say that I've just covered the topic of staying customer-focused during a presentation. "Quick, show of hands — how many of you have had a prospect walk out during your presentation? . . . Of course not! But can they reach for their smartphones or mentally check out if they feel like you aren't speaking their language? They do it all the time. That's why it's so important to keep that customer-focus throughout your presentation — to maintain your prospect's attention."

4. Introduce the next agenda item.

Move to the next agenda item with a simple transitional statement like "Now we're going to talk about how your prospect's problem came into being by identifying that trigger event."

5. After you finish that agenda item, go back to the agenda and invite interaction.

After you cover the next agenda item, repeat Steps 2–4, being sure to vary your interaction each time to keep attention high. For example, if you've asked a question after your first agenda item — like in the previous example — try using a prop or telling a story for the next one.

6. Repeat for each agenda item until you've gone through the entire agenda.

Nonlinear agenda

A *nonlinear agenda* is ideal when it doesn't matter what order you deliver your agenda items in, or if you want to have more flexibility to discuss topics in the order that the conversation flows. Here's how to build a nonlinear agenda:

1. Create hyperlinks on your slides.

In order to jump from your agenda to the topic you want to cover and back to your agenda, you need to create some hyperlinks on both your agenda slide and the first and last slide of each topic section. Here's how:

  1. In PowerPoint Normal view, select the first agenda item on your Agenda slide — it can be either text or an object.

  Figure 8-1a is an example of a full agenda.

  2. In the Insert tab, click on Hyperlink.

  3. In Link To, select Place in This Document.

  4. Select the first slide in the section for the agenda topic to be covered and click OK.

  See Figure 8-1b of the first slide of the section covering agenda item #2.

  5. In Normal View, go to the last slide in the section for the agenda item covered and select an object or text.

  Figure 8-1c is the last slide of the section covering agenda item #2.

  6. In the Insert tab, click on Hyperlink.

  7. In Link To, select Place in This Document.

8. **Select the Agenda slide and click OK.**

   Figure 8-1d is the agenda slide that you will return to.

9. **Repeat this process for all agenda items.**

2. **Follow steps 2-6 in the previous section.**

   To encourage interaction, you can let the conversation dictate which order you show your agenda items in or ask your audience to choose.

Figure 8-1:
Examples of an agenda slide with one completed agenda item (a), a first slide in an agenda topic section (b), a last slide in an agenda topic section (c), an agenda slide with two completed agenda items (d).

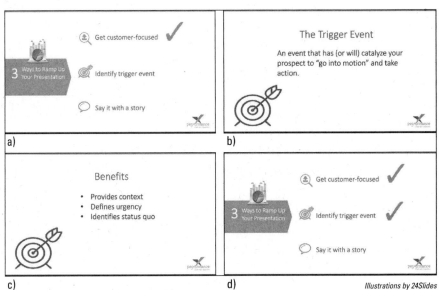

Illustrations by 24Slides

Keeping your agenda on track

Consider a few important things as you plan and prepare to deliver your agenda:

✔ **Keep it simple.** A busy or too-detailed agenda can give the impression that your presentation or product is complicated or hard to understand. Aim for no more than five main topics.

✔ **Be quick.** Remember, an agenda is an overview, not a deep dive. The goal is to assure your audience members that you plan to cover key issues as well as pique their interest, not give it all away up-front. A quick sentence or two on each topic is sufficient.

✔ **Be consistent.** If you're going to use an agenda, refer back to it at consistent intervals, such as after you've finished wrapping up one topic and before you move on to the next. If you do it for the first two topics and then forget it for the next two, someone in your audience may notice, which can make you appear disorganized or distracted.

✔ **Summarize with your agenda.** Using your agenda as a guide and a way to interact with your audience is great, but don't forget about it after you cover the last topic. Remember, it may have been an hour or more since you covered the first topic. Use it as a quick final summary of what you covered before you move into your close to help reinforce the topics in your prospect's mind. You don't need to belabor it because you'll have already discussed each point, so just a quick sentence about the topic and how it benefits your prospect will do.

Building Credibility with Your Introduction

Many salespeople don't realize that your introduction — letting the audience know who you are and why you're qualified to speak on the topic — is a part of your presentation. In fact, it's not just *a* part of your presentation. It's the *first thing you say to your audience* prior to your opening. Despite that fact, most salespeople don't prepare for their introduction until the last moment and often end up adlibbing on the spot. Unfortunately, most people can't consistently pull off adlibbing, and their introduction comes across as awkward and makes their audience uncomfortable. A combination of nerves and being too close to the subject makes it a risky bet for even the most seasoned salesperson whereas new salespeople struggle with what to say in their introduction or what tone to strike.

A well-planned introduction can be a powerful way to give you an immediate shot of credibility at the start of your presentation — when you need it most. Credibility is that quality of being believable and worthy of your audience's trust. Because credibility and first impressions are so critical to the success of your presentation, make sure that you do a good introduction.

The following sections will help you to plan and deliver (or have someone else deliver) a sharp, to-the-point introduction that will enhance your credibility, project a professional image, and get your prospect excited about hearing your presentation.

Planning your self-introduction

Don't expect a great introduction to just come rolling off of your tongue. It requires some planning and practice. Consider how much time you spend planning your actual presentation opening, whether it's a story, an insight, or another type of hook. Spending a little time focusing on the introduction that comes *before* your opening only makes sense. After all, it's something you will use again and again. Chapter 5 shows you how to create an opening.

Here are some ways to plan and practice a good introduction that starts you off on the right note.

- **Pick highlights.** Because your presentation isn't a job interview, your prospect doesn't need to know your entire career history or where you went to college. Think of your introduction as creating a highlight reel of key points that support why you're qualified to advise them on this topic.

- **Limit it to three or four points.** Keep your introduction short and pertinent. An introduction is no time for a long monologue, so focus on and prioritize what's really important to establish up-front.

- **Avoid too much information.** Strive to be friendly and open but don't make your audience uncomfortable by oversharing. The fact that you just spent a year sipping sangria across Spain may be interesting to your friends, but it can cause your audience to question your reliability.

- **Deliver an informal mission statement.** If you're a new salesperson or a recent college grad, you probably won't have an extensive resume to draw upon, so don't worry. Most prospects won't expect you to come in and wow them with all your experience. What they really want to know is can they trust what you're saying and can they count on you to deliver. This requires a certain level of confidence.

Apologizing for your lack of experience or drawing undo attention to it by highlighting your college achievements isn't the way to get it. Instead, give them an informal mission statement. For example, you can say, "As an account executive with Global Corp., I have the opportunity to work with a wide variety of small to midsize companies, helping them navigate the new healthcare landscape and provide Fortune 500 benefits to their employees." This information is just enough to give your prospect reassurance in your ability as a valuable member of the team.

- **Strike a professional tone.** Your introduction also sets the tone for your presentation. A too casual or flippant attitude can come across as arrogant to your audience members or cause them to place less importance on the rest of your presentation. Although you may well be friends with some of your prospects, they're making a business decision and as the expert there to guide them, you need to act the part.

> ✔ **Practice.** Having to practice your own introduction may seem silly, but doing so can serve you well. Treat your introduction as any other important element of your presentation. Practice it for content, continuing to edit and fine-tune until it's crisp and clear and then work on making it as conversational as possible.

Knowing what to include in your introduction

Like benefits, your introduction isn't really about you. It's about what you can do for your audience. Therefore, the fact that you're the reigning Words with Friends champion probably isn't relevant. Here are some things that you may want to include

- ✔ Current position and title
- ✔ Length of time and responsibilities
- ✔ Industry accreditation or recognition
- ✔ Specific experience working with others in your client's niche or industry
- ✔ Experience helping other clients with similar challenges

Add in only things that are relevant to this particular prospect or opportunity. Lead with your strongest fact. For example, if your prospect is a bank and you've worked in the banking industry, start with that. If you have several strong points, use the most current.

Although you may want to include an interesting personal fact later on in your presentation when you've established credibility and built up rapport, it's risky to start off too personal or off-topic with a business audience during your introduction.

Here's an example of a relevant introduction:

> "For those of you who don't know me, my name is Anita White. As an account executive at EMJ Solutions, I've had the opportunity to work with a variety of companies like yours who have grown to a point where their old tools simply aren't able to keep up with new demands. In fact, I faced many of the same challenges you're experiencing in my former career as a financial analyst. It gives me great pleasure to help companies like yours find ways to continue to grow while controlling costs and minimizing risks in a constantly changing market."

Employing a prospect introduction

Speaking about yourself is awkward for both you and your audience. Most people (yes, even salespeople) are uncomfortable blowing their own horn. Talking about yourself in these circumstances is difficult without coming across as either arrogant or self-conscious. To compensate, salespeople either say too little or deliver uncomfortable stream-of-conscious style introductions. Neither approach builds credibility, and in fact, may hurt it.

The best type of introduction is to have someone within your prospect's organization introduce you, which has the added bonus of borrowing credibility from your customer. This introduction works because humans are much more likely to trust the opinion of a third party with no personal stake in a company's success, as opposed to someone associated with the company (as in you, the salesperson). In fact, many people frequently use this third-party principle. Millions of people regularly rely on reviews from people whom they've never met to guide them before shelling out hard cash for goods or services. Think of the many such services and sites online. Using someone within your prospect's organization to introduce you sets the expectation of the audience and gives you an instant boost of credibility — before you've even opened your mouth.

Consider this example of a prospect introduction, delivered by your sponsor within the prospect's organization or the highest-level manager in the room.

> "I'd like to introduce you all to Bob Simmons. Bob is a senior account executive at Java Industries where he's worked with mid-size financial organizations like ours for the past three years. Prior to that he worked in data processing at a community bank, so he has a good firsthand understanding of the challenges we face. Bob is going to talk to us about how we can increase the efficiency and accuracy of our reporting and ultimately make our jobs easier. Now I'll turn it over to Bob."

In order to write your own prospect introduction, follow these steps:

1. **Type out a short introduction for yourself.**

   Use a large font — so the person who introduces you can easily read it — that includes two-three relevant points about why you're qualified to talk to your audience.

2. **Ask the highest-ranking member of your audience to introduce you.**

   Tell him to simply read the page, not memorize it. Have him look over your introduction beforehand to go over any tricky pronunciations. You want to save both of you the embarrassment of having him mispronounce your name or company.

3. **Invite (and encourage) your prospect to add any opening remarks or instructions.**

   Your prospect may like to frame the meeting by telling the audience why they are there or remind them to turn off cellphones and laptops. He can then simply read the introduction just as it's written.

4. **Thank your prospect and jump right into your presentation.**

Reimagining the Company Overview

Remember getting cornered by that guy at a networking event who went on and on about himself immediately after you were introduced? Unfortunately, you may be that guy if you're still opening your presentation with a typical company overview like this one.

> "Before we start, I want to tell you a little bit about our company. We started as a small data management company in Wisconsin with ten employees. By 2004 we had grown to 1,000 employees across five time zones. Here's a picture of our current office in Stamford which we purchased last year to make room for everybody–and it's already getting cramped! On this next slide you can see some of the over 500 customers we've helped, including IBM, Sunkist, P&G."

Are you still awake? Good. This paragraph consists mostly of facts — bone–dry, boring facts. Nuggets of information that, as delivered, have little direct connection or interest to your customer.

This staple of the typical sales presentation needs an overhaul to be effective with today's savvy decision-makers. Here's why:

✔ **Your audience is educated.** At one time, before the Internet (yes, that's how dated the company overview is) this section of a sales presentation served an important purpose — to provide prospective buyers with information about your company to help them determine if you were capable of addressing their needs. Assuming that your prospects have access to the Internet (of which three billion people do, so the odds are high), more than likely they already have a good deal of information about your company. In fact, studies show that nearly 80 percent of Americans research a product or service online before buying. Your website or other publically available information may have gotten you on the short list to deliver this very presentation. Do you really want to spend the crucial first few minutes repeating what they already know? Probably not.

✔ **Nobody cares . . . yet.** People don't care what you sell until they know that you care. Nothing says the company and you care like opening your presentation by engaging and connecting with your audience and making them feel like the star of the show. Talking about how many locations you have or your growth strategy misses on both counts. Of course, you do want to highlight or reinforce relevant points and there's a place for that, but it's not at the very beginning of your presentation. Company strengths and capabilities helped to get you in the door. Now that you're *in* the door, focus your energy first on giving them a reason to pay close attention by letting them know that the presentation is about them first, not you.

✔ **It doesn't differentiate you.** You have some unique features and capabilities, but the fact is that almost any salesperson is able to reel out a list of facts, quotes, and accomplishments about her company. Although it would be refreshing if someone stood up during a presentation and said, "We had a few rough years, lawsuits, bankruptcies, and bad investments, but we're bouncing back" or "We can't touch our competition in terms of product launches and service times, but we're quite a bit cheaper," it's likely not going to happen anytime soon. Because every vendor can and will pull out its best quotes, stats, and charts, don't count on your overview to set you apart, because it won't.

✔ **It can hurt your credibility.** Paradoxically, sharing your company's achievements too early in the presentation can actually damage your credibility rather than enhance it. Today's decision-makers can be understandably skeptical. They've heard and seen hundreds of business propositions, and a few may have even burned them with more promises than they could deliver. Leading with your accomplishments opens you up to that skepticism and unfavorable comparisons. Earn the right to talk about your accomplishments with today's business audiences. Focus on delivering value in the beginning and your credibility will build quickly and naturally.

Recognizing what to include in a company overview

You want to reinforce or make sure that your audience knows some key points or facts about your company. At the same time, you want to avoid the potential tune-out factor or rehashing of the same territory.

A typical company overview includes some or all of the following:

✔ History

✔ Locations

- ✔ Mission statement
- ✔ Products/services
- ✔ Target markets
- ✔ Executive team
- ✔ Major accomplishments/industry awards
- ✔ Accreditation
- ✔ Customers
- ✔ Partners

Are all of these things relevant to your prospect? Probably not. Even if they are, will the audience members remember them all? Definitely not. This is not a case where more is better. These sections offer some tips to help you decide what to include in your company overview, including using the WIFM test.

Evaluating relevance

Include only those items that most directly link to the case you are building for your prospect. Review your objectives (refer to Chapter 2 for more on objectives) and see which company facts support your goals. For example, if one of your objectives is to address your audience's concern that you haven't been in the industry as long as some of your competitors, then point out other happy customers and industry awards. If audience members have a CEO who is part of an organization that your firm is accredited by, by all means, draw their attention to it. But be selective. Pick two to five key facts that you think are important to highlight for this particular customer.

Applying the WIFM Test

The fact is that facts don't sell themselves. Be grateful. If they did, your job would be obsolete. To avoid delivering the equivalent of a factual sleeping pill, sit in your prospect's seat and put the facts you want to include to the WIFM (What's-in-it-for-me) Test.

The WIFM Test ensures that each fact you're considering including about your company can be seen as a benefit for the prospect by answering the question "What's in it for me?"

Consider these facts taken from the earlier example in this section:

Fact: "We started as a small data management company in Wisconsin with ten employees."

WIFM Test: What's in it for your prospect? Unless your prospect is a big cheese-head, then it's hard to say. Remember, most companies are proud of their roots, but most customers couldn't care less.

Fact: "By 2004, we had grown to 1,000 employees across five time zones. Here's a picture of our current office in Stamford that we purchased last year to make room for everybody — and it's already getting cramped!"

WIFM Test: What's in it for your prospect? Plenty, if your prospect is in the market for an office building in Stamford, Connecticut. Otherwise, not much. Companies seem to think showing prospective customers a picture of their office building is impressive, but it's more like showing pictures of your high school graduation on a first date.

Focusing facts on customers

You may need to reposition or expand on each fact that you include, making sure that your overview is more customer-focused. Take the extra step to quickly tell them *why* each fact is meaningful to your prospects by thinking about the following three questions as you apply the WIFM test:

- ✔ **How can you make this interesting to your audience?** Think about how you can connect this fact to your prospects' business or industry. Use words or phrases that let them know not to expect the same old dry facts.

  For example: "Before we get started, I'd like to tell you a little bit about our company *that may surprise you.*"

  Now, instead of telling your prospects that it's time for a quick nap, you've given them a reason to pay attention. Just make sure that you follow through on what you're promising. (For example, the fact that you have 1,000 employees is not surprising to your prospects, unless they thought you were a one-man firm.)

- ✔ **How does this relate to your prospect or her business?** Look for areas of shared interest or history between your companies. This may be something you discovered in your research or a conversation with someone in your prospect's organization. Are they a similar size or geography, or do they share a common mission? Use that information now.

  For example, "*Like you,* we started out in the Midwest as a very small, ten-person data management company and have made it a priority to maintain those midwestern values as we've grown."

  You've now established a connection by relating your company's roots and values to theirs.

- ✔ **Does this provide a benefit?** On their own, most facts aren't benefits. Think about how you can turn a fact into a benefit for your prospects by asking yourself, "What benefit would my prospect derive from this fact?"

  For example, "By 2004 we had grown to 1,000 employees across five time zones, which means we always have someone available to take your calls."

  This revision to the example lets your prospect know why it matters that you have 1,000 employees.

Don't make your prospects do all the work. Make it easy for them to connect what you're saying to their business by applying the WIFM Test. If it's not readily apparent what's in it for them, ask yourself whether it needs to be said at all.

Positioning your company overview

Most sales presentations start with the company overview right smack up front before or after the agenda. I discuss various reasons why it's ineffective, not the least being that everyone else does it in the "Reimagining the Company Overview" section earlier in this chapter. Here are some tips for placing your company overview where it can provide the most value to your audience:

- ✔ **After your first benefit:** Place your overview slide after you discuss your first agenda item and discuss the benefit. See if you can tie the benefit to the first fact in your overview, which is even better, as shown in the next point. By waiting until you get through the opening and deliver some value, your audience will be more open to hearing about your accomplishments because you have started to establish a relationship and built some credibility.

- ✔ **Distributed throughout:** Instead of dumping all of your company information on one or two slides and lumping it all together at the beginning of your presentation, distribute a few key facts or accomplishments near the subject they pertain to. For example, if you're talking about why your prospects need customer support, bring up the fact that you've provided more than 500 customers with ongoing support for 26 years. Placing the fact and the benefit closer to the subject increases the impact of your message.

Keeping your audience engaged during your company overview

After picking your key points and making your company overview customer focused, you can hold your audience's attention while talking about your company in these additional ways:

- ✔ **Keep it short.** Remember, most of this information isn't news to your audience, so don't belabor it. To avoid losing attention, keep things moving along at a brisk pace.

✔ **Make it conversational.** Reading slides to your audience is a bad habit, but reading your company overview is an especially egregious crime. Resist the urge because nothing will cause your audience to disengage faster. As you highlight a particular point on your company overview, focus on connecting with your audience through eye contact or movement as you tell them what it means to them. (Check out Chapter 11 for ways to use eye contact.)

✔ **Build a story.** To make your company overview more interesting to your audience, think of structuring it like a story, with an attention-grabbing opening, a body that builds tension, and an ending that resolves conflict. Refer to Chapter 12 for more information about building a story.

Chapter 9

Designing a Winning Presentation

*A*pproximately 350 PowerPoint presentations are estimated to be given every second, so more than likely your prospect has seen a few. In fact, he may be watching one right now. Slides are the most popular visual aid for your message — and visual support plays a critical role in focusing your prospect's attention, engaging emotion, and improving recall. The quality and relevance of your presentation material reflects on your product, your company, and you. Endless bullet points, competing fonts, dizzying animations, and cheesy graphics can give your product, your message, and your credibility a beating.

If you're like most salespeople, you put a good deal of time into creating your slide deck, but with little training, it can still fall short of the mark. Shoddy or generic decks give your prospect reason to doubt your ability to perform as a company or deliver on your proposal — a concern you can't afford in a competitive market. Make sure the quality of your design matches the quality of your content.

In this chapter, you find out why you should incorporate some form of visual element and then determine which one is right for your presentation. I help you understand the difference between software presentation programs and how to apply the one-slide/one-idea concept to keep your story flowing. I also introduce the ten rules for designing great slides as well as graphic tools like photos, videos, and animation for making your presentation pop. I finish this chapter with a checklist to make sure your slide deck is designed to keep your prospect engaged and involved in your presentation.

Figuring Out What Presentation Materials to Use

Salespeople who tell me that they just want to have a conversation with their prospects usually have had too many near-death-by-PowerPoint experiences. Your presentation material doesn't have to be a boring barrage of bullet points that distances you from your prospect; in fact, good presentation material can fire your prospect's imagination, trigger emotion, and enhance and focus conversation. These sections explain the impact visual support can have on your prospect and help you choose the right option for your presentation.

Understanding why you need visual aids

Eighty percent of the information a person's brain takes in comes through their eyes, making the visual component of a presentation extremely valuable in fostering and focusing a conversation. There are many other reasons to include a visual aid in your presentation:

✔ **Engaging your audience:** Your slides can entertain, inform, and with the right graphics, dazzle. With longer presentations in particular, having a variety of tools for refocusing your prospect's attention is necessary. Slides, whiteboards, or even flipcharts, can add a nice break to a verbal presentation or a product demonstration.

✔ **Adding emotional impact:** Visual representations allow your prospect to experience your message through more than one sense, which activates more areas in the brain, making your message more powerful.

✔ **Simplifying complex ideas:** People want to quickly be able to grasp a concept or make sense of information. That's part of why infographics have taken off so quickly. A visual expression of the idea takes the mental work out of it for your prospect. Figure 9-1 shows a graphic that makes quick sense of data (outbound call results).

✔ **Improving recall:** No matter how compelling your delivery, spoken words aren't as powerful as when they're combined with visual images. Research shows that people remember only about 10 percent of what they hear just one week later, but that percentage jumps to 65 when a visual is associated with that message, which is a compelling case for using some sort of visuals in your presentation.

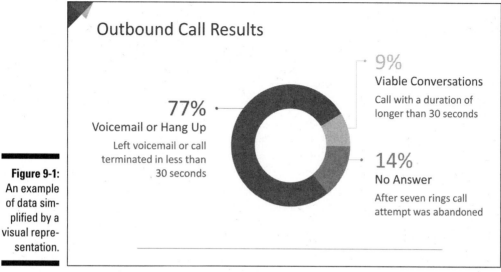

Figure 9-1:
An example
of data sim-
plified by a
visual repre-
sentation.

Choosing your visual aid: Your options

When selecting a medium to bring your presentation to life visually, you have many things to consider. You have to consider how large your audience is; are you presenting to one person, ten, or a virtual audience? You also need to know your presentation environment — web, boardroom with projector, or across a desk. You also have to consider how formal or informal it is. All of these factors influence which type of the following visual aid that you use:

- **Slide decks:** Slides are the medium choice for most presenters. Because slides are so common, I devote a large chunk of this chapter to them.

- **Whiteboards:** Using a dry-erase board is a great tool on its own or in addition to slides to capture ideas in the moment and communicate in a nonlinear fashion.

- **Handouts:** Many people still like to have something physical to look at and take notes on in a presentation. For best practices on using handouts in your presentation and creating a custom handout, flip to Chapter 7.

Table 9-1 compares the pros and cons to your three choices.

Table 9-1	Comparing Your Visual Aid Options	
Option	*Pros*	*Cons*
Slide decks	Versatile	May be too formal for a one-on-one presentation
	Easy to create and to change	Reliant on technology
	Easy to capture attention when needed	The expected choice — can blend in with competition
	Allow you to visually support key messages within your presentation with graphics, charts, text, and movement	Difficult too give nonlinear presentations
Whiteboards	Useful when message is nonlinear and presentation requires collaboration	Hard to convey complex ideas
	Grab audience's attention, especially C-level executives	Can be difficult to read — especially if handwriting is bad
	Easy to change	Presenter has back to audience while writing
Handouts	Audience can follow along and take notes	Easier to lose control of your prospect's focus who can tune out
	Serves as memory aid for prospect	Not easy to make last-minute changes

Weighing In on Presentation Software for Your Slides

It may surprise you, but several alternatives to slideware are available. The list continues to grow, and I explore a few of the major contenders in the following sections.

Ultimately you should choose the format that best fits your purpose (telling a linear story versus building on the fly), your resources (PC, Mac, or web), and your content (graphic or video heavy). And no matter which software you choose make sure it's the highest quality.

Because PowerPoint owns about 95 percent of the presentation software market as of this writing, I focus the remaining design concepts in this chapter on PowerPoint; however, good planning and design principles are consistent across platforms.

All of these programs are simply tools. They have yet to invent a software that can fix a weak case, poor structure, or unclear messaging.

PowerPoint

Love it or hate it, it's the 1,000-pound gorilla in the conference room. Although its success may have more to do with the fact that Microsoft bundles PowerPoint with other programs than its unique capabilities, it's still the go-to solution for telling a linear story, which is ideal for most sales presentations.

PowerPoint is user friendly and provides a decent selection of design styles, animations, and builds. Built for a PC, you can get a version for your Mac, but as with any PC-Mac conversion, miscommunication is possible, which can result in inconsistent layouts, fonts, and animations. Because it's linear, PowerPoint doesn't have the flexibility for jumping around to accommodate audience interaction like Prezi, and it creates some very large files when you add images and video, making sharing your presentation more challenging. Check out *PowerPoint 2013 For Dummies* by Doug Lowe (John Wiley & Sons, Inc.).

Keynote

Apple's presentation software is for Mac users only. Although Keynote has many of the same features as PowerPoint, it's more media-based and offers better sound, image manipulation, and video integration. It includes more ways to introduce entertaining animation effects all with smooth transitions between slides. It has an easy, clean interface but, as with all things Apple, the program doesn't play well with other programs, which can cause problems in a predominantly PC world.

Prezi

Unlike PowerPoint, Prezi is ideal for a nonlinear presentation, allowing you to create a presentation starting with a blank canvas and branching out from there. Prezi's unique differentiator is its zoom function and its ability to jump from one part of the presentation to another, allowing you to focus in on areas as needed. Its distinguishing features are also its downfall; the zoom function can make your audience a bit dizzy and overshadow your message. Prezi also has limited backgrounds and pre-chosen fonts/colors that can't be changed. If you want to discover more about Prezi, read *Prezi For Dummies* by Stephanie Diamond (John Wiley & Son, Inc.).

SlideRocket

One of several online presentation options, SlideRocket has a good interface and allows you to easily add content from the web. It doesn't do a lot of the fancy animations or graphics as the big boys, but for web presentations it's worth considering.

Determining Slide Content

Before you choose what to *show* you must be absolutely clear on what you want to *say*. Many salespeople make the mistake of starting with the sales deck and building messaging and structure after that. Slide decks should be the result of all your discovery, planning, structuring, and messaging.

The best decks tell a story, and like any well-told story, it needs to follow a logical path. You need to be fanatical about connecting the dots and selecting only content that helps you illuminate and build your story. Each slide needs to seamlessly follow the one before it, staying focused on your message and highlighting key points along the way. The way to ensure this is to start on your deck only after you have your message and structure down.

Slides are there to help your audience understand and remember your message. They are not *the* message. Your message is the star. Your slides are the supporting cast. They're there to reinforce your message, call attention to it, and help the audience remember it. The following sections explain some guidelines for deciding what to include on your slides.

A good sales deck shouldn't be self-explanatory. It requires you, the presenter, to give it context and meaning.

Refer to www.dummies.com/cheatsheet/salespresentations for a checklist you can follow to help you design a slide deck.

Choosing which messages to support

Understanding which elements in your presentation would and wouldn't benefit from visual support is important. Not every message deserves a slide. Nothing in your slide deck can be gratuitous. Every slide needs to earn its right to be there. Too many slides have the same negative effect as too much information on one slide. Go through your written presentation or outline and pick out the key messages you want to visually support. This preliminary step is easy to skip, but doing so is critical for keeping you organized and on message.

Here are some elements you may want to visually support in your presentation starting with the opening of your presentation through the close:

✔ **Opening hook:** The attention-grabbing device used in your opening is an ideal place for visual support. Use the same visual when you close to reinforce recall. Check out Chapter 5 for tips on hooks.

✔ **Stories:** Whether it's an anecdote, a customer story, or a personal story, a picture or graphic can enhance the impact and make it memorable. Find more on storytelling in Chapter 12.

✔ **Value proposition:** A visual aid can reinforce for your prospect the benefit that he will derive from your solution. See Chapter 3 on value.

✔ **Agenda:** Providing a list of topics to cover that you refer back to lets your prospect know where you are and give them a sense of progression. You can find tips on creating an agenda in Chapter 8.

✔ **Features:** Those unique things that your product or service can do often can be more powerful when your prospect can visualize them. Chapter 6 has more on features.

✔ **Benefits:** Graphics that show how improved your prospect's situation will be after using your solution provide a strong emotional trigger. Chapter 3 discusses benefits.

✔ **Supporting data:** If you have facts and figures that help make your case, a graphic representation can greatly enhance your prospect's understanding and recall. Find more on supporting data in Chapter 7.

✔ **Call to action:** Make it easy for your prospect to take the next step by visually supporting what it is you want him to do. Chapter 7 has tips on coming up with a clear and specific call to action.

Identifying the idea that you're communicating

Each slide should focus on one idea or concept. Overloading your slides with too many ideas can overwhelm your audience and water down your message. The good news is that slides are free (in most cases), so use another slide if you have more than one idea to communicate. For each slide:

- ✔ **What is the one thing?** What is the single idea you want your prospect to take away from this slide? It can be specific, as in "we can increase your bottom line by 5 percent," or conceptual, "bigger is not always better." Although statements of fact can often be effectively represented by text, a conceptual idea is often better expressed through graphics.

- ✔ **What is the tone?** Is it light or humorous? Is it emotional? Is it serious? The tone of your message helps you determine whether to use text (for more serious messages), pictures (for lighter or more emotional content), or graphical representations (for facts or data) to support your message.

- ✔ **How can you say it visually?** Instead of just putting the words on the slide as most salespeople do, consider whether something graphic can communicate your idea more effectively. For example, if your topic is time management, you could use an image of a clock, a watch, or an hourglass.

Picking a template

Whichever presentation software you use, you'll have a variety of *templates* — pre-developed slide layouts — from which to choose. Templates are important to ensure that your design remains consistent through your presentation. Some considerations when choosing a template are as follows:

Know your audience

Make sure that you know your audience members and what kind of presentation to give them. Are they C-level executives or the people who will be using your product or service? Is it a formal or informal presentation? Are they in a creative industry like architecture or a more reserved industry like finance? These questions help you decide on an appropriate template. For example, you probably want to steer clear of whimsical designs and comic fonts for finance executives and let your inner designer shine for prospects in architecture or fashion industries.

Present the right image

Your slides are a reflection of you, your company, and your product so consider what type of image you want to portray and choose your design accordingly. Is it one of professionalism, security, or collaboration? You probably want colors and designs that support those ideas. If your prospect is looking to be more innovative, get creative and don't go in with the same old boring presentation template that he has seen a hundred times.

Make your slides readable

You need your prospect to be able to quickly read and understand your slides. If you make your prospect work too hard, he'll tune out. Some templates look great from an artistic perspective, but in practical terms they're difficult to read. Some examples include dark backgrounds with light type, busy graphics, or fancy, scripted fonts. Never sacrifice the clarity of your message for design. Figure 9-2 shows examples of two slides — one with low readability and one with high readability. The slide on the left has a dark background and weak contrast. The slide on the right has a white background and sections are clearly defined with icons. Check out the later section, "Fostering readability" for specific ways to do it.

Figure 9-2: An example of two slides, one with low (a) and high readability (b).

a)   b)

Illustration by 24Slides

Be original

Approximately 95 percent of the world uses PowerPoint, so your prospect has probably seen many of the program's themes. Part of the value of a theme is its ability to provide visual impact. Using a common theme removes much of that power and makes it more difficult for your prospect to differentiate you from your competition. Your prospect should feel that you have carefully chosen every slide for him.

Here are some options for finding an original theme for your presentation:

✔ **Mix it up.** If you use a standard PowerPoint theme, changing an element within that theme — such as font, color, or layout — can make it look fresh and new.

✔ **Create your own.** You may find it easier to build your own template by creating the design elements in Adobe Illustrator or Photoshop first before exporting it into a basic PowerPoint template and editing it further. If you need more help, Canva (`www.canva.com`) gives you access to hundreds of pre-designed templates so you can start creating your own. You can reach out to freelance designers on `www.fiverr.com` or `www.upwork.com`.

✔ **Use a professional design service.** Many online services can provide you with quick, original themes or help you to create your own. For example, 24 Slides (`www.24slides.com`) can take your ideas and quickly — often within 24 hours — design or redesign a concept much better and faster than you could do on your own. The company is fast, experienced, and reasonably priced.

Following the Ten Rules of Visual Presentations

Although a great slide deck can be a work of art, you don't need to be an art major to create one if you follow these simple design rules.

Considering your environment

Where and how your presentation will be viewed is important to the design. Take into consideration whether it will be projected on a screen to a large group, delivered on your iPad to a single prospect, or viewed on a computer monitor. Take into account the following as you determine design:

✔ **Using a projector:** If you're using your prospect's projector, be prepared for less-than-ideal-viewing circumstances. Weak lighting combined with a bright room can make your images and text fuzzy and hard to read. Think about using more contrast between colors and shapes as well as a larger type size. Better yet, bring your own portable projector and you won't have to worry.

✔ **Using computer screens or tablets:** On a smaller screen the impact of any movement becomes multiplied and can be distracting. Limit your animations to simple builds or wipes. Refer to the later section, "Recognizing the types of animation" for descriptions and usage.

Having a hierarchy

Although the concept is one idea per slide, you may have more than one element on your slide — multiple bullet points, heading, image, and so forth. The information on your slide has a hierarchy, which means that some things are more important than others.

Think of your slide as an advertisement. Most advertisements are broken into three parts: Headline, subhead, and details. Give more weight through size, color, movement, or space to the more important elements on your slide to ensure that your audience quickly gets the main point.

Incorporating white space

Keep your slides simple so they're a quick read. Hence you need some *white space,* or a portion of the slide left unmarked. Your prospect should be able to follow what you're saying and take in your visuals at the same time. If the slide has too much information, your prospect will tune you out until he has finished processing the point of the slide, so leave off the big logos, added boxes, or cutesy graphics. The more white space you create — the stronger the visual impact. Think headline, maybe a few bullet points, and/or an image.

Figure 9-3 shows an example of how the use of white space can affect the readability of a slide. The slide on the left is cluttered and has too little white space. The slide on the right has less copy and more white space making it easier and more inviting to read.

Figure 9-3: An example of slides with limited white space (a) and sufficient white space (b).

a)   b)   *Illustration by 24Slides*

Using contrast

You want your prospect to be able to quickly grasp the intent of each slide. If everything blurs together, your prospect won't know what to focus on. To make certain elements stand out, make the contrast between them more distinct through the use of placement, space, color, or size.

Being consistent

Too many different sizes, fonts, colors, alignments, or transitions can make your presentation look like Frankenstein's monster. Keep design elements consistent within your presentation from slide to slide. A good template can help you accomplish that. See earlier section on "Picking a template" for tips on how you can select a template.

Creating alignment

A well-aligned slide is easy to read and won't distract any OCD members in your audience. An easy way to achieve alignment is to use the grid feature in PowerPoint to help you lay out different elements and keep them looking neat and organized. Align text from left or right as opposed to centering it, which is more difficult to read.

Figure 9-4 shows a slide with the grid feature enabled in PowerPoint. The horizontal and vertical lines help you to more precisely align the text which makes it easier for the prospect to read.

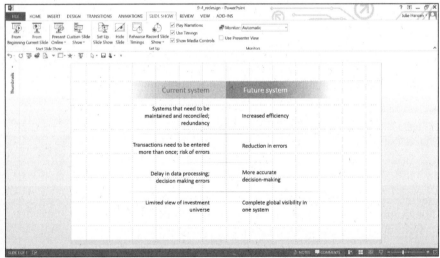

Figure 9-4:
The grid feature aligns your slide content.

Illustration by 24Slides

Grouping

Art displays often group like items in threes to form a whole. Think about grouping similar elements in your presentation together to create a unified message as opposed to multiple messages. For example, grouping together several images of your product being used can create a message about over-all usefulness as opposed to focusing on individual features.

Fostering readability

You're frugal with your words to make the strongest statement, but if people can't read your text in the back of the room or it's too fancy to decipher, you've missed the moment. Here are some tips to ensure readability:

✔ Always use at least an 18-point font on your slides so that your prospect doesn't have to struggle read it.

✔ Use a sans serif font like Arial, Helvetica, or Calibri for body text.

✔ Save decorator fonts for slide headers.

✔ Use dark text on a light background. Black slides are cool, but they're difficult to read.

✔ Limit your use of ALL CAPS. Let your delivery provide the emphasis.

Balancing text

If at first glance, your slide looks like a page from the dictionary, your pros-pect will likely bale out when trying to read it. Try not to exceed eight lines of text per slide and keep it balanced on the slide to make it easy to read. Figure 9-5 compares unbalanced and balanced slides. Figure 9-5 shows a slide that has too much text unequally distributed (on the left) and a slide that uses less text more evenly distributed (on the right.)

Keep your sentences from looking too choppy or too verbose by follow-ing the guidelines of six words per line with 30 to 40 characters (including spaces) per line.

Figure 9-5: Examples of unbalanced text (a) and balanced text (b).

a)

Designing your future

Technical expertise
- Well-managed team effort and strict quality control
- Every project is executed by a streamlined process
- Principals are personally involved with guidance and review of each project
- Familiarity of building codes and their applications

Innovative, quality design
- Highest attention to detail and client communication
- Collaborate on the best possible solutions
- Portfolio of nationally recognized projects from chains to multi-purpose buildings
- Commitment to sustainable solutions

b)

Designing your future

Technical expertise
- Well-managed team effort and strict quality control
- Every project is executed by a streamlined process
- Principals personally involved with guidance and review of each project

Innovative, quality design
- Highest attention to detail and client communication
- Collaborate on the best possible solutions
- Portfolio of nationally recognized projects from chains to multi-purpose buildings

Illustration by 24Slides

Design renaissance with Apple and Pinterest

Follow the leaders to see how design has changed in the last ten years. Two places to look are Apple and Pinterest.

✔ Apple's simple, clean style extends from its products to its advertising and even into its apps. Apple is the ongoing leader in how to design simple, beautiful interaction.

✔ Pinterest entered the scene in 2011 and quickly began influencing the design of

everything from websites blogs to home interiors. Viewers interact with design and tell stories with pictures. It's a great source for inspiration — if you know where to look. Because Pinterest has no hierarchy — one picture isn't more important than another — focus on following some popular pinners to find inspiration. Here are a few worth checking out: Joy Cho, Sean Booth, Chad Syme, and Carolina Beiertz.

Giving bullets a rest

You can easily fall into the bullet point trap — slide after slide of bullet points and sub-bullet points — in PowerPoint and Keynote templates. Overusing bullets is boring for your audience and discourages interaction. Consider whether you need to use bullet points at all — or if a graphic may be a better choice.

No one remembers a bullet point, but they do remember a smart graphic. If you do use bullet points, make sure each one supports your key message. This forces you to weed through your bullet points to find the one thing that you absolutely have to share with your clients. If you have ten one things, then you need ten slides.

Picking the Best Graphics

Graphics are simply visual words. The only reason to use them is to increase the impact of your presentation. Graphics either move your message forward or are a distraction. Because no one can stare at bullet points for thirty minutes without needing transfusions of coffee, graphics are necessary attention getters. After you decide to use graphics, you have a variety of options to choose from. You can use almost anything — in moderation. Don't limit yourself to one category, especially if you have a long presentation. These sections point out a couple of options to consider.

Don't load up a slide with words *and* graphics unless your goal is to give your audience a headache.

Using photographs

Photographs are the most commonly used graphics in a presentation because of the sheer quantity available to choose from and the ability to quickly convey an idea. Before you just head to a stock photo site, you may want to consider the different types of photos you can use to create variety:

- ✔ **Your company photos:** If your business is a service company, like an architectural or construction firm, you have a lot of pictures from job sites. If you're selling a product, like office machines or vehicles, you have photos of people interacting with your product. Original photos are always better if appropriate, but be wary of turning your presentation into "all about us" with photos of your work.

- ✔ **Stock photos:** Buying stock photos is a great option when you know what type of photo you want, and you're short on time and money. You can choose from many different stock photo companies online. If you want it, you can find a picture of it. They vary in cost from free to quite pricey for more original, high-quality pictures.

Steer clear of overused stock photos or clearly staged photos. You can recognize many of them from social media sites and blog posts. A dead giveaway is exceptionally beautiful people having way too much fun at their jobs. Often the first idea you come up with is the most generic and thus most overused (for example, a handshake for team work). Overused photos instantly weaken your message so think outside of the box.

- ✔ **Your own digital photo:** You have a camera, but do you have an eye? A homegrown photo can look amateurish if it's not done well. Always make sure your photos are as polished as the rest of your presentation.

- ✔ **Manufacturer photos:** Big money was probably spent to create product photos and it's great to use them — sparingly. A product brochure type of presentation can be as dull as nonstop bullet points. If you do need to feature a few products, focus on a great headline to put the energy back into your presentation.

- ✔ **Advertising artwork:** Many stock art sites have pieces of a familiar ad or the ad itself that can be used for comparison points.

- ✔ **Hire a photographer:** If you know the look you're going for and the experience you want your customers to feel, spend the money to have a professional photographer capture it. Having your own original art can be a huge boon. You can't be copied and you've custom built your message.

Take advantage of all the options. If you are using more generic photography, focus on the headline to stay original.

Keep diversity in mind when choosing photos. Consider your prospect's organization and customer base and try to represent it accordingly.

Showing an idea with illustrations

Sometimes a photograph can't fully capture an idea, and an illustration may be your best bet. An *illustration* can be a drawing or a sketch, and it can be done by hand or with the help of programs like Adobe Illustrator.

Illustrations can have an amateurish feel to them and be reminiscent of old clip art if they aren't done well. If you need to have a specific concept visualized, a designer may be able to capture it in a fresh way with an original illustration. For example, Fiverr is a great resource to find reasonably priced graphic artists to help you achieve your desired effect. Figure 9-6 demonstrates an example of an illustration to communicate a complex idea.

Explaining with graphs

Using graphs to show or compare data is much more effective than just listing or rattling off a bunch of numbers. But a graph can be equally confusing if your audience doesn't understand it because too much information is jammed into the wrong format.

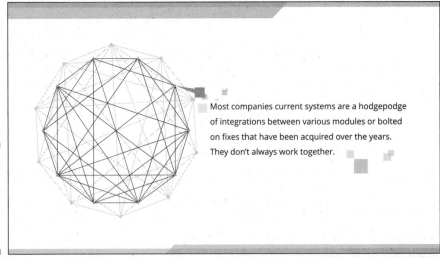

Figure 9-6: An illustration can help communicate an idea.

Most companies current systems are a hodgepodge of integrations between various modules or bolted on fixes that have been acquired over the years. They don't always work together.

Illustration by 24Slides

Manipulating photographs

In some instances, you may want to use a photograph in your presentation but change something within it to achieve a specific look or feel.

You can manipulate your photos in many ways to add originality. You can play with the size or crop the photo for interest. You can enlarge the entire photo or just a portion to hone in on a key detail. You can increase or decrease the amount of light or saturation to create a mood or fit your presentation environment. Choosing a high brightness level can change the emotion, but if you are presenting in a ballroom or a bright boardroom it can get washed out. Check out your surroundings ahead of time if possible, but if you're not sure, duplicate your presentation and change the brightness so that you have two options.

Here are some things to keep in mind when using graphs:

- **Choose the right graph.** Select your graph based on what is most important to highlight. Think about design elements, such as color and contrast, two-dimensional or three-dimensional, or horizontal or vertical. Your choices should be based on how your prospect can easily understand your data. Here are some uses for the basic graph types:

  - **Column:** Compares the differences in individual values vertically by time period or other data categories. For example, comparing the total number of orders each month for the past year. Columns are good for comparing multiple categories and data points.

  - **Bar:** Shows the differences horizontally. Use a bar chart to highlight results from one or two questions. Bar charts get confusing and difficult to read when you start adding more categories or the differences between categories are slight.

  - **Pie:** Graphically representing the percentages of each segment of a whole as a part of a pie is an easy way to grasp something visual that quickly gets everyone on the same page. A pie chart is good for a single question or data point.

- **Use strong contrast.** Make the difference between categories instantly clear and avoid any confusion by opting for strong color pairings. Think opposites, like green, red, yellow, as opposed to staying within the same color family, such as pink, purple, and violet.

- **Pick a strong title.** Be clear about the heading for your graph. Opt for a simple title with one to two sentences that summarizes the data.

- **Be consistent.** Decide on a design format for your graphs, such as two-dimensional or three-dimensional, color scheme, and font style, and stick to it to make your presentation appear more unified and polished.

The good news is that all of the major presentation formats PowerPoint, Prezi, and Keynote have graph building software included. Most of these tools more than meet your needs. Your job is to match the layout to the purpose and the information. You want your one idea to stand out as opposed to charts of information so convoluted your meaning gets lost.

Turning Video Into An Asset

Video is a powerful force. If you walk into a store, a bar, or a lobby where the TV is on, you're automatically drawn to it. Video is being embedded into all forms of communication. Today it's the norm not the exception. Using video in your presentation can break up your content and energize your audience. However you don't want the video to steal the thunder. Make sure that it doesn't tell the whole story or make your main point — that's your job. Use it to back up your message.

Using short, high-energy bursts of video that are in-line with your topic can support your point, shed light on your message, and re-engage your audience. Here are some tips for incorporating video effectively in your PowerPoint presentation:

- ✔ Upload the video in your slide deck. Don't count on having Internet access to pull up clips from the web.
- ✔ Limit video clips to two to three minutes.
- ✔ Edit the video so that it starts and ends precisely where you want it to.
- ✔ Make sure that your sound is set to an appropriate volume level and test the speakers out before your presentation. The impact of your video is greatly lessened when your audience can't hear it easily.
- ✔ If you need to stop the video early, simply hit ALT Q.
- ✔ Be quiet when your video is playing. You want your audience to focus on the screen, not you.

If you're going to use video in your presentation, invest in a portable speaker. You can't count on your prospect having one, and most computer speakers don't provide adequate enough volume to fill the space.

Using Animation to Create Movement

Many of today's presentations use animation to make content more memorable and dynamic. Unlike video, animations are usually quick amplifiers for your slide where an object moves and or a sound is added. An effective engagement tool, animations are one of those tricks that can get old fast if you're not careful. The next sections help you understand when it makes sense to animate and show you various types of animation.

Animating with purpose

More often than not, every presenter is tempted to incorporate animation into sales decks, but sadly, the concept of animation is often much better than the reality. Unless the animation serves a very specific purpose, it's likely to come across as childish, foolish, and unprofessional, undoing much of the goodwill you may have built up.

Here are some ways to make sure you are animating purposefully:

- ✔ **Expand on a great idea.** A simple way to add some dynamo to your deck is animating your transitions — how you enter and close out of each slide. Whether it's the basic fade to black or dissolve, explore all the options, but settle on just one or two. Less is always more with animation.

- ✔ **Reveal a point.** When you want to add some suspense to your presentation and hold back on a key message or punch line, timing is everything. Using animation to reveal your point at the right time can be very effective.

- ✔ **Focus on one message at a time.** If you have a list of bullet points or group of items and don't want your prospect to jump ahead, building out or revealing the bullet points or items one at a time is an effective way to keep your prospect focused.

Recognizing the types of animation

If and when you add animation, do so judiciously. What you want your prospect to see when you start and end the movement on the slide matters. The longer it takes for the graphic to finish its dance the more tiresome and confusing for your audience. Don't use animations on every slide. Stick to the most subtle and professional. All animations are available on the "Animations" menu in PowerPoint. The most common choices to create movement inside the slides are as follows:

- ✔ **Reveal:** An object appears in its final place with no additional movement.

- ✔ **Slide:** Visuals move across the screen falling into their final position.

- ✔ **Divide:** Slides images into boxes and simultaneously reveals the graphics from left to right or top to bottom.

- ✔ **Dissolve to black:** This makes a graphic or type slowly disappear to add drama.

- ✔ **Lengthen:** The graphic expands outward from a starting point at the center line of the final point.

- ✔ **Rotate:** The graphic moves around a central axis before coming to a stop in its final position.

- ✔ **Zoom:** It hones in on a small piece of a graphic from either a spot centered on the final position or from the slide center, depending on the settings you set until revealing the graphic in its entirety in its final position.

- ✔ **Wipe left to right:** The feature reveals a sentence or object from left to right, which is how people read. Good for bullet points.

Part III
Delivering an Impactful Presentation

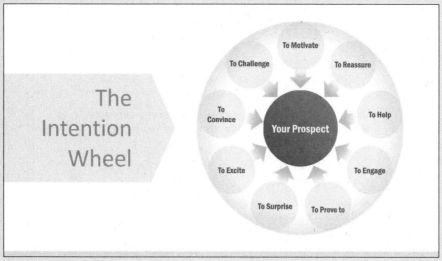

© John Wiley & Sons, Inc.

One of the most powerful ways to make an impact on your prospect is through the use of storytelling. Download the seven secrets to telling a great sales story at www.dummies.com/extras/salespresentations.

In this part . . .

✔ Understand the impact that presence has on your prospect and how to expand your presence with credibility, connection, and confidence.

✔ Use your voice and body language to bring your presentation to life and focus your prospect's attention on key points.

✔ Discover how to get to your vocal and physical best for your presentation with a solid warm-up and effective practice tips.

✔ Find out how to use your stage, move with purpose, and eliminate distracting movements that detract from your message.

✔ Know when to use stories in your presentation to trigger emotion, increase recall, overcome objections, and shift perceptions.

✔ Keep stage fright from stealing the show with helpful tips from the pros.

Chapter 10

The Presenter's 3 Cs: Credibility, Connection, and Confidence

A perfectly targeted, well-written presentation can fall on deaf ears if you're unable to make an impact your audience. The most effective presentations are a marriage between presentation and presenter; as the presenter, you're the lightning rod that connects the message to your prospect. Great actors, politicians, and presenters share a quality referred to as *presence,* a quality that draws people in and makes them sit up and pay attention. Whether your stage is a conference room, a living room, or a computer screen, you need to have presence if you want your prospect to give your proposal the attention and consideration it deserves.

In this chapter you find out how to develop your own brand of presence by leveraging a winning combination of ingredients. You discover several ways to earn credibility during your presentation. You find out how to connect and build rapport with your prospect. I also introduce you to some techniques for delivering your presentation with confidence — even when you don't necessarily feel it. Finally, you find some practical ways to increase your presence during those critical first few seconds when your prospect is forming a first impression of you.

Understanding Why You Need Presence

Presence is an energy, an attitude, or a bearing that makes other people want to connect with you and hear what you have to say. Although that may sound vague, the impact of presence is very clear. People with presence are able to move other people. Presence is a vital and often overlooked component in sales where your success depends on engaging and motivating a prospect to take action.

George Clooney, Oprah, Jimmy Fallon all have it; although defining presence isn't easy, people know it when they see it, and they most often see it in celebrities. Though you may think of famous people as having an exclusive hold on presence, you probably have people in your life — family members, coworkers, teachers, and coaches — who you can point to as exhibiting that quality. The truth is if you're alive and taking up space, you have presence. The question is how much presence do you have and how are you using it? Do you have enough presence to command the attention of one, two, or 20 people? For how long? Ten seconds? Twenty minutes? Two hours? Obviously having enough presence to connect with your entire audience for the full length of your presentation is important. And with the declining attention span of today's decision makers, you need an extra boost of presence to keep them engaged. That mysterious quality of presence that you bring to a room or a group of people can be broken down into three qualities — the three Cs:

- ✔ Credibility
- ✔ Connection
- ✔ Confidence

Boosting Your Credibility

Credibility is the power to inspire belief or trust in others. In a presentation, credibility is how much trust your prospect places in what you're saying. If the trust is low, your every statement can be subject to scrutiny and skepticism. If trust is high, you're given the benefit of the doubt in most instances. Being perceived as credible is critical to the success of your presentation; therefore, it deserves some thoughtful consideration and planning.

Credibility often has to be earned, which can be difficult when you may be meeting some of your prospects in person for the first time. Here are some tips for boosting your credibility in your presentation:

✔ **Use a reference.** Receiving the thumbs up from others in your propect's company or industry can give you a great deal of credibility. Weave these stories into your presentation early to establish credibility, or if you have an internal advocate, leverage that connection with an introduction, which you can read more about in Chapter 8.

✔ **Share qualifications.** Think about what qualifies you to present on your topic and work it into your introduction or when discussing a related subject. Some things to consider include

- Your title or accreditations
- Length of time in your position
- Experience with the subject or industry
- Professional achievements or awards

✔ **Show congruency.** Credible people's words match their actions. If your words say one thing but your body says another, your audience will pick up on it. For example, saying you welcome questions and then rushing through your topic without leaving space for input doesn't inspire trust.

✔ **Keep your word.** Being credible and trustworthy is all about doing what you say you're going to do. You can display that in simple ways during your presentation, for example, by starting when you say you're going to start, ending on time or early, and following up on all questions. Nothing makes you more credible than talking the talk and also walking the walk.

✔ **Prepare like crazy.** Even if you have little credibility to begin with, an insightful, well-prepared presentation can go a long way toward improving your credibility with your audience. Make sure you have everything you need to support your case, including numbers related to your product/service, sales and industry figures, and examples.

✔ **Stay authentic.** Most people can spot a phony. Own who you are and what you have to offer. If you are okay with that, chances are your audience will be as well.

Establishing a Connection with Your Audience

When is the last time you were really moved by an actor's performance? You probably can think of at least one recent example. Now, when was the last time you were really moved by a business or sales presentation? Not so easy, is it? Great actors make an emotional connection with their audience, drawing them in and inviting them to come along on their journey. Great salespeople do the same thing. Instead of talking at their audience, relying on the information to make the connection, they establish an emotional connection with their customers or prospects. As a result, they're able to inspire them to think about something in a new way or motivate them to change their behavior. The following techniques help you form a stronger connection with your audience:

- ✔ **Focus on others.** When you're interested in others, they become interested in you. Prospects can sense when you're truly interested in them or when they're just serving as a means to an end. Of course, you're there to make a sale, but you're also presumably providing a product or service that will improve your prospect's circumstances in some way. Approaching prospects with a genuine interest and curiosity about them, their needs, and how you can help is contagious. And you can't do it if you're too busy talking about yourself or your company.

- ✔ **Have a vision.** People are drawn to others who have a clear *vision* of where they're going and what they're trying to achieve. That visionary quality is consistently seen among leaders in business, politics, entertainment, and sports. Knowing what you can accomplish and communicating it in a way that helps your prospect visualize it is a compelling quality that makes your prospect want to connect.

- ✔ **Be in the moment.** Many opportunities to connect with your prospect come in those unplanned moments of your presentation, yet most salespeople miss them because they're not in the moment. Like an improv actor, you must focus fully on the present in order to connect and respond to your prospect. Giving each moment your full attention — not ruminating over what you just said or worrying about the next slide — gives you a heightened awareness that is compelling to your prospect. You're actively listening and responding, making discoveries at the same time as your prospect. Being in the moment doesn't mean that you don't have a plan; on the contrary, you know your plan so well that you're able to let go of it when needed and really focus on connecting with your audience. Doing so makes your prospect feel like she is experiencing the wonder of how the future could look right along with you for the first time.

- ✔ **Be vulnerable.** It means being transparent enough to let prospects get to know you. (Don't worry; you don't have to overshare or break down in tears.) Especially in personal businesses like real estate or any type of direct sales, buyers want to know with whom they're embarking on a business relationship. Being vulnerable means being open enough to share (appropriately) and confident enough to admit when you're wrong or don't know the answer. Personal stories are a great way to let your prospect gain some insight into who she'll be working with, while at the same time delivering a message that reinforces your key point. Chapter 12 has more on storytelling.

- ✔ **Break the fourth wall.** In the theater, the *fourth wall* is an imaginary wall that the actor projects on the audience to maintain privacy and separation. When an actor stops and suddenly talks directly to the audience, it causes the audience to sit up and pay attention. During a sales presentation prospects are typically very passive, partly because that's how they're trained, but also because salespeople often slip into autopilot as they deliver their presentations — standing just distant enough from their audience to make them feel safe enough to, say, read a text, write down a quick reminder, or simply let their thoughts wander. See the nearby sidebar for examples of breaking the fourth wall.

By breaking the fourth wall with your prospect, you can create a stronger connection and avoid falling into the autozone. Here are some ways to break the fourth wall:

- Speak directly to your audience.

- Ask a question.

- Walk toward — or into — your audience.

- Ask an audience member to participate by writing down something.

Breaking the fourth wall in film and TV

There you are comfortably snuggled into your couch watching a movie when suddenly the main character seems to look past the camera, directly at you, and begins speaking to you. If you're like most people, you can find this a bit unsettling. This theatrical technique called *breaking the fourth wall* originated in live theater but has become a popular device used in film, television, and even video games. Here are some popular examples of breaking the fourth wall that you may recognize:

- ✔ *House of Cards:* Kevin Spacey's character Frank Underwood often addresses the camera to let the audience in on his schemes.

- ✔ **The Wolf of Wall Street:** Leonardo DiCaprio as former stockbroker Jordan Belfort confesses to the audience how a nice guy like him got in over his head.

- ✔ *Ferris Buehler's Day Off:* Matthew Broderick as Ferris talks directly to the audience throughout the film, even scolding them for staying through the credits at the end.

- ✔ *Goodfellas:* During the dramatic courtroom scene, Ray Liotta suddenly stands up in the witness box and walks up to the camera to tell his side of the story while everyone else in the scene freezes.

- ✔ *High Fidelity:* The audience plays therapist to John Cusack as he tries to figure out where he went wrong in past relationships.

- ✔ *Annie Hall:* Woody Allen famously vents to the audience during this cinematic class.

- ✔ *Kiss Kiss, Bang, Bang:* Robert Downey Jr. gives a master class on how to break the fourth wall, right up to thanking the audience for coming at the end.

- ✔ *Modern Family:* Part of the hilarity of this Golden Globe winning series are the mockumentary-style interviews the characters have with the camera.

Being intentional

Feeling like you're connecting with your prospect isn't enough if your prospect doesn't feel it. Selling is very intentional and based on impacting your prospect's feelings, attitudes, and eventually behavior. From a communication standpoint, it's more than just sending out words; it's sending out feelings as well. To accomplish this, you need to have a very clear and strong intention.

To begin to put intention into action you need to understand what intentions are and the potential impact they can have on your prospect.

Knowing what an intention is

Intentions are the driving force under all of your words and actions. Much like expectations, intentions influence how you say things and accordingly, how people respond to you. In the performance world, actors consciously choose strong, specific intentions to direct their actions and words and create a specific effect on their audience.

People with real presence know precisely what they want and it's evident beyond just their words. Many salespeople have vague, inconsistent, or simply hopeful expectations that don't strongly impact their prospect. When you get clear and focus on communicating with your prospect in an intentional way in an effort to impact her feelings, attitude, or behavior, then you're well on your way to becoming a great communicator and a great salesperson.

Here is an example of a typical presentation intention:

> Presenter just finishing an accurate but boring presentation.
>
> Me: "So, what was your intention?"
>
> Presenter: (Looking momentarily confused.) "I'm trying to sell them." ("Duh," I believe he whispered under his breath.)
>
> Me: "Of course that's the overall goal," I said. "But in this specific section of your presentation, what are you trying to accomplish?"
>
> Presenter: "I'm trying to tell them how our solution can help them."
>
> Me: "Ah!" I said. "Well, I certainly feel 'told,' just not 'sold.'"

We all know that telling isn't selling when it comes to the *content* of your presentation (for example, features with no benefits), but the implications of that statement on the *delivery* of the presentation is rarely discussed. Few salespeople consciously consider what their intention is or what intention would be most effective in any given circumstance, which means when they're in a situation where they need to get information across to a prospect, their default intention of telling kicks in.

Think about how many times a day people tell you something. It's not particularly compelling, is it? The same goes for inform or educate. These words have no particular passion, energy, or power of persuasion, which can be transferred to your audience. Now, imagine if my intention were to excite you about something. I guarantee you that it would have a much greater impact on you simply because I have chosen a stronger intention. Refer to Figure 10-1 for examples of strong intentions.

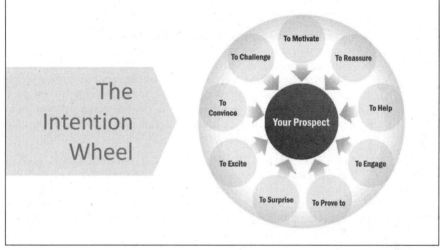

Figure 10-1:
The intention wheel.

© John Wiley & Sons, Inc.

Displaying Confidence

Confidence is attractive and reassuring. It's a quality most people want and expect in leaders, celebrities, and professional athletes. Fans don't want to hear their star player say "I'm not sure we're ready for this game," just as prospects don't want to hear you say "So I gave this my best shot, but let's see what you think." Prospects want to feel like the person they're going to spend money with, venture into a partnership with, or take a risk on, has *confidence* (a belief in your ability or power). And that confidence — or lack of confidence — is on display the moment you step in the room.

Here are some proven ways to increase your confidence:

- ✔ **Believe you provide value.** If you don't think that you have something of value to offer, neither will your prospect. Even the toughest customers want to believe that you can help solve their problems. Having a strong focus on the value you bring reassures nervous prospects and gives you an inner strength that can lessen any self-consciousness or nerves that may surface.

✓ **Assume a peer-to-peer dynamic.** Apologizing for taking up your prospect's time, excessively thanking her, or being overly deferential can make you appear insecure and give you a perception of lower status. Always be courteous and respectful at a level appropriate for a respected peer or trusted adviser.

✓ **Be an expert.** When you're well armed on the topic, on your prospect's situation, and on any potential questions that may come up that you're presenting, being confident is easier. The more expertise you can demonstrate, the more credible you are in the eyes of your prospect and the more your own confidence increases.

✓ **Prepare your instrument.** Professional athletes don't show up for the game without stretching and professional singers don't go on stage without vocalizing. As a professional salesperson, don't go onto the business stage without first warming up your instrument — your voice and body. Breathing, releasing tension, and creating energy before your presentation are all practices that give you confidence when you're in front of prospects. Chapter 11 has some easy warm-up exercises to help you prepare for your presentation.

✓ **Act as if.** Despite all of your planning and preparation, sometimes you simply don't feel confident. Maybe the prospect is especially challenging or you could have used more preparation time. *Acting as if* is a way to feel confident from the outside in. Much like forcing yourself to smile when you don't feel like smiling can make you feel happier, willfully acting confident can make you feel real confidence. Here's how to act as if:

   • Identify what confident behavior looks and sounds like for you. For example, you may stand taller, be more open with your gestures, speak louder, and hold eye contact longer.

   • Apply these confident behaviors during your warm-up (or even in your conversations before your presentation). Push through even when it feels awkward and uncomfortable.

   • Maintain that confident behavior in your presentation and continue to act as if. You should soon find that you have slipped into actual confidence, but in the mean time, your audience won't know you ever doubted yourself.

✓ **Express your passion.** Salespeople who are otherwise very passionate about their product or service often fail to convey that passion in their presentation due to nerves or a lack of confidence. I've heard salespeople tell a prospect that she'll save six figures with their solution with the same enthusiasm as telling her that she can get her parking validated. Tamping down your passion doesn't pay off. If you're not passionate and enthusiastic about the results you can provide, why should your prospect be? Don't dilute your passion.

✔ **Own your stage.** One surefire way to exhibit confidence is to be comfortable in the space that you're given. Hiding behind your laptop doesn't broadcast confidence. Whether it's an office, a conference table, or an auditorium stage, using your space to its fullest implies ownership and power. Owning your space doesn't, of course, mean aimlessly bounding from one side of the room to the other. Strive to inhabit whatever space you're in as if you're quite comfortable standing in the spotlight. See Chapter 11 for more tips on using your stage to connect with your audience.

✔ **Strike a power pose.** Research has shown that holding your body in a *power pose,* for example, standing with legs and arms stretched wide, for at least two minutes, can make you feel and act more confident. It increases your level of testosterone — the hormone responsible for power and dominance — and decreases cortisol — the hormone responsible for the stress you often feel before a presentation or big event. Do a power pose in the parking lot or sneak into the bathroom before your next presentation to ensure your confidence is at its peak.

Bringing Presence to Your First Impression

Most people fail to make a strong first impression, and salespeople are no exception. It's not that salespeople aren't interesting, charming, or knowledgeable. They often don't convey that quickly enough, which makes them forgettable. And to be forgettable in your presentation is a mistake that you can't afford to make.

Salespeople often hold back when they first start their presentation until they've gauged the room temperature. But if you don't give a strong first impression, you may be out of luck. Research shows that people make snap decisions about the type of relationship they want (or don't want) with someone they just met. And then they act accordingly. So if your prospect decides you're likeable, she will be more receptive to your suggestions, listen to your ideas, and be more open with their responses. If she decides that you're not likable, she'll quickly pick apart everything you say, distrust your predictions, and find ways to eliminate you from the running.

Because first impressions happen so quickly, most first impressions are based on nonverbal cues. In fact, when you first meet someone, up to 60 percent of her first impression of you happens before you even open your mouth. Knowing this and leveraging that knowledge with these tips can give you a great head start to making a strong first impression:

Create a strong moment before

A good actor is fully in character before the curtain rises or the director shouts "Action!" This fullness of character includes knowledge of where her character has been, what she has done, and what she's going to do. This gives her character an energy and an attitude that effects how she enters the room and how she says her first line. You too are influenced by your preceding events. Whatever happened just before you enter the room influences the energy and momentum you bring to your presentation. What happens if you have a series of crummy preceding events — a traffic delay, a spilled cup of coffee, a headache? You can take control and create your own moment before by keeping these steps in mind:

1. **Determine what emotions and/or state of being you want to project.**

   For example, you probably want to express positive emotions like confidence, excitement, or happiness.

2. **Identify what immediate preceding circumstances would lead you to feel this way.**

   Ask yourself what would have to happen to make you feel that emotion. For example, receiving a call or email from a customer telling you how happy she is with your services and her new purchase or winning a close deal.

3. **Visualize as many details of the circumstances as possible to make it as real as possible for you.**

   Imagine that phone call as specifically as you can. What is the customer saying? Where are you? What is your response?

4. **Find an image or object that helps you picture your moment before.**

   Find something that can physically connect you to that moment. Perhaps it's holding the phone in your hand or seeing your customer's picture. The more real you can make it for yourself the more effective it will be.

Elevate your expectations

Everything you do and say is based on your expectations. You text a friend and expect to get a response. You call a prospect and expect to get voicemail. Are you surprised sometimes? Sure. Sometimes the friend doesn't text back or the prospect picks up the phone. But your expectations — right or wrong — almost always effect your actions. There is a distinct difference in your tone, your attitude, and your behavior when you believe your prospect is looking forward to your presentation as opposed to just tolerating it.

Your expectations create a physical shift in the way you act, and in turn, in the results you get. Approach each presentation with the expectation that your prospect can't wait to hear how you can solve her problem, improve her business, or be a valuable resource, and you're more likely to feel confident and make that expectation a reality.

Leverage body language

From how you stand to how you gesture or walk across the room, your physicality sends constant signals to your prospect about who you are. Knowing what your strengths and weaknesses are and working on them can improve your first impression dramatically. Here are some best practices for body language. You can also check out Chapter 11 for tips on how to use your body to support your message.

- **Stand up straight.** Just like your mother told you: Slouching affects how people perceive you and makes you appear subordinate.

- **Look but don't linger.** You know the importance of making eye contact. However although eye contact is important, relentless staring at your prospect can make her uncomfortable and cause you to forget your words. Strive to maintain eye contact with your prospect long enough to complete a thought or a sentence. Refocus your sights on a natural transition. Or if it's easier, maintain eye contact at least long enough to identify the color of her eyes — but not long enough to propose marriage.

- **Use full gestures.** Extend your arms beyond your torso. Smaller gestures make it look like you're trying to protect yourself.

- **Commit to your movements.** Half-hearted gestures or movements come across as insecure or indecisive to your audience.

- **Smile.** A smile conveys warmth, confidence, and approachability. Everyone knows the power of a genuine smile. And you've probably been told that even a phony smile has the power to change someone's mood.

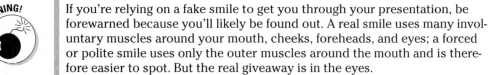

If you're relying on a fake smile to get you through your presentation, be forewarned because you'll likely be found out. A real smile uses many involuntary muscles around your mouth, cheeks, foreheads, and eyes; a forced or polite smile uses only the outer muscles around the mouth and is therefore easier to spot. But the real giveaway is in the eyes.

Try it for yourself in the mirror. Think of something that really makes you smile: your significant other, your dog, closing a big sale. Now think of something that makes you unhappy and force yourself to smile. Would you invest money in that person with the phony smile staring back at you? If you've done a proper warm-up and prepared a positive moment before to launch you into your presentation, you shouldn't have to fake your smile. Even if no one else in the room is smiling and it's a very serious subject, smile. It's contagious — maybe your prospect will get the bug.

Speak with animation

No, I don't mean speaking like a cartoon character. I'm referring to the pre-Disney definition of animated: *full of life, vivacity, and spirit.* You want your words to come forward with life and spirit and urgency. In order to have that, be clear on three things:

You have something important to say.

It must be said now.

You must say it.

Mirror

People tend to like people who are similar to them. *Mirroring* is a proven behavior in which one person imitates the gestures, movement, or pattern of speech of another. This happens all the time on a subconscious level, whether it's with a smile or a yawn or a gesture. Conscious mirroring of certain behaviors of your prospect — gestures, vocal pace, eye contact — can help prospects feel a stronger rapport with you. Just make sure to use sparingly so you don't fall into imitation or mockery.

Chapter 11

Leveraging Your Voice and Body for Impact

*P*erhaps you've sat through a presentation where the presenter spoke in a slow, monotone voice, his only movement to advance to the next slide. Or conversely, the presenter seemed to be speaking in ALL CAPS as he ping ponged from one side of the room to the other. One style had you reaching for coffee, the other for some motion sickness medicine. Either way, the presenter failed to achieve his goal of drawing you in and inspiring you to change your thoughts, beliefs, or behaviors.

A well-crafted message is a critical component of your presentation, but you can't rely on your content to do all the heavy lifting. After all, even an award-winning script can bomb at the box office if the actor fails to deliver it convincingly. Great presenters make average content better and good content exceptional. In a competitive market where differences between products and services are getting smaller and messages easily blur in a busy prospect's mind, how you deliver your presentation can mean the difference between winning and losing a sale.

This chapter explains just how much your voice and your body language affect your audience's attention, the perception of your product or service, and the impact of your message. You discover how to strategically control your voice and body with the skill of a performer to connect with your audience and drive home key points. You start to identify and eliminate vocal and physical habits that can send your prospect straight to his smartphone. I provide specific tips on how to use your stage and move about with confidence. I also examine the importance of warming up and you can take away some simple exercises to ensure that you're communicating at your persuasive best in every presentation.

Unleashing the Power of Your Performance Tools

Two actors read the same script, and one actor wins the role over another. He earns it obviously not because of the words because both actors read the same script. He wins because of the meaning, the connection, and the quality that he brings to those words. His winning audition doesn't require any high tech tricks, fancy graphics, or animations. He simply uses his performance tools — his voice and body — in a way that brings the script to life, captures his audience's attention, and sparks their imagination.

Like an actor, you can access those same tools to win a role in your prospect's business. From the sound and the quality of your voice to the way you stand or move across your stage, you affect how your audience perceives you, your company, and your solution. Use your tools well and your prospect is drawn into your message and enticed by the picture you're painting. Use them poorly, and your prospect may not remember or even hear your message. Utilizing your voice and body to focus your audience's attention, keep them tuned in, and transfer powerful emotions can give you an unfair advantage over your competition.

The following sections explain just how much your voice and body can influence your prospect and what it takes to master these secret weapons to gain a winning edge in your presentation.

Impacting your audience with voice, body and words

No doubt about it, the words you use play a critical role in the success of your presentation, but the influence that your voice and body have on how your audience receives and perceives your message plays a much larger role than you may realize. In fact, a study revealed that people receive communication in the following way:

✔ 38 percent vocal tone

✔ 55 percent body language, facial expression, and so on

✔ 7 percent spoken words

When 93 percent of the initial impression you make on your prospect comes from your vocal tone and body language, you don't want to concentrate on only the words. Obviously if your words are gibberish, or just plain wrong, it doesn't matter how commanding your body language or melodious your voice is. Assume your content is good, your proposal is sound, and your value proposition is compelling. That likely puts you on a pretty level playing field in today's competitive market. That's why you want to gain an advantage over your competition and use your voice and body strategically.

Focusing on what you can control

Although you don't have control over some things, such as technical difficulties, agenda changes, no-shows, and delays, your voice and body are to some extent within your control. Making a conscious decision to leverage their power can dramatically affect your win ratio.

You may be thinking, "That sounds great, but my voice is my voice." Yes, you're born with a certain amount of raw material to work with, a set of vocal cords, some muscles, and cells that make you, uniquely you. But within your framework you have a choice over many things. For example, you can use your full vocal range and add variety and inflection to keep your audience engaged. You can carry yourself with confidence and move about the room to connect better with your audience. You can eliminate poor vocal and physical habits that may be sabotaging your message. The road to regaining control of your voice and your body in your presentation requires three commitments:

✔ **Developing awareness:** Recognizing what good vocal and physical practices are and determining where you improve is the starting point to mastering any new skill. Refer to the next section for some specifics.

✔ **Ditching bad habits:** You've been speaking and moving for a long time and more than likely you've developed a few bad habits along the way. Getting rid of those things that separate you from your audience dramatically increase your presentation power. Check out the later section, "Eliminating Five Vocal Bad Habits" for more information.

✔ **Practicing new habits:** Developing any new habit takes repetition and consistency to make it part of your natural repertoire. The later section, "Warming Up for a Winning Performance" has some simple exercises for you to continue to work on areas that need improvement.

Keeping Your Audience's Interest with Vocal Variety

Your voice can play a symphony, yet most presenters settle for chopsticks.

Your voice is a powerful instrument with the potential to bring your message to life or cause it to fade into oblivion. The way you use your voice can affect the attention, perception, and ultimately opinion of your audience. Your voice takes on even greater significance when you're doing virtual or phone presentations and lack the physical piece to support your message.

Many factors contribute to the way you sound and the way you draw in your audience (or shut them out), but part of the key is in variety. The way you use your voice, the number of notes you play, and when, go a long way toward keeping today's attention-challenged audiences attentive, interested, and ultimately moved to take action.

Here I take a look at the different ways you can use your voice to engage your prospect, highlight key messages, and refocus attention.

Adjust your volume

Speak too quietly and your prospect may misunderstand or just plain miss your message. Projecting at full volume all the time can simply wear them out. Your voice should be easy to hear without the feeling that you're straining it. Don't count on your audience members to let you know if your voice is too soft or loud either. They'll simply tune you out. In a larger room, audience members in the back row should be able to clearly understand you and the front row shouldn't have to cover their ears.

Here are some tips for varying your volume:

- ✔ **Check your breath.** Quiet voices can be powerful, but if you're constantly being told to speak up, your audience may be missing valuable information. You possibly may not be getting enough wind power. Taking deep breaths from the diaphragm before you speak and doing some breath work or exercises including yoga breathing can greatly improve your ability to project.

- ✔ **Get quiet.** If volume has never been a problem for you, find some moments to soften it. Most people get louder when they're excited or making an important point. Getting quieter (though not so quiet you can't be heard) as if you're letting your audience in on a secret is a very effective way to draw them in.

✔ **Check acoustics.** Every room has different acoustics, so be sure to check out the idiosyncrasies of your space before your presentation if possible. Especially in a larger room, make sure that back row of the audience can hear you by doing a sound check prior to people arriving. Have someone move around the room and let you know if he can hear you and adjust accordingly. Keep in mind that a full room absorbs more sound so you may need to amp it up a little more or use a mic if you have a large audience. See Chapter 19 for tips on presenting to a large group.

Mix up your pace

How fast or slow you talk (your *pace*) plays an important role in your audience's attention and comprehension. Speak too quickly and you frustrate and eventually lose them. Talk too slowly and you try your prospect's patience.

Cultural and geographical influences as well as anxiety and the complexity of your words affect pace. Although there's no perfect pace, you want to stay within the range that most people find acceptable, which, according to studies is somewhere between 150 and 170 words per minute.

Speeding up when you're nervous or excited is only natural, but beware that you may leave your audience in the dust. If you're talking fast because you're nervous, relaxation and breathing exercises prior to your presentation can help. If you're excited, channel that energy into getting your message across as accurately as possible by slowing down and articulating your words, rather than letting your words run away from you. You can even pretend you're speaking to an audience who use English as a second language.

Here are some easy ways to make sure your pace doesn't get stuck in first gear:

✔ **Pause.** Rapid, nonstop speech is exhausting for your audience — and you! Avoid this audience drainer by taking an extra beat at the end of each sentence. Doing so gives both you and your audience a chance to catch up.

✔ **Mix it up.** The same steady pace over an hour can work like a metronome on your audience, lulling them into a trancelike state. Try varying your pace during key sections of your presentation. For example, speed up as you deliver features and slow down to call attention to benefits.

Chances are that you already know if you're a fast or slow talker, but if not, ask your friends or using your smartphone, talk at your normal pace for one minute. Then use an app like Evernote to convert your speech to text. Paste the text in a Word doc and count the number of words, which is your words per minute.

Emphasize emphasis

You want to stress certain key points and words in your presentation, but remember: *If you emphasize everything, nothing stands out.* Following are some guidelines for when and how to use emphasis in your presentation:

- ✔ **Highlight key words.** Determine what main points or key words you want to call out in your presentation and then practice hitting them naturally. The secret is you have to really feel like they're important or the emphasis will feel like a phony afterthought.

- ✔ **Throw away a line.** All punch lines and no throw-away lines can feel relentless to an audience. Much like getting quiet, purposely de-emphasizing an important line can actually draw attention to it. Steve Jobs was a master of this. During his much anticipated presentations he would save the big product reveal for the very end and announce it with a casual aside that was in sharp contrast to its value.

Focus on clarity

Ask Idina Menzel, introduced by John Travolta at the Oscars as "Glom Gazingo" whether clarity matters. You may empathize with John. Many business phrases used today, like "customer engagement optimization," or "empowering actionable intelligence," don't exactly roll off the tongue.

You've worked hard to clearly define your message. The last thing you want is for your audience to misunderstand it. Mumbling through or tripping over your words can make you appear unconfident or unprepared. Although you don't need to speak like you're in a speech class, you also don't want to be too casual about it either. Good, clear articulation never goes out of style.

Here are some easy ways to improve your articulation:

- ✔ **Say tongue twisters.** Tongue twisters are a very effective way to improve your articulation as well as warm up for your presentation. For example, warm up with "Sally-sells-seashells- by-the-seashore," "Unique New York," and "Worldwide Web." Refer to the later section, "Warming Up for a Winning Performance," for more preparation tips.

- ✔ **Practice.** Try reading your presentation aloud while overarticulating every word with your tongue and lips. This exaggerated practice can help you to hit them perfectly after you're in front of your prospect.

- ✔ **Visualize.** When you come across a word you normally slip up on in your presentation, imagine seeing it spelled out in front of you before you pronounce it.

Take a pause (or two)

Not using the voice is an important vocal technique — and one that is seriously underused in business. Don't be afraid of silence. Used strategically, a pause can be a powerful tool for focusing the attention of your audience.

For example, pausing before revealing an important point builds anticipation, whereas a pause afterward gives the audience a chance to process it. A pause after a question gives your prospect a chance to think about an answer, and it keeps you from using unnecessary filler words or phrases.

Eliminating Five Vocal Bad Habits

You've probably heard some people speak whose voices were so distracting that it was difficult to focus on what they were saying. You probably have some less glaring vocal habits that may be detracting from your message and may even be creating a negative impression with your audience.

Here are five common vocal habits that can ring the death toll for your presentation. Do you recognize yourself in any of them? No worries. I include a fix for each.

Monotone Mary

Mary delivers every word of her presentation at the same level. It's like a song played entirely on the note of C or a steady dripping faucet. Either way, it quickly gets tiresome. The audience can't differentiate between what's important and what's not, because it all sounds the same. Tune-out danger is extremely high.

The fix: Stretch your range. Many presenters use a very limited section of their full vocal potential, which is a big problem during virtual presentations or presentations lasting longer than ten minutes — in other words, almost every presentation. Like most vocal habits, if you're monotone in your presentation, you probably are outside of your presentation as well.

You have ample opportunities to work on it. Here's how:

> ✔ **Run scales.** Think of your voice as floating on a scale. Your goal is to increase the number of notes that you play, both in the upper and lower end of the scale.

- ✔ **Read Dr. Seuss.** Reading children's books out loud in as animated a voice as possible delights your kids and exercises your voice. If you don't have kids, you can still read children's books. Doing so stretches your voice *and* you may discover something new.

- ✔ **Get deliberate.** Look for natural places to add variety in your presentation. For example, when you want to call attention to a particular point, change your intonation, volume, or emphasis. Although it may seem inauthentic at first, it becomes more natural with practice. Your words come alive with meaning when you use variety.

- ✔ **Practice at your local coffee shop.** Make an effort to stretch your range as you go through your day. "I'll have a med*ium pep*permint mo*cha* with an *extra* shot, please." You get a vocal workout, and I guarantee your barista will remember your drink!

Speed-talker Sean

Sean's prospects are impressed by his natural enthusiasm and his ability to speak at length without oxygen. Unfortunately, this steady stream of information eventually becomes too much, and they shut down, often well before Sean gets to his main point.

Speed talking is also a one-level delivery problem, and that level is set to stun! If, like Sean, you find yourself racing through your presentation, take it down a notch to let your audience catch up. Remember, you may have said your presentation a dozen or more times, but your audience members are hearing it for the first time so slow down and give them a chance to take it in and digest it.

Consider the following to fix this problem:

- ✔ **Put a period on it.** When you're finished with one thought, put a period on it and pause. Let the impact of what you've said stick with the pause before moving on.

- ✔ **Use silence.** If you leave space for your audience, they may actually tell you something you wouldn't have otherwise found out had you rushed ahead to your next point.

- ✔ **Catch a cue.** Wait for a nonverbal response from your listeners: a nod of the head, a blink of the eyes, or anything that suggests they have it, before you move on.

- ✔ **Mix it up.** Alternate a quicker pace with a slower pace when you transition to a new section. Doing so gives your audience a much-needed chance to catch up.

- ✔ **Prioritize.** Attempting to cover too much ground in too little time can often be the culprit for rushed speech. Never try to squeeze too much content in too little time. Prioritize sections so that you can leave out the less important ones instead of sacrificing overall clarity.

Filler-word Franny

So, like, you know . . . Franny's presentation is peppered with these filler words. So much so that her prospect is more focused on counting the number of likes than the actual message she's trying to convey. Filler words serve no purpose, yet they have starring roles in many sales presentations.

Fortunately, there is help. To fix this problem, follow these tips:

✔ **Record yourself.** Hearing how many filler words you actually use can be a very unpleasant revelation, but don't kick yourself too hard. Most people have their pet words and aren't even aware of them. Listen to the recording and simply note which ones you're particularly fond of and then vow to banish them from every conversation, not just your presentation.

✔ **Check out Toastmasters.** Although having a bell go off every time you use a filler word may seem like some sort of sadistic aversion therapy, Toastmasters' system of stopping you the moment you use a filler word is extremely effective in breaking you of the habit. Refer to www.toast masters.org to find your local chapter.

✔ **Pause.** Filler words are commonly used to fill space because you haven't quite formulated your next thought. Figure out how to get comfortable with pausing instead of opening your mouth before you're ready to speak. Even though a five-second pause seems like an eternity to you, your audience won't perceive it as unusual and may actually welcome the break!

The word *so* may be the most commonly used word at the start of a presentation or an introduction into a new topic. This tiny two letter word weakens an otherwise powerful opening or point and becomes a real crutch. To ensure that you don't fall prey to its power, memorize your first line and take a moment to pause before you start.

Newscaster Nancy

Nancy has a warm, bubbly personality that all but disappears during her presentation. Instead, she goes into presenter mode that would make her a welcome addition to the local news team. Talking about a new feature is delivered with the same level of enthusiasm as warning you of a pending snowstorm. In business, most people (and salespeople are no exception) don't speak with as much energy or personality as they do in their personal lives.

This tendency to stuff down both the good and the bad alike produces a bland, one-dimensional delivery that eliminates valuable opportunities to engage and connect with your audience. Presenter mode can strike anyone, but it's especially common among experienced salespeople who have delivered a presentation a number of times. Fighting presenter mode is important because without proper inflection your meaning may get lost on your audience. After all, even though you may have delivered your presentation 25 times, it's the first time that your audience has heard it.

To fix this problem, use these pointers:

- ✔ **Connect to your words.** Just like an actor has to keep a performance fresh night after night, so do you have to connect with your material anew each time. Connecting to your material requires really thinking about the meaning of what you're saying. For example, if you're telling your prospect about a benefit that is going to save him time or money, make it obvious with the tone of your voice that it's good news even if your audience speaks another language.

- ✔ **Go big.** Practice by doing an over-the-top version of your presentation. In other words, pack in as much energy, personality, and excitement as you can muster — and then go even bigger! Take that energy with you as you go into your presentation, and you'll find yourself land at a nicely energized, connected level using your normal (indoor) voice.

Pitchy Paula

Paula's message is right on target, but her breathy, high-pitched voice has her audience questioning her credibility. It's not fair, but people with higher-pitched voices are considered less powerful and more nervous than people who speak in a lower-pitched voice. Although you don't need to sound like Harvey Fierstein, you can give your voice greater gravitas.

Incorporate the following to fix this issue:

- ✔ **Hum a few bars.** You may not be speaking in the best pitch for your voice, which can strain and even damage your vocal cords. Try putting your lips together and saying, "Um hum, um hum . . . " to find the best pitch for your voice.

- ✔ **Take a slide.** Get to know the full range of your voice by practicing vocal slides. Take a deep breath and start at the highest note you can find, make an open vowel sound, like "ahh," and on an exhale, slowly slide down the scale to the bottom of your register. Inhale and repeat. You can even get fancy and try sliding up and down all on the same breath, like a rollercoaster.

- ✔ **Stop ending statements with questions.** Make sure you aren't ending your sentences on an uptick? Like this? Doing so makes a statement sound like a question? This habit is hard to break so you may need to enlist some help.

Communicating Effectively with Body Language

To be a persuasive and credible presenter, you need to communicate with more than just your voice and words. You need to get your entire body into the act. Before you utter your first word, you're sending a steady stream of information to your prospect. How you carry yourself, the gestures you use, the facial expressions, eye contact, and so forth, all contribute to your prospect's perception of you, and by association, your product or service.

Even in a virtual presentation where your prospect can't see you, your body plays an important role in how you're perceived. Consider how differently you speak to someone when you're slouched in a chair as compared to standing up, shoulders back, feet firmly planted.

You can easily get lost in the many rules of body language, but if you know these four key principles you can start to understand how and why to apply them:

- ✔ **Congruency:** If I said "Hey, great to see you!" with my arms tightly wrapped across my chest, you would probably question whether I was truly happy to see you. Good body language is always *congruent* — in synch with your voice and words. When a person's words say one thing and his body says another, your subconscious picks up on it and you instinctively don't trust that person. Trust is an integral part of the buyer-seller relationship. After it's damaged, repairing it is difficult if not impossible, so make sure your body isn't betraying you by aligning your words and your body.

- ✔ **Authenticity:** Some people are big gesturers, some aren't. Some people like to move, some don't. Trying to be something you're not can appear inauthentic to your prospect, which can give him cause to question the sincerity of what you're saying. Although you don't want to turn into someone you're not and be someone you're not, like most people, you can probably afford to push yourself beyond your comfort zone and still remain true to yourself. How you move and gesture when you're telling a story or talking to good friends is the level of animation you want to achieve. If you're falling short of that, you're capable of greater expression than you're allowing your audience to see. Check out the later section, "Gesturing with authenticity" for some tips.

- ✔ **Purposefulness:** When you first recognize the power of body language, you may be tempted to move around or add gestures anywhere you can, but slow down. Gestures, smiles, movement, and so on should be purposeful and connected to a thought or an intention. In real life, you don't gesture just to gesture. You do it because you want to point to a picture or underscore a point. You don't move just to move; you move because you want to write down something or connect with another person. Disconnected movements ring a false note with your audience every time.

✓ **Relaxation:** This isn't the lying-on-the-couch-with-a-bag-of-chips kind of relaxed, but the loose-and-physically-ready-to-react kind. The key to being in this alert state of relaxation is getting rid of tension. Tension interferes with the free flow of communication and therefore is a big problem for anyone who gets in front of an audience. The warm-up exercises in the "Warming Up for a Winning Performance" section later in this chapter are helpful in releasing and redirecting tension so that you can communicate at your best during your presentation.

Following Some Easy Body Language Guidelines

What do you do with your hands? How long should you look at a person? When should you move?

Of course the easy answer is simple — when it feels natural! Unfortunately, natural impulses can get lost or drowned out by nerves when you're standing in front of an audience. Here are some tips to help you reconnect with your natural ability to communicate physically.

Gesturing with authenticity

Gestures can add a powerful punch to a point or a needed wake-up call to a drifting audience. Unfortunately, if your gestures aren't real or you look uncomfortable using them, gestures can have a negative effect on your audience. When to gesture as well as how to gesture are common questions presenters have. Here are some suggestions on how to liven up your presentation with purposeful gestures:

✓ **Tell a story with your body.** Look for places where a gesture would help you physicalize an action (tossing, ducking, or weaving), describe an object or person (he was *this* big, or it went from *here* to *there*), or make a key point (saving you *50* percent per year!).

✓ **Connect to a thought.** All movement should be purposeful, and that includes gestures. Everything should be connected to a thought or intention. Don't just gesture to gesture.

✓ **Commit to it.** If you're going to gesture, go all in. When you're half-committed or unsure, your gestures appear vague and unsure, which conveys a lack of confidence.

✔ **Have a limit.** Don't overload your presentation with gestures lest they steal the show. Too many gestures can be distracting and even cross the line into annoying.

✔ **Keep gestures size appropriate.** Small gestures are lost in a big room. The bigger the room, the bigger the gesture. As with your voice, think about gesturing large enough so that members in the back row of your audience can see you with ease.

✔ **Be precise.** Aim for accuracy and specificity when you gesture. Don't tell your audience something is five feet tall and have your hand at waist height.

✔ **Avoid T-Rex arms.** Nerves can cause you to draw inward and protect yourself by keeping your arms close to your chest. Being able to use your full range of motion and extend your arms fully is more engaging and shows an openness and confidence that is contagious to your audience.

✔ **Watch the tempo.** Strive for large, slow movements as opposed to small, jerky ones. Unless you're making a rapid gesture to illustrate a point, jittery moves can be hard to read and make you appear nervous.

✔ **Be consistent.** If you start listing points by holding up fingers, don't suddenly stop halfway through your list. Inconsistencies pull your audience out of the moment and detract from what you're saying.

✔ **Use open body language.** Body language experts suggest using open arms and palms to indicate you aren't hiding anything.

People who use a greater variety of gestures are seen in a more positive light. According to research people who gesture actively and naturally are seen as warm, agreeable, and energetic. People who gesture mechanically or move very little are perceived as logical, cold, and analytical.

Using your face

People like and remember people who smile at them. In fact, smiling at others directly influences how they respond to you. But smiles aren't the only expression in your toolkit. Some things are inappropriate to say with a big smile on your face, such as "This decision is costing you nearly five million dollars a year in lost revenue."

Here are some tips for smiling, frowning, and every mood in between.

✔ **Look for places to smile.** You may be addressing a serious challenge or problem, but making everything doom and gloom can become awfully heavy for your audience. Balance it by looking for opportunities to lighten things up with a smile. Benefits are good, right? How about growth or savings? Let your face express that to the audience, not just your words.

✔ **Keep it real.** You want to express concern, surprise, frustration, and even anger at different times within your presentation. Pasting on a phony smile or look of concern rarely fools anyone. Connect with the real emotion behind the words by thinking about what you're saying and what it really means for your prospect. You need to be internally connected to the emotion you want to express. If you're not sure what the emotion behind a statement is, put yourself in your prospect's shoes and explore what he may be feeling. Refer to the section on "Gaining an outsider's perspective" in Chapter 6.

Relying on effective eye contact

One of the benefits of doing a live presentation is the ability to make eye contact with your audience. Eye contact allows you to read your audience as well as make your audience feel more connected to you and your message. In some parts of the world, eye contact is considered rude. In other places like the United States, Europe, and Australia, businesspeople expect eye contact 50 to 60 percent of the time.

Here are some handy guidelines for gazing at your audience:

✔ **Notice eye color.** Looking at an audience member just long enough to note the color of his eyes is a good general rule.

✔ **Refocus on a transition.** Finish your thought while looking at one person before you shift to the next. Doing so keeps you from racing around too quickly, which can appear shifty.

✔ **Look away to process.** Looking away while thinking or processing information is natural so go ahead and glance away once in a while. Just be sure to bring your focus back to your audience as soon as you've collected your thoughts.

✔ **Don't look down.** Looking down can convey a lack of confidence — unless you have to pick up your marker.

Don't overdo eye contact. The goal is to connect, not do a Vulcan mind-meld. Maintaining constant eye contact with someone is unnatural for you and uncomfortable for your audience. Look just long enough to determine the color of your listener's eyes.

Applying Guidelines for Movement

Because humans are hardwired to respond to anything that moves, movement is an especially powerful tool for gaining an audience's attention. Unfortunately it's a tool that many salespeople rarely use effectively in most sales presentations. You've probably sat in presentations where the present-er's movement — or lack of movement — was a distraction. Randomly pacing about or standing immobilized behind your laptop is still quite common in sales presentations.

The following sections examine how and when to incorporate movement in your presentation as well as how to get rid of any movements that may be distracting to your audience. You also find out how to coach yourself to use movement more strategically and naturally.

Moving effectively

Even more experienced salespeople can struggle with when, where, and how to move. Here are some guidelines for incorporating movement effectively in your presentation:

- ✔ **Move on transitions.** Like shifting eye focus, moving at the end of a thought or the start of a new one is a logical place to change positions, approach your audience, or walk to the other side of the screen.

- ✔ **Use your space.** No rule says that you have to remain standing at the front of the room for your entire presentation. Variety is an effective engagement tool, yet often salespeople get fixated on one or two audi-ence members and miss the opportunity to connect with others. Mix it up. Use your space to circulate and make sure you connect with each audience member at least once.

- ✔ **Find a reason.** You can easily get stuck behind your laptop. To avoid doing so, create reasons to move throughout your presentation. Place a whiteboard on the opposite side of the room or stash a handout near the audience.

- ✔ **Just do it.** If you're going to move, commit to it fully. Avoid those weird little half steps or side moves that make you look unsure of yourself and make your audience jittery.

- ✔ **Plant yourself.** After you arrive at your destination, plant yourself firmly on the ground and speak from this position. Don't be so quick to leave.

Getting rid of your go-to-move

Everybody has a *go-to-move* — that thing you do with your hands, your feet, or your face when you're nervous or tense. If you're unsure what your go-to-move is, record yourself or ask someone who's seen you present.

Although your go-to-move may feel like a comfy old sweater, it can distract your audience and draw their focus from your message. Here are some of the top offenders:

- Pointing, *steepling* (holding your hands palms together with your finger tips up touching), or making other repetitive gestures
- Adjusting your clothing
- Thrusting hands in your pockets
- Shifting your weight from one foot to the other
- Playing with your hair or jewelry
- Obsessively checking your slides (no, they haven't moved)
- Folding your arms across your chest
- Pacing at random

The good news is that after you're aware of your go-to-move, you can start to eliminate it and replace it with more effective behaviors. Here's how:

- **Get rid of tension.** Warming up before your presentation helps eliminate some of the nerves that are at the base of these go-to- moves. (Refer to the section, "Warming Up for a Winning Performance" later in this chapter.)
- **Ground yourself.** When you find yourself tempted to reach for your pockets or shift your weight during your presentation, stop and place one hand on a nearby table, desk, or laptop until the urge passes.
- **Adopt a power stance.** If you're a wanderer, figure out how to get comfortable with just standing still, feet planted, weight equally distributed, arms by your side. Stay there until you have a good reason to move or gesture again.

To sit or stand? That's the question

The answer to "To sit or stand?" depends upon your space, your audience, and the formality of the presentation. Standing is usually preferable because it provides you with more control and greater opportunities to express yourself and connect with your prospect. It also endows you and your presentation with more authority and power. However, if just you and two prospects are in a small office, then standing can be awkward. If you do end up sitting, don't take it as an invitation to get too relaxed. Maintain good posture and place your feet flat on the floor.

Who says you can't do both? Placing a chair or stool near your stage so you can take a seat when doing Q&A can help you to connect more intimately with your audience, add variety, and give you an occasional break.

Recording yourself

Getting a true picture of how you appear and sound to your prospect is an invaluable tool toward better presenting. Unless you have a good relationship with a prospect or client, you probably need to record a dry run or set up a staged rehearsal.

Here are some tips for getting the most out of your recording:

- ✔ **Use a simple camera.** You don't need fancy equipment; your phone or your laptop will do. Just make sure that you can get as much of the area that you'll be using as your stage in the screen and that the sound is adequate.

- ✔ **Set the stage.** Use duct tape to mark off the perimeter of your stage and stay within those guidelines. Place the camera in a central location or where the main decision maker will be.

- ✔ **Keep it real.** Deliver your presentation with full vocal, physical, and emotional commitment. Interact with invisible audience members. Pause when you ask a question and listen as you would if you were receiving an answer. You want to get as accurate a picture of yourself as possible. You could also invite co-workers to sit in the audience and ask you questions. Refer to the upcoming section "Practice and then practice some more" for more tips.

Analyzing your performance

Just like a coach preparing for the big game, you need to watch the tapes to know what you're up against. First, get a piece of paper and draw two columns. Write *plus* on the top of one side and *minus* on the other. Then, view your video three different ways:

- ✔ **First run:** Watch for an overall sense of how you come across. Simply note the things you did well in the plus column and things that didn't work in the minus.

- ✔ **Second run:** Turn off the sound and focus on your movements. You may see a go-to move jump out at you or a real reluctance to move. Add these to your minus column. Also look for the good moments. Analyze where you did move or gesture well. Notice how your smile and eye contact was. Add these to your plus column.

- ✔ **Third run:** Listen to it without the video. See if you can pick up any distracting speech patterns, use of filler words, poor articulation, or a too fast or slow cadence.

Make a note of all the areas for improvement on your sheet. See Figure 11-1 for an example of a performance evaluation form.

Performance Evaluation

Category	+	−
Overall		
Eye contact		
Facial expression		
Movement		
-Too much/too little		
-Purposeful		
-Variety		
-Go-to-moves		
Gestures		
-Too much/too little		
-Purposeful		
-Full range		
-Specific		
-Consistent		
Voice		
-Variety		
-Volume		
-Pace		
-Emphasis		
-Clarity		
-Use of pauses		
-Filler words		

Figure 11-1:
A performance evaluation form.

© *John Wiley & Sons, Inc.*

Many people hate to watch themselves on video. When you watch yourself on video, keep an objective view and focus on the major issues, not the minor flaws (don't worry how your eyebrows move), or things you can't change that likely only you notice.

Practice and then practice some more

After you identify the areas where you have some room for improvement, you're already miles ahead of most of your peers. Don't stop there. Now put that knowledge to use and start on a course of action:

✔ Review "Keeping Your Audience's Interest with Vocal Variety," and "Following Some Easy Body Language Guidelines" earlier in this chapter for suggested improvements.

✔ Commit to doing the recommended exercises for 30 days. Consistent efforts produce consistent results.

✔ Record yourself again after 30 days and compare the two recordings, noting all improvements and redoubling efforts on continued trouble spots.

✔ Tell a manager or team member the specific habits or techniques that you're working on and ask him to help by pointing them out to you.

✔ Do the recommended warm-ups in the next section before each presentation.

Warming Up for a Winning Performance

Going from zero to 100 on the spot is impossible, yet that's what most salespeople attempt to do when they give a presentation. Do yourself a favor and give yourself time to ramp up to your optimal state by warming up before you present. Those first few moments in front of your audience are critical. Don't waste them working out the kinks in your delivery or finding your zone.

The following presentation warm-ups help settle nerves, increase confidence, and have you communicating at your highest potential for each presentation.

✔ **Take some deep breaths.** Communication starts with the breath so make sure that you're breathing properly before you take the stage. Do some deep yoga breaths or try the following:

- Inhale deeply from your diaphragm, hold for four counts, and exhale for eight.

- Repeat four times to oxygenate your body and brain

✔ **Release tension.** Tension is energy that is stuck in your body, energy that could be going into your performance. Here is a technique for ridding yourself of unwanted tension:

- Scan your body for any hidden tension.

- Tighten the muscle group where you feel tension.

- Hold for ten seconds, then release.

- Continue tensing and releasing, paying special attention to areas where you feel tension.

✔ **Express yourself.** Free up the facial muscles to improve your ability to express yourself. To do so, try these exercises:

- Move your eyebrows up and down rapidly, hold, release, and repeat.

- Open your mouth as wide as you can and extend your jaw like you're making a big yawn. Hold and release.

- Laugh.

✔ **Warm up the mouth.** Your mouth has numerous working parts. Warm them up one area at a time by repeating the following consonants:

- For the lips: Ba-ba-ba-pa-pa-pa

- For the tongue: Ta-ta-ta-da-da-da

- Back of the throat: Ka-ka-ka-ga-ga-ga

✔ **Stretch your range for vocal variety.** In order to have access to all the various notes in your voice, you need to warm up and expand your range before your presentation. Here are the steps to open up your range:

1. **Take a deep breath and on an exhale make a long vowel sound, like "ah."**

2. **Starting at the highest note you can hit, slide down the scale to the lowest point as you complete your exhale.**

3. **Reverse and start at your lowest point and slide up the scale.**

4. **Repeat.**

✔ **Try tongue twisters to improve articulation.** Say each of the following quickly five times in a row. Overenunciate for precision.

- Sushi chef

- Worldwide web

- Green leather, yellow leather

- Unique New York

✔ **Stretch it out.** Reach for the sky, do side bends, or touch your toes.

✔ **Shake it out.** Shake your arms, your wrists, your legs, and your feet.

✔ **Get energized.** Dance. Do the hokey pokey. Whatever you do, be sure to move loosely and fluidly and engage your whole body. You can even kill two birds with one stone and do vocal exercises while you move.

Chapter 12

Increasing Emotional Engagement through Storytelling

*Y*ou build a logical case for why your prospect should buy your product or service, but logic alone won't move your prospect to take action. You need to engage your prospect emotionally, and storytelling is one of the most effective tools available to do that. Telling a story can gain emotional buy-in in a way that presenting countless facts and data simply can't. Stories have many other super powers as well; they can gain attention, soften a hardened stance, overcome objections, and differentiate you and your product or service in a memorable way.

A smartly crafted, well-delivered story is a powerful vehicle for making a persuasive case. On the other hand, a long, irrelevant, or poorly told story can cost you attention, credibility, and undo any goodwill that you've managed to establish. More salespeople are starting to embrace the idea of using stories in their presentations; however, not a lot of them are doing it well because they're missing one or more of the elements critical to an engaging, purposeful sales story.

In this chapter I examine the science behind why stories work, when and how to use them in your presentation, and what the ingredients are that go into creating a persuasive story. I introduce different types of stories you can use in your presentation and the elements of drama for maximum effect. I also discuss specific tools for crafting an effective story with examples and tips on when and where to use them in your presentation. Even if you don't consider yourself a natural storyteller, by the end of this chapter you can discover the secrets to delivering a persuasive sales story with confidence.

Understanding Why Stories Work

There's so much buzz about storytelling in business lately that you may think it was the latest app. In fact, long before the written word, stories were used as a vehicle to pass down information (don't feed the dinosaurs), interpret events (what did that meteor mean?), instill values (Noah and the ark), and make sense of the world (the stars are the gods frozen in the sky), and of course, entertain.

Stories work for many reasons. Not only are stories a traditional form of communication, but in the following sections you also see how stories actually impact your prospect's brain. You see how stories can help you do more showing and less telling, as well as create associations that increase understanding and recall of your message.

Impacting the brain with stories

Science has been studying the effect that stories have on people. Overwhelming evidence shows that they can do more in your presentation than just break up bullet points. Stories stimulate different parts of the brain and form a powerful connection between storyteller and listener:

- ✔ **Engaging the brain:** Brain scans reveal that stories activate certain parts of the brain that don't get activated by just delivering data or information. Most information goes into the language-processing area of the brain, and it processes language, that's all. Stories activate the language-processing area as well, but they go a step further and stimulate other areas of the brain, which is why the experience of hearing a story is so much more vivid and memorable than just hearing a bunch of facts.

  For example, a story that talks about how something feels stimulates your sensory cortex. A story that talks about how something moves triggers your motor cortex. Most sales presentations focus almost exclusively on the language-processing area of the brain, leaving the rest of the brain disengaged. By using a story, you capture greater mindshare and make a bigger impact on your prospect.

- ✔ **Synching storyteller and listener:** Recent research also indicates that during the telling of a story the brains of both the storyteller and the listener can actually synchronize. What it really means is that the part of your brain that is activated when you tell a story will likely be activated in your listener's brain. A nice way to be more simpatico!

Showing with stories

Just like you, prospects are told things all day long: "We're the best . . . . You should do this. . . . Here's how this works . . ." Stories allow you to *show* your message, solution, or results in action which is much more effective than barraging them with a list of facts.

For example, telling your prospect about all of the amazing things your product can do may create a healthy amount of skepticism. Telling a story about a customer's positive experience with your product is much more likely to make your prospect a believer or at least intrigue them.

Talking in stories

Storytelling is a natural way for people to communicate. If you really stopped to look at the content of the conversations you're having with friends, relatives, and co-workers throughout the day, you may be surprised to find that much of it is in the form of stories. In fact, a recent study found that personal stories and gossip account for about 65 percent of people's conversations. To not include storytelling in your presentation is almost, well, unnatural.

Associating with stories

Through a story you can help your prospect quickly understand and remember your message by associating it with something familiar. Because the human brain is very receptive to stories, people try and understand them. When you hear a story, your brain searches for a similar experience to relate it to. Finding that relationship helps you associate a new story with something familiar; in other words, you find a spot for this new information in your brain. This is especially helpful when you have a product or service that is new.

Leveraging Storytelling Super Powers in Your Presentation

Like a great movie, a great sales story can change the minds and hearts of audiences, differentiate you and your solution, and inspire action. But that's not all. The following sections explain some of the other super powers that make it a must to include in your presentation.

Engaging emotion

Logic alone is never enough. Engaging your audience emotionally is critical for a persuasive presentation; storytelling is one of the most effective means of doing that. Stories can bring emotion into your presentation by putting a face and a name on a subject or explaining what those numbers mean and why that meaning is important.

Notice in political campaigns how often the candidates use stories of ordinary people to illustrate and drive home their points. (Bob, the auto worker from Detroit who had to take a second job in order to feed his family or Carol, the retired widow from New Hampshire, who had to go back to work in order to make ends meet . . .) They don't present only the facts and the statistics because smart pollsters know that facts and figures are cold and unemotional abstracts. People care more about individuals than they do about abstractions. Stories can draw in prospects and get them emotionally involved in a way that just hammering them with numbers won't.

Creating memories

Because stories can create emotion and emotion plays a critical role in your ability to remember, they're vital in presentations that have a lengthy buying cycle or involve multiple decision makers. Many salespeople of more complex solutions don't walk out of a presentation with a signed contract.

Decision makers may not get together for days or weeks to discuss your proposal. In the meantime, they're likely to see other vendors and be presented with other options and priorities to handle. Using a story to frame a key point in your message is an effective way to make information stick in your prospect's mind after you walk out the door.

Influencing opinion

An old Navajo expression says, "Those who tell the stories rule the people." The real secret to the power of stories is that they can influence and change minds by allowing the prospect to draw her own conclusion. Butting heads and telling a prospect what she should believe leads to debate, judgment, or criticism — if not verbally, then certainly mentally. The right story can get a prospect off of a sticking point or shift her perspective by allowing her to weigh the story and form her own opinion.

Disarming an audience

One of the most powerful and proven ways to increase attention and recall is to do something unexpected. Using stories effectively and creatively in your sales presentation — beyond the standard business case or happy customer story — is still relatively uncommon. Take advantage of that fact to differentiate yourself and gain attention by having a few good stories up your sleeve.

Defining Purposeful Storytelling

Storytelling itself is the art of conveying an event, a thought, or an idea to another person by using language, images, or physicality. Much like in any conversation, you have different reasons for telling a story. Stories can be used to entertain, educate, inspire, or warn, but to be effective they must have a purpose. And like any element in a sales presentation, the purpose of a story is to move the sale forward, which means it must be related to why you're there. Stories that lead nowhere and that are used to grab attention and nothing else can do more harm than good with busy decision makers.

Although telling a story just because it's interesting or funny is fine for everyday conversations, a sales presentation is no everyday conversation. It's a purpose-oriented, heightened conversation. Many stories fail in presentations because they don't incorporate either one or both of these qualities.

The next sections show you how to create a purposeful story that rises above the everyday to engage your prospect. You also recognize when to use stories in your presentation and discover three key questions that can ensure your story is on the right track.

Heightening your story

Whatever story you choose to tell, keep in mind that it must be a heightened event. Stories about an everyday event — shopping for groceries, taking in your dry cleaning — where nothing really unusual happens are going to leave your audience yawning. To rise to a heightened state, something extraordinary must take place. By extraordinary, I don't mean aliens landing, but rather, something out of the ordinary that gives your story a twist and creates conflict. For example, "I was shopping last minute for groceries for an important dinner party, and they were out of the one thing I knew how to make — salmon." A heightened story includes the elements of drama, which I discuss more in the later section, "Incorporating the Elements of Drama in Your Story."

Giving purpose to your story

Whatever story you tell, it should entertain and inform; however, in a presentation, entertainment can't be its primary purpose. An effective sales story needs to be relevant or tie back to the reason that you're there or the topic that you're discussing; otherwise your prospect may well feel like you're wasting her valuable time.

For example, consider how this story told at the opening of a presentation leads into a subject that's relevant to the prospect.

> "How many people have kids in college? Probably no surprise to you that tuition has doubled in the last decade. Cable? Tripled. Cost to service loans? Quadrupled. Few things have increased as dramatically in cost and from what you told us, it's keeping you from focusing on your core competencies and limiting your ability to grow. We're here today because our core competency — providing loan services — can complement what you do and allow you to focus on doing what you do best, providing excellent services to your clients. Let's get started."

This example illustrates how you can heighten and weave a story into your presentation in a purposeful way. Certainly the opening is a great place to use a story but I explore some other areas where a story may be just what's called for in the next section.

Recognizing when to use stories

Stories can be a powerful tool, but like any tool, you need to know when and how to use them to be effective. Before you start putting a story together, first consider why you're using it.

Here are some conditions where storytelling can be one of your go-to tools:

✔ **Gaining attention:** Using a story to open your presentation is a great way to pull your prospect's focus away from her phone, laptop, or thoughts and onto you and your message. But because attention isn't a constant, at other times you also need to regain your prospect's attention within your presentation. Using a story to frame a new topic or agenda item or highlight a feature or benefit is good way to wake up your prospect's brain at key moments. See Chapter 5 for ways to use a story as an opening hook.

Your prospect's attention naturally starts to wane after spending 10 minutes on any particular subject. A story is a great option to consider for those times when you need to reengage your prospect.

✔ **Changing a misconception or strongly held belief:** Often you may find yourself faced with a prospect who has a well-established — and conflicting — opinion on a subject. For example, she has been using your competitor's product for years and believes — incorrectly — that it's superior to yours. To approach this type of resistance head-on is a losing strategy. No one likes to be told she's wrong or misinformed. Rarely will you hear, "Thank you for correcting me."

Your prospect is much more likely to get defensive and draw a bigger line in the sand — either through arguing back verbally or in her mind. With the right story you can soften a hardened position and open a prospect's mind to a different perspective. By telling a story that presents an alternative outlook in a nonconfrontational manner, you allow your prospect to reevaluate and re-form her opinion without feeling like she is having her arm twisted.

✔ **Simplifying complex ideas:** People typically don't want to buy something that sounds complicated or difficult to understand or use. The problem is that many products and services today have complex features or processes, which can make your product sound complicated. Using a story in this situation — particularly a metaphor or analogy — is an effective way to make what your product or service does quickly understandable to your prospect. Here's an example:

Assume that you're selling a system that allows your prospect to operate many of her business processes remotely. You could explain how the system collects, sorts, prioritizes, and transfers all the data. Or you could compare what your product does to the instrument panel on an airplane that allows the plane to safely go from point A to point B without manual input. With the second option, your prospect now has something familiar to associate your product with. Much like a good infographic, stories, especially metaphors and analogies (like the previous airplane example) — can give your prospect a quick mental picture of some pretty complicated ideas.

✔ **Addressing an objection:** Presentations aren't always a smooth ride. You want to anticipate objections that may arise as part of your preparation efforts and have a strategy for addressing them. A story is one way to effectively diffuse an objection. Whether it's a service or feature you don't provide or a price or value issue, a well-crafted story specific to that objection is a handy tool to have. For more tips on handling objections, see Chapter 15.

✔ **Reinforcing a message:** You want to shine a light on some points within your presentation — a competitive advantage, a benefit, a value proposition — so that your prospect doesn't miss them. Building a story around any key message or point is a powerful way to grab attention and improve recall of your message. .

> ✔ **Inspiring action:** Your presentation goes well, everyone is in agreement and then . . . nothing happens. Time passes, other priorities pop up, and the deal gets stalled. Stories are a great way to create urgency for your prospect to take action — either by highlighting the pain of postponement and/or the benefits of taking quick action.

Planning a purposeful story

The tendency when using a story is to start with the story and then retro-fit it into your presentation. Sometimes that strategy works, but often it feels forced or misses on some level. Before you jump in and come up with stories for your presentation; take a few minutes to answer the following three questions. They help to ensure that you're using the right story at the right time.

> ✔ **Why are you telling a story?** As the previous section explains, a purposeful story must satisfy some need beyond to entertain or inform. Define what your purpose is. Is it to overcome a misconception? Illustrate how a feature works? Shift perspective or create urgency? Starting with your purpose gets you headed in the right direction as you start to consider story options.

> ✔ **What's the point or lesson?** The lesson in your story is the outcome you want your prospect to connect to your message. For example, if I'm telling a story because my prospect is afraid of change, the lesson in my story would be that change brings good things or that not making a change can be riskier than change itself.

> ✔ **How do I want my prospect to feel?** Stories are about triggering emotions so consider what emotion you want to convey. Is it joy, relief, fear, pride? Defining how you want your prospect to feel at the end of your story influences the tone, the nature, and the type of story that you will tell.

Determining What Type of Story to Tell

Deciding on what kind of story to use is also important. Following are several types of stories that can be effective in a sales presentation. Reading the descriptions can help you decide which type of story is right for your specific situation.

Highlighting happy customers: Business case

The most common type of story used in a presentation, a business case example or a *happy customer story* as they're often called, showcases an existing customer's results from using your product or service. Pointing out a happy customer can be especially helpful when you need to establish credibility, as in the case of new companies or products, or existing companies expanding into new industries or markets.

Select a customer that has some relevance or similarity to your prospect. For example, you can use a customer in the same industry or even a different industry experiencing similar challenges as your prospect. Either way, you want to point out the pain of where your customer was, how you helped her, and where she is today. Because this type of story is so common in sales presentations, it doesn't have the attention-grabbing power of other types of stories that I discuss in the following sections, so you need to work a little harder to make it interesting.

Here are some tips for using business case stories successfully:

- **Pull out relevant quotes.** An interesting quote from your customer along with a picture can give a business story some needed personality.

- **Use metrics.** *Metrics* are measurable results that companies use to judge performance, like an increase in sales, reduction in turnover, improved ROI. Using a case study allows you to introduce these figures with a little color and context so don't be shy about showing off those results. Give those figures a memorable boost by having them on a slide or writing them on a whiteboard or flipchart. Figure 12-1 shows an example.

- **Add a personal touch.** Because a business story typically has less of an emotional aspect to it, consider how you can personalize it in some way to make it real for your prospect. Did you work with the customer? Are there any quick, interesting details or anecdotes you can add to make this story come to life?

- **Include dramatic elements.** Because these stories are similar in content to the rest of your presentation, make them stand out by including dramatic elements like conflict and raising the stakes. You can see how to do it in the upcoming "Incorporating the Elements of Drama in Your Story" section.

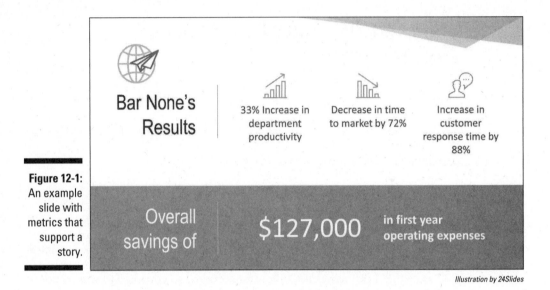

Illustration by 24Slides

Figure 12-1:
An example slide with metrics that support a story.

Sharing about a day in the life

This type of story is an effective way to explain the application of a particular feature or capability of your product or service. In a *day-in-the-life* story you put yourself into the role of a person using your product who needs to accomplish a specific task or solve a problem. By using this type of scenario your prospect is able to more directly see and understand how and when she would use your product in her own job. For example:

> "Let's say I'm Jean a new HR person, and I'm told we need to hire a new engineer. I would first go into the system and find out what the salary range is for that position. Even though I'm unfamiliar with the system, I can easily find what I need by looking at the options on my dashboard. After I get that information, I would look for the job description . . . "

Showing with a metaphor or analogy

Metaphors and *analogies* are popular literal devices used to compare one or more things to something else in an attempt to explain or entertain. People use metaphors all the time — the 800-pound gorilla, the elephant in the room, that's a slippery slope. They're like shorthand for communication because they quickly create a visual picture in your listener's mind. Now you may no longer create a visual picture when someone says the elephant in the room because you've heard it so many times, but fresh, new metaphors and analogies can do a good job of communicating something quickly that you want the prospect to visualize. Here's an example of an analogy:

> "How many of you have a smartphone? But think back to before you had a smartphone. If you wanted to make a call, you needed a phone. If you wanted to send an email, you needed a computer. If you wanted to play music or watch a DVD, you needed a device for that, too. When the iPhone first came out, it was ground breaking for many reasons, but primarily because a single device replaced the need for a lot of those additional products. It was faster, easier, and more efficient. This reminded me of your organization because currently you're using multiple systems to accomplish your job. What I'm going to show you today is how you can create a seamless end-to-end customer experience and achieve that goal more efficiently by using one system."

A complex idea quickly conveyed in an easy to understand package. That's the power of metaphors.

Here are some good rules to follow when using a metaphor in your presentation:

- **Don't overuse them.** A metaphor about a ship, a volcano, and then a football game will have your prospect busy trying to keep the metaphors straight — and potentially miss your point entirely.

- **Be creative.** Avoid overused, such as "She was pale as a ghost," or mixed metaphors, such as "Run it up the flagpole and see if it sticks."

Finding just the right metaphor is often the trick. Here are some tips for designing your own metaphor:

- **Identify the subject that you're trying to describe.** Know whether it's a feature, a benefit, or a concept — for example, 24/7 service and parts.

- **List the characteristics of that subject you have identified.** Write down all of the words or phrases you can think to describe your subject, including what it does, how it makes you feel, and what senses does it involve — for example, easy and fast access or worry-free buying.

- **Brainstorm ideas of things that also share these same characteristics.** Looking at your list, write down all of the different types of things that share those same qualities — for example, gas stations, convenience stores, concierge service, and warehouse stores.

- **Write a sentence that compares your topic to the ideas you came up with.** Create a comparative sentence connecting the two topics with the word *like* or *as* — for example, "Our service center is like having a private concierge for your business 24 hours a day."

- **Run it up the flagpole.** Tell your metaphor without explanation to several people to find out if it makes immediate sense. If you have to explain it, it probably isn't a good metaphor.

Revealing something personal

When done well, telling a personal story — something you've experienced, witnessed, or learned — is one of the most powerful elements you can add to your presentation. Personal stories contribute to the success and growth of everything from 12-step groups to religious organizations to political candidates. Telling a story from your perspective or experience allows your prospect to see the person behind the salesperson and helps forge a stronger connection as she steps into your shoes. Here's an example of a personal story used at the opening of a presentation:

> "I recently decided to remodel my bathroom. Because I consider myself a fairly handy person, I decided to save some money by doing it myself. After two weeks and $1,000 to get the right design and find all the materials, I was ready to start. Unfortunately, I realized that I needed some special tools. So back to the hardware store to spend another $200. When I finally started, I accidently cut a pipe and things got worse from there. I didn't order enough tile, and the fixtures didn't fit. After the bathroom had been off limits for a month, my wife had had it. What began as a fun little side project quickly turned into a much more costly and time-consuming job because frankly, it wasn't my specialty. I finally hired a contractor, and he finished it perfectly in two days. The reason I tell you this is I know you're considering using internal resources to do this project. Like me, I think you'll find that it's much less risky in terms of money and time to work with specialists."

Many salespeople worry that a personal story is inappropriate for a business audience. Although a personal story may indeed be considered out of place in certain cultures, don't be too quick to assume your audience fits into this small category. Your audience is made up of people — the same people who watch movies, read books, and tell stories to their children. Just because they're at the office doesn't mean they don't appreciate a good story. That being said, telling a personal story isn't without risk. You must be very cognizant of several things:

✔ **Don't make yourself the hero.** If anything, you want to share some lesson you learned or shortcoming you were able to overcome like the previous example.

✔ **Make extra sure that it's relevant.** An irrelevant story will really have your prospect's head shaking. Be on point and on time.

✔ **Commit to it.** To be successful delivering a personal story, you must go all in. If you don't appear confident (notice I said "appear" — see Chapter 10 for tips on gaining confidence) or come across as uncomfortable or uncertain, your prospect may dismiss your story as untrue or trivial and question your credibility.

Going with an anecdote

Unlike a personal story, an *anecdote* is a story about someone — or something — else. It's not the friend-of-a-friend story (that no one believes), but rather something that you have a connection with, whether it's through interest, knowledge, or experience. Stories about famous people, companies, and events are common subjects for anecdotes. Here's an example:

> "There are many things we now take for granted that at one point were revolutionary. Take the high jump. You're probably used to seeing athletes jump over on their backs. But it didn't used to be that way. In fact, up until 1965, high jumpers cleared the bar by using a straddle jump, which meant the big, burlier athletes were better equipped for it. Dick Fosbury was a slender jumper and invented this backward J style to help him clear the bar easier and at a greater height. This style, called the Fosbury Flop, won Fosbury the gold in the 1968 Olympics. It was by looking beyond what had always been done that Fosbury forever changed that sport. In the same way, we're going to ask you to look beyond what you've been doing and consider a new, faster, leaner approach to running your business . . . "

When choosing an anecdote for your presentation, keep your eyes open for these potential issues:

- ✔ **Stay away from heavily trafficked areas.** You can bet your prospect has heard the story of Apple or Microsoft's beginnings, Henry Ford's invention of the assembly line, and Michael Jordan's success. If you're going to visit popular ground, look for a different take on the same old story.

- ✔ **Avoid controversial subjects.** Religion, politics, sex, global warming — any of these could offend someone with a strong opinion. If you're unsure whether your story crosses the line, total abstinence is your best bet.

Incorporating the Elements of Drama in Your Story

Stories are a form of drama, yet most sales stories I see are uniformly devoid of this quality. In an effort to appear more real or professional, salespeople often cut out anything resembling drama in their stories, which results in some really professional boring stories. Drama is certainly nothing to shy away from, especially in a story, here's why:

Drama is all about action. It incites emotion and attracts interest. As the movie industry can attest to, drama can keep people in their seats and hold their attention for as much as three hours at a time.

Now aren't those qualities — the ability to incite emotion and attract and hold attention — qualities you want to have in your presentation? Drama is a powerful magnet. It helps you to identify with and care about the people in the story. Instead of leaving prospects flat with another lifeless and forgettable story, apply the following elements of drama and take your prospect on a dramatic journey that engages them, gets them invested in the outcome, and sticks with them long after your presentation is over.

Following are some key elements of drama that can take your story from straight-to-video to box office hit. Use the story planning guide (see Figure 12-2) to make sure you don't miss any of these critical elements.

What is the purpose?				
What is the point or lesson?				
What type of story is it?	Personal	Anecdote	Business case	Analogy
Who is the hero?				
What is the conflict?				
What is at stake?				
What are the key details?				
Where does it open (action!)				
How does it end? (payoff)				
Can I use a prop?				
How can I use my voice/body?				

Figure 12-2: A story planning guide.

© John Wiley & Sons, Inc.

Pick a hero

Every story needs a hero also known as a *protagonist* that an audience can identify with. The hero can be your solution or your prospect, but avoid making yourself or your company the hero as it comes across as arrogant.

Add conflict

Conflict is a vital part of a story and necessary to engage an audience. Thousands of movies and television shows rely on the fact that people are intrigued by conflict and tension and curious to know how things are going to turn out. If your story is just one happy romp from start to finish, you haven't given your prospect much to hang on to. Stories require conflict and tension before ultimately coming to a resolution, so give your story the "So what?" test. If it doesn't pass, you may need to escalate the dramatic tension with the next technique.

Raise the stakes

If the hero doesn't find the bomb by midnight, the city will be destroyed. If the city is destroyed, the country will go to war. If the country goes to war the . . . You've seen this movie, right? The stakes keep getting higher until the audience members are on the edge of their seats! Contrast that with most stories where little is at stake. "I had to choose between a red car and a green car." Ho hum.

You can't expect your prospect to care about a story where there are no consequences. If you want to have your prospect on the edge of her seat instead of slumped over the table, raise the stakes in your story. If in your story the consequence of making a wrong decision is only a minor inconvenience, your prospect won't care. However, if the consequence for a wrong decision were a $10,000 fine versus a $10,000 reward for the right decision, you'd have a better chance of piquing her interest. Stories should be a heightened reality; in other words, something important must be at stake. Make sure you know what is at stake in your story — money, pride, love, security?

Make the stakes as high as possible to increase engagement. No, it doesn't have to be thousands of dollars or certain death, but if you do some digging, you can probably find more is at stake than you first realized. Here's an example of a sales story with high stakes.

> "Recent clients of mine also needed to sell their house very quickly. They had twin girls going into their senior year in high school when the city announced they were redrawing boundaries, placing their current home just outside of their school district. After much searching, they found a house within the new boundaries and their offer was accepted, so they quickly put their house up for sale by themselves. After two price reductions their home finally went under contract, but a week before deadline the buyer backed out. My clients were either going to be stuck with paying two mortgage payments — which they couldn't afford — or telling their girls that they'd be spending their senior year at a new school, leaving their friends of 12 years behind. Working together we were able to price their home right and market it effectively to qualified buyers and had an offer within three days. They were able to move into their new home in time for the girls to start their senior year with their friends."

You can raise the stakes in the following ways:

- ✓ **Brainstorm the consequences for your hero.** Explore all the various consequences of making a wrong decision or no decision. Don't limit yourself, and get creative.

- ✓ **Raise the stakes.** Continue to increase the dramatic tension by asking yourself after each consequence, "And then what would happen?"

- ✓ **Include the stakes in your story.** Highlight very clearly in your story what the highest stakes are for your hero so that your prospect stays engaged in the journey.

- ✓ **Hold the final outcome until the end.** Tension and curiosity is what keeps your prospect hooked so don't give away the results until the end of your story.

Pick your details

Consider which details are necessary to move your story forward. Details are necessary to bring your story to life for your prospect, but providing too many details can make your story too long and quickly overwhelm your listener, creating tune-out. When first crafting a story, get all the elements of the plot down on paper. Read it aloud several times and continue to edit out those details that aren't necessary or don't add significant value or interest to your story.

Be specific

Clear and precise language is always more compelling than vague language to your listener. Select a few key elements in your story to describe in detail. Use sensory language when possible — for example, "it smelled like just after a rain" or "it looked like the surface of the moon." Quantify when you can. For example, "99 percent" rather than "most" or "five" instead of "several" will be more meaningful and clear to your prospect.

Start with the action

Where you begin your story is a key factor in gaining and holding your audience's attention. The reason most stories are too long is because the salesperson doesn't recognize where the real story begins, and he errs on the side of including too much backstory before getting to the point. This is the kiss of death with today's busy decision makers.

To start the story at the right point, think about where the action starts and provide just enough context to give your prospect some bearing. Here's an example of a story starting with the action:

> "In 1986 Jack Nicklaus was a long shot to win The Masters. He hadn't won a title in 10 years, and there were lots of new, younger players on the tour. But he surprised the odds makers by winning his sixth Masters that year. It was his crowning achievement. Why did he win? Because he knew the course better than anybody. He knew what it took to win better than anybody. He had experience. And experience plus professionalism is always the best bet. In the same way, we recognize there are new players in the industry, and it makes sense for you to evaluate them. But in the end, we believe that you'll realize that experience is the winning bet when it comes to taking your business where you want it to go."

Now I could have started that story talking about Jack Nicklaus's esteemed career, his rivalry with Arnold Palmer, or his successful golf course design business — all of which would take up valuable time and keep me from getting to where the story really starts — winning the 1986 Masters — and the real point of the story — experience is a winning bet.

Like well-written TV shows, assume your audience is smart and start where the action is. Certainly use enough detail to get your prospect oriented, but start with that attention-grabbing action scene and you'll have your prospect hooked.

End with a payoff

Many stories fail because the ending is telegraphed way in advance. If your prospect sees it coming a mile away, there is no reason to stay tuned. Give your prospect clues, build your story to its climax, and when you've made the stakes as high as possible, reveal the outcome. Doing so gives your prospect a sense of completeness. The ending is the payoff, and the more tension you create beforehand, the greater the payoff at the end for your prospect.

Sharing Your Story with Skill and Confidence

A story is only as good as the storyteller. When it's done well, storytelling looks incredible easy, but make no mistake, it requires planning, practice, and keen attention to timing and purpose to get it right. Even if you don't consider yourself a natural storyteller, you can improve your storytelling skills dramatically by mastering a few of the following techniques from great storytellers for bringing a story to life:

- ✔ **Just start.** Don't put your audience on notice that you are going to tell them a story. For example, "I'd like to share a story with you . . ." That sentence alone gets their defenses up: ("I don't have time for a story! I want to hear how you're going to help me.") If your story is interesting, succinct, and relevant to your audience, they won't have time to think these negative thoughts, so just begin.

- ✔ **Keep it short.** In a world of increasing demands and expedited communication, your story needs to be short and to the point — think two to three minutes max. If you've followed the previous suggestions in this chapter about fleshing out a few key details and starting with the action, your story should be fairly concise. If it's not, consider whether you're trying to get too much across and take the time to edit down to the essence of what you're trying to say.

Aim for keeping your story fewer than two minutes to avoid tune-out or impatience.

- ✔ **Be descriptive.** Think in terms of word pictures. In the previous section, "Impacting the brain with stories," I discuss how your brain interprets stories that use sensory words, which can help your listener experience the story in a more three-dimensional way. Be careful not to go adjective crazy. Pick and choose only those descriptions that help color or advance your story.

By using sensory language you activate those areas in your listener's brain. More brain activity means a more engaged audience.

- ✔ **Incorporate your voice and body.** A story is an opportunity to use more of your personality and express it through your voice and movement. Consider how you can vary the tone, volume, or pace of your voice as you tell your story. Incorporate dramatic pauses. Use gestures to describe things for your audience. For more tips on using your voice and body, see Chapter 11.

- ✔ **Use your stage.** Don't hide behind your laptop when telling a story. Imagine you're telling a story to a friend rather than a speaker at the pulpit delivering an address. Connect to your prospect as you tell your story by using your stage to move toward her or position imaginary objects in your story on the stage with you and refer to them. See more on how to effectively use your stage in Chapter 11.

If you're placing imaginary objects on the stage with you, be consistent and clear with your locations when you refer to them so that you don't confuse your audience.

✔ **Consider props.** Think about how you can bring your story to life for your prospect. Perhaps there's a picture you can show or an object, like a book, tool, or piece of clothing you can reveal. Even a small effort in this area goes a long way to making an impact on your audience. Chapter 14 looks into using props.

✔ **Own your story.** A half-hearted attempt to tell a story will fail. Be fully committed to sharing this story with your prospect. If it doesn't come out exactly how you anticipated, keep going as if that's exactly how you planned it.

✔ **Rehearse well.** Telling a story with impact takes a lot of practice, so don't wait until the night before to start rehearsing your story. Practice saying your story aloud several times a day for at least a week before your presentation to make sure you have it down. If you find new ideas while you're rehearsing, that's great. Jot them down and incorporate them into your story, but beware of the length because you may have to eliminate something else. Having a good story ready to go gives you greater confidence and frees you up to really focus on your prospect.

Chapter 13

Managing — and Surviving — Stage Fright

*Y*ou don't have to be performing on Broadway to experience a first-run case of stage fright. Whether you're giving your presentation to a group of three or 300, *stage fright* — performance anxiety — can strike, leaving you uncomfortable and derailing your plans. Symptoms sound like a punch line to a joke about the side effects of a popular advertised medication: shortness of breath, dry mouth, racing heart, shaky voice, sweating, trembling, and even nausea. But they're no laughing matter when your presentation is on the line.

Most actors have that nightmare of being on stage and not knowing their lines — even though they have spent weeks and months rehearsing them. Forgetting a line or two on stage isn't uncommon, just like forgetting parts of your presentation isn't uncommon. Even though the actual event is rarely as devastating as you imagine it will be, you can lessen the chance of stage fright occurring by taking some preventative measures.

You may always feel butterflies just as you're about to step in front of a group. But you don't have to let those jitters negatively impact you. By applying the proven techniques in this chapter that performers have been using for years you can go from stage fright to stage excite.

This chapter helps you understand what happens to your body when anxiety strikes and how getting rid of nerves all together may actually be a mistake. You discover some tips for decreasing the likelihood of stage fright from occurring as well as practical tools and exercises for managing stage fright when it does strike.

Comprehending Stage Fright

A case of nerves can strike anyone — new or experienced, young or old — at any time. Professional actors, speakers, performers, and business leaders — anyone who has to perform in front of others is a potential victim. Why do you get anxious before or during a presentation? Stage fright usually stems from one or more of the following causes:

- ✔ **Fearing judgment:** Not unlike an actor who gets nervous knowing a critic is in the audience, being in front of people who can influence the outcome of your presentation can be nerve-racking. Unfortunately, the truth — you're being judged — does little to alleviate that fear.

- ✔ **Projecting a negative outcome:** Expecting something to go wrong can turn into a self-fulfilling prophecy. An actor worries about forgetting a line, and sure enough, he does. You worry that the prospect won't be interested, you pull back and give a lackluster presentation, and the prospect forgets your presentation the minute you walk out the door.

- ✔ **Being hyper self-conscious:** When you're aware of being observed by an audience, it's natural to start observing yourself as well. I'm sure you've experienced that detached out-of-body sensation of watching yourself do something frightening. This self-examination takes you away from your audience and multiplies your symptoms by shining a light on them. The slightest tremble in your voice or surge of anxiety takes on monumental proportions, and you become even more involved in your self-analysis and less in your message and your audience.

- ✔ **Lacking confidence in your knowledge or ability:** Stage fright has a much greater chance of creeping in if you aren't feeling fully prepared. Although common among newer salespeople, stage fright is every bit as much an issue for experienced sellers who struggle to stay on top of new features and products that their company puts out, developments in their industry, and changes in their client's organization.

Realizing what's really happening in your mind and body

Even though anxiety starts in your mind, its effects are very real on your body. Anxiety triggers your sympathetic nervous system, dumping adrenaline into your blood stream and signaling your body's *fight-or-flight reaction* (a physiological reaction that causes a person's body to either prepare to stay and fight or flee a perceived threat) — which explains why you feel like running for the exit when it strikes.

So you think you have stage fright . . .

Actors are no strangers to stage fright. Adele has actually vomited on people. Carly Simon passed out on stage. As a young comedian, Jim Carrey was put off performing for two years after a painful stage appearance. Later in her career, Barbra Streisand developed such debilitating stage fright after forgetting the words to a song at a Central Park concert that she couldn't sing in public for almost three decades. Hayden Panettiere, Megan Fox, Brian Wilson, the list of performers who struggle with stage fright is long. Most have come to accept that it's part of the package and learned ways to manage it and channel it into a successful performance.

If excitement and anxiety were on the elemental chart, they would be right next to each other because they produce similar symptoms in the body. Both result in an increase in tension, or energy; however, when you're anxious, you tend to use that energy to become more inhibited as the body tries to protect itself. That's why your movements get smaller and closer to your torso. When you're excited, you become less inhibited and your movements become more expansive.

Recognizing the upside to stage fright

Attempting to eliminate your anxiety entirely is unrealistic and unwise. Many actors who have attempted to cut out nervous energy all together have found that it also drains all of the enthusiasm and energy out of their performance. Instead of dreading performance anxiety, they use it to give them a heightened level of awareness and energy to kick-start them into a more dynamic performance. You can do this too by relabeling those nervous feelings as excitement and pleasant anticipation rather than fear and dread.

Doing so turns your energy outward, and you become more engaged in your presentation and your audience, which starts to build your confidence and help you overcome those nerves. In the following sections I introduce some techniques from the performance world to help you do just that.

Reducing the Likelihood of Presentation Jitters

The good news about stage fright is that maintaining an intense level of anxiety for an extended period of time is difficult. The bad news is that stage fright is usually worse in the beginning of your presentation, and your opening is critical because it sets the stage and creates your first impression. Actors generally suffer the most while waiting backstage to go on. But after they get through their first few lines (which most all do), their rehearsal preparation kicks in and they're able to ease into their role. Make sure that you take steps to reduce the onset of stage fright and performance anxiety well before you arrive at your presentation.

Here are some tips that can prevent — or at least lessen — the onset of anxiety:

- ✔ **Boost confidence with preparation.** Preparation can go a long way toward preventing stage fright. When you're secure in the knowledge that you know your presentation and you're ready to deliver it, anxiety is less likely to hit, or if it does, anxiety is less likely to hit as hard. Knowing your presentation allows you to focus on connecting with your prospect, leaving less room for fear to creep in. Here are some ways to ensure that you're prepared:

  - **Understand what you're saying and why you're saying it.** Go beyond just memorization and strive for a deeper understanding of your content. Building your presentation on a logical flow and progression can help you get back on track if you should get lost.

  - **Role-play.** Reading your presentation quietly to yourself isn't enough to either prepare you for your presentation or give you enough confidence to offset any nerves that crop up. Set up a simulated presentation space, even placing imaginary audience members in specific locations and allowing them time to answer. Then give your presentation with full vocal and physical commitment.

  - **Rehearse.** Take it a step further and do a full dress rehearsal in front of real people — friends, team members, or family members. Give your audience some background on who they are and ask them to stay in role to make it as real as possible. Invite feedback afterward.

- ✔ **Channel anxiety into positive energy.** Instead of getting rid of stage fright, try channeling it into positive energy that can work to enhance your performance. A simple way: Relabel anxiety as excitement. Although the symptoms are similar, when you're anxious, your tendency is to shut down and become smaller and more inhibited. When you're excited, you open up, becoming more extroverted — obviously a preferable state for a presenter.

By redefining those nervous feelings as excitement or anticipation instead of fear, you can shift your mind-set and start to turn this energy outward, which allows you to become more engaged in your presentation and your audience and increase your confidence. Try this exercise the next time you're excited:

- Notice what symptoms you're experiencing.

- Compare those symptoms to the symptoms you feel prior to a sales presentation.

- Notice those similarities and when they crop up and use the positive expression of those symptoms — like excitement instead of anxiety, or anticipation instead of fear — to describe how you're feeling.

✔ **Assume the audience likes you.** Imagining you're walking into a trial by fire can certainly get your blood pumping. Even if you anticipate a challenge, adopt the attitude that the audience members like you — or at least — that they want to hear what you have to say. Expectations affect how you act and in turn how people respond to you. Assuming an attitude of "they like me, they really like me!" and considering the audience a friendly group of peers who wants you to succeed, not a royal court whose recognition you aren't worthy of receiving, can help keep anxiety from overtaking you.

✔ **Stay in the moment.** "*What if I forget my opening? I wish I hadn't just said that!*" Most fear is located in the future or the past, not the present. Staying in the moment and focusing on everything that is happening right now, as opposed to projecting into the future or reviewing the past, can keep negative thinking from taking over. Doing so also can allow you to communicate and respond fully by being mentally and physically present for your prospect.

✔ **Visualize success.** Many books have been written about the power of visualization to impact your success. Professional athletes, performers, public speakers, politicians, all have benefited from the practice of visualization before a performance. Here are some steps to take to visualize a successful presentation:

1. **Get into a relaxed state.**

2. **Create a picture in your mind of the presentation environment you'll be in.**

   Use as much detail as possible. Identify the colors, the sounds, and the smells.

3. **Imagine yourself entering the room feeling confident, prepared, and happy.**

4. **Imagine the first words coming out of your mouth with ease and your audience nodding in response.**

5. **With the image strongly planted in your mind, slowly open your eyes.**

6. **Continue to practice visualization leading up to your presentation to reinforce those positive pictures.**

✔ **Use a strong moment before.** Anxiety is typically at its worst right before you start. To ensure that nerves don't take over and negatively impact your opening, use a strong *moment before,* which is an acting technique in which you imagine a set of circumstances that put you in the emotional and physical state you want to project. For example, if you want to project confidence, you may imagine just getting a call that you've closed a deal that you've been working on or been asked to speak at a prestigious event. Using a powerful and positive moment before can give you the positive focus and momentum you need to carry you into your opening and through those critical first few minutes of a presentation. Find steps for creating your own moment before in Chapter 10.

✔ **Nail your opening.** Nothing gives you greater confidence than delivering a great opening. Spend the extra time necessary to really master your opening. Practice it out loud under a variety of different circumstances, not just in the privacy of your home or office. You may receive some funny looks if you say it out loud in a crowded place with a variety of distractions, but it can give you the confidence to know that you can pull it off no matter what. Starting strong is the best anecdote to combat most of the anxiety you're initially feeling. After you get off a good opening, your preparation will kick in and you'll be able to relax into it. For more on creating a strong opening, see Chapter 5.

✔ **Move your body.** If you feel like jumping out of your skin before your next presentation, take the leap! If you watch athletes before a competition or an actor or musician before a performance, more than likely you'll see them moving around, stretching, and shaking it out. They're focusing all of their pent-up anxiety and energy pulsing through their bodies and giving it a much-needed release. Even if your presentation doesn't require a lot of physical movement, moving your body beforehand — especially the large muscle groups — is one of the best things you can do to relieve pre-performance anxiety. Moving your body energizes you and makes you feel loose and ready to go, free to focus on your presentation and your audience and free of paralyzing nerves. Check out the warm-ups in Chapter 11.

✔ **Use your breath.** Breathing is a miraculous thing people do with little thought about 15,000 to 20,000 times a day. Changing your breathing can produce millions of biochemical reactions in your body. Proper breathing can release relaxing substances, like endorphins, and inhibit anxiety-producing substances like adrenaline and toxins. Often anxiety causes your breath to quicken, which triggers those negative substances to be released.

Here's a quick exercise to do before your presentation to slow down your breath and reduce stress:

1. **In a standing position, press your thumbs into the soft spot below your rib cage and above your pelvis.**

2. **Place your fingers so they're pointing toward your belly button.**

3. **Inhale for four counts as you focus on expanding your abdomen, back, and sides, while maintaining the pressure of your thumbs and fingers around your abdomen.**

4. **Exhale for 8 counts as you squeeze (don't pinch) your fingers and thumbs together.**

5. **Repeat until you feel more relaxed.**

6. **Release your finger pressure and exhale.**

Handling Stage Fright When It Takes Hold

You're waiting for your prospect and a bad case of nerves hits. Or, you're in front of your prospects and anxiety comes out of nowhere. Suddenly, you find yourself short of breath. Your voice sounds high and unnatural. You feel hot and can't remember what the next slide is. How can you stop the spiral of anxiety when it takes hold? Keep the following pointers in mind to help:

✔ **Stop the chatter.** When pressure strikes, you may recognize a few unfriendly voices in your head predicting disaster and telling you that you're not prepared and that you're going to screw up. Those voices are lies. Stop and ask yourself, "Is it really true?" Unless you just got a copy of the presentation handed to you, more than likely you're as prepared as you can be. Could you have prepared more? Of course, if you had nothing else on your plate, which I'm guessing isn't the case. Don't believe those voices in your head when anxiety strikes. They aren't your friends.

✔ **Focus on an activity.** Demonstrating a feature, presenting a case study, writing on a whiteboard — all of these activities or props offer opportunities to direct your focus *on* a presentation-related activity and *off* your performance. The more involved the activity, the busier your mind is and the less time you have to take your emotional temperature. Here are some props and activities to place your focus on:

   • Show a video clip.

   • Demonstrate a product or feature.

   • Use a whiteboard or flipchart.

   • Provide a handout.

   • Engage your audience in an activity.

   • Ask a question to get the audience involved in a discussion.

✔ **Having a destination.** Actors can feel awkward on a stage if they don't have a physical destination. If your body doesn't have a reason to move and a place to move to, you're likely to feel awkward and self-conscious. Without a reason to move you can easily be overcome by a sense of self-consciousness and panic that eventually leads to a poor performance.

Unfortunately the response to this awkwardness is often falling back on habitual or protective movements, like rocking back and forth, folding and unfolding your arms, or adopting what you assume are natural positions, which suddenly feel anything *but* natural! The problem is your movements have no real justification.

You can solve this by predetermining some spots within your presentation where it makes sense to move. After all, no rule says that you have to stand in one place to deliver a presentation, but on the other hand, you don't want to wander aimlessly. Knowing your first destination can boost your confidence. If your body feels purposeful, your mind will as well. See Chapter 11 for more tips on purposeful movement and using your stage.

✔ **Applying the Marsha Brady technique.** In the "Driver's Seat" episode from *The Brady Bunch*, Marsha is attempting to get her driver's license, but she becomes so overcome with anxiety that she chokes before she even pulls away from the curb, failing the test. Before she retakes the test, Mike Brady suggests that she visualize the instructor in his underwear to overcome her fear. When she starts to panic, she takes his advice, the fear passes, and she passes the test with flying colors. You don't have to picture your prospect in his underwear — which may be more terrifying — but you can imagine that you're speaking to him under less formal circumstances, like in a coffee shop, or that he is an old friend of yours, which may relieve some of your fear and anxiety.

Here are other ways to handle stage fright in different circumstances.

Dealing with large groups

A special kind of anxiety can affect you when speaking before a large group of people. Most people have had this situation in mind when they voted public speaking a greater fear than death. The size of the audience doesn't matter — whether large to you means 10 people or 200. Although the sheer size of your audience can induce terror, here are some proven ways to limit that fear from taking over:

✔ **Create privacy.** With a dozen or more eyes staring at you, not feeling a bit self-conscious like you're on display is difficult. And yet, in an increasingly crowded world, most people have become experts at creating privacy in some pretty un-private places, a busy coffee shop, a crowded restaurant, riding on the bus, and so on. They're able to block out others enough to focus on an activity or sometimes engaging in a fairly intimate conversation within earshot of others without thinking twice about it. How is it that possible? By focusing so intently on what you need to do or communicate to another person, you're able to block other distractions out of your awareness.

This skill is useful in front of a large group to lessen your self-consciousness. With a concentrated focus, you don't have to worry about what others are thinking of you at the same time. By increasing your focus on communicating your message to your audience and making it your sole purpose to get through to them, you'll feel less like a reality show contestant and more like a professional with a mission to accomplish. Try it yourself before you give your presentation:

- Visit a crowded restaurant or coffee shop with a good friend or co-worker and try and hold a private conversation. (You may or may not want to tell them what you're doing.)

- Increase your focus on your partner until you realize you have blocked out the other conversations around you.

- Bring that level of intense focus to your next presentation and see if it doesn't reduce your anxiety.

✔ **Narrow your focus.** When giving your presentation, the stage, lights, and audience can easily overwhelm you, making you self-conscious and causing you to lose your bearing if you aren't focused. One technique designed to help actors combat this tendency to get distracted by an audience is to have them start their focus small and then slowly build it.

By placing your focus on one or two people and waiting until you feel grounded before you expand your focus to include more people, you can slowly work up to feeling comfortable with the entire group. This technique allows you to stay relaxed as you continue to enlarge your focus. Here's how you can apply this technique with a large audience:

1. **Place your initial focus on one or two people in the audience and speak directly to them.**

2. **When you're comfortable, expand your focus to include one or two more people.**

3. **Continue enlarging your circle of attention until you have included most of the room.**

4. **If you find yourself getting nervous at any point, go back to placing your focus on a small subset of your audience and start the process over again.**

When you do this, try not to obviously exclude others by turning your back to them or talking too quietly for other audience members to hear. Just focus on one person and in a short amount of time you should be comfortable taking in the entire room.

Using beta-blockers to deal with stage fright: Yes or no?

Some people suffer such severe stage fright or performance anxiety that it keeps them from doing their jobs. For these unfortunates, beta-blockers, a class of drugs used to treat everything from hypertension to heart attacks to tension headaches, may seem like a quick fix. Beta-blockers slow down the heart rate, fight off stress hormones, and put a lid on that part of your brain that controls emotion.

Although they can indeed calm that fight-or-flight reaction that inhibits many performers,

beta-blockers aren't without their detractors. Banned by the Olympics, some say they give performers and athletes who take them an unfair advantage. To many, they seem to dull a performance. Invariably the decision should be made between you and your physician. Although beta-blockers can be helpful on occasion, like anything else, though, they can become a crutch. Consider other more sustainable programs to alleviate anxiety, including biofeedback or behavioral therapy.

Believing that you'll recover

Even if your anxiety causes you to make a mistake, know that you will recover. You may find that after you actually face what you fear, the actual event itself is rarely as bad as you imagine it will be. Mastering some tools to help you rebound when anxiety strikes and impacts your presentation can give you confidence as well. Head to Chapter 21 for ten great tips for recovering from these so-called presentation "disasters."

Part IV
The New Rules of Engagement: Interacting with Your Audience

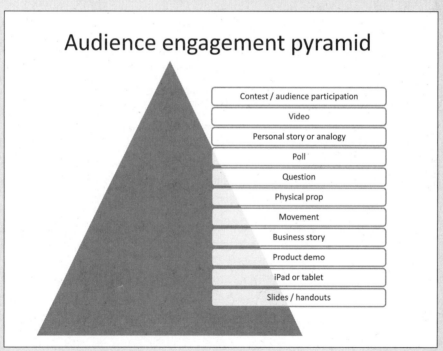

Illustration by 24Slides

Maintaining your prospect's attention during your presentation is every salesperson's challenge. Explore how gamification can help you engage your prospect at www.dummies.com/extras/salespresentations.

In this part . . .

- ✔ Understand why and how often you need to reconnect with your audience in order to maintain attention.

- ✔ Explore a variety of props and interactive activities to keep engagement consistently high during your presentation.

- ✔ Manage your time, your Q&A session, and your audience to keep your presentation on track.

- ✔ Identify objections that may come up during your presentation and discover effective strategies for pre-empting them.

- ✔ Get unstuck from any objection by applying a powerful rule of improv.

Chapter 14

Engaging and Managing Your Audience

*Y*ou can easily blame a lack of interaction on your prospect, but the truth is that interaction isn't your prospect's responsibility. It's yours. The battle for attention is one of the greatest challenges salespeople face around the world regardless of product or industry. Yet few salespeople put much thought or planning into making sure their prospect is consistently engaged throughout the entire length of their presentation. Although they may have a strong opening, it can only hold a prospect's interest for so long. The result? Much of the meat of their persuasive case isn't delivered to a fully attentive prospect.

Engaging today's busy decision makers isn't easy and doesn't just happen by lobbing a few questions their way. In fact, asking unclear or leading questions can be worse than trying to interact at all. Poorly handled Q&A sessions cause many presentations to end on a sour note.

Fortunately salespeople have many more tools available to them than they had in the past. By putting some thought, creativity, and planning into how and when to use them, you can give your presentation the best possible chance to be heard and acted upon.

In this chapter I introduce a wide variety of tools for engaging and reengaging your prospect before her attention reaches the point of no return. You discover how to encourage audience participation through props, interaction, and staging. You see how to put together an engagement plan to help you use the right tool at the right time. I also introduce some effective tactics for keeping your presentation on track and on time by using proven audience management and Q&A techniques.

Engaging Your Audience and Why Interaction Fails

Maintaining your prospect's attention is a challenge. Certain audience members show no signs of shame or hesitation when it comes to texting, emailing, or talking while you're presenting. Although you can complain about the disturbing state of manners in society — and I will join you — you have to find a way to work with all types of audiences if you want your proposal to have a fair chance. Engagement and interaction are critical in order to drive the sort of behavior change that you're asking your prospect to make. But even those who aren't busy texting and emailing are prone to tune out during your presentation if you don't take some proactive measures. Here's why:

- ✔ Attention spans have declined 50 percent in the last decade.

- ✔ Sustained attention is between 5 and 20 minutes.

- ✔ Attention is at its highest at the start of your presentation and drops to its lowest point within 10 minutes.

You need a plan for dealing with the realities of today's attention spans. You need to understand where you're in danger of having your audience tune out and what adjustments you can make to reign in prospects that stray and keep those who are tempted to stray from starting.

Many salespeople make attempts to interact with their prospects — sometimes they work, mostly they don't. This hit-or-miss strategy is something you can't afford in today's competitive marketplace. Here are some common reasons why interaction attempts fail for salespeople:

- ✔ **Waiting too long to interact:** Most prospects come into a presentation expecting to be a passive audience member. You can't blame them. People are creatures of habit. Put them in front of a screen and they're ready to sit back with their popcorn and watch the show. If you want more interaction, you have to reset your prospect's expectations early. Within the first few minutes of your presentation, you're teaching your prospect what level of interaction you expect from them. Give a 20-minute monologue before engaging your prospect and you can expect to hear nothing but crickets.

- ✔ **Interacting too infrequently:** Most presentations are structured around how long it takes a salesperson to explain a certain topic or feature — not how long a prospect's attention span is. For example, although you may take 15 minutes to talk about project management, your prospect's attention span is well past its low point at 10 minutes, which means much of what you say won't make the impact you're hoping for. Just like other biological needs require breaks, your prospect needs an attention break to reboot. Ignoring the restraints of human nature is a common mistake in presentations — and one that you can easily avoid with some awareness and planning.

✔ **Lacking variety:** Humans quickly adapt to patterns. If all of your attempts to engage your prospects are the same, such as asking a question or writing on a whiteboard, your prospect quickly adapts, and those techniques will lose their power to engage her.

✔ **Leaving no space for their audience:** Too many salespeople ask questions without giving their audience enough time to respond. Of course, letting a question hang there in silence is nerve racking, but if you answer your own question too quickly, your prospect will happily let you answer the remainder of the questions yourself as well.

✔ **Using the wrong tool:** Examples of using the wrong tool include presenting on your iPad when you have more than two prospects, passing out a text-heavy handout at the start of your presentation, and asking questions that inspire heated debate. As important as it is to use a tool, the wrong tool can fail miserably and get you hopelessly off track. You need to take into consideration your audience, your venue, and your message before you choose an engagement tool.

Considering Different Engagement Tools

You can engage and interact with your prospect in many ways, yet most salespeople stick to the same one or two: slides and questions. Lack of variety is one of the biggest reasons engagement efforts often fail to produce results so consider all of your options and find a few that are appropriate for your purposes. I focus on four major categories of engagement tools as follows:

✔ Engaging at an emotional or intellectual level: You can engage with a *hook* — an attention-grabbing device like a quote, question, story, insight, or shocking fact. I discuss them in Chapter 5 for openings, but don't be shy about using these techniques in the body or closing of your presentation as well. Keeping your audience emotionally and intellectually engaged throughout your presentation is crucial.

✔ Using props

✔ Interacting with your prospect

✔ Staging

The rest of this chapter examines the last three categories in greater depth.

Using Props to Move the Sale Forward

A *prop* is something that supports, reinforces, or clarifies your message. Props can enhance your presentation in a way that words alone can't. Much in the same way that an actor uses a prop to help support his character and move the action of the play forward, a prop in your sales presentation can help support your message and move the sale forward. Keeping this goal in mind will help you determine what is and isn't useful to include in your presentation.

In a digital age, most salespeople rely on PowerPoint or their product demo as their prop. Although PowerPoint or a demo certainly provides value over no prop, slides and demos really just put you on a level playing field with your competition. Introducing something new into your presentation can renew your prospect's attention. I have seen salespeople use simple items including coins, phones, and books to great effect. To differentiate and increase the lasting power of your message consider using a physical prop along with your slides.

The following sections help you understand the power of props to engage your audience, how to choose the appropriate prop for your presentation and audience, and how to get the most mileage out of your prop.

Comprehending why props work

There are many good reasons to consider incorporating a prop in your presentation. Props can do the following for your presentation:

- ✔ **Increase listener retention.** According to Toastmasters International, on the average, listeners only retain 10 percent of what they've heard one week later. This percentage increases to 67 percent when visual aids are added to the equation. If you want a prospect to remember what you've said, a prop can be extremely valuable.

- ✔ **Emphasize key points.** If your entire presentation is on PowerPoint, each message has equal weight. By adding a prop to a key message, you can make that particular message stand out in your prospect's mind.

- ✔ **Prove capabilities.** Often there is no greater sales tool than the product or service itself. A demonstration, sample, or model adds not just a visual component, but a tactile one as well. See Chapter 18 for tips on delivering a winning product demonstration.

- ✔ **Simplify or clarify information.** Some products or features are quite complex. Even if your prospect is familiar with it, she can get lost in the sheer volume of data. Providing a visual shortcut or reference, like an illustration or a handout, can help your prospect more easily understand the information and follow along.

✔ **Break up the monotony.** No matter how compelling your presentation is, research shows that a listener's attention starts to wane after about 7 to 10 minutes. Introducing a prop at these key intervals is one effective way to reengage your audience.

Exploring types of props

Surprisingly, you don't have to look far to find great props to help add to or reinforce your message. These sections examine some of the more popular props you can use in your presentation.

In Chapter 5 you can see an example of using a prop in an opening. The prop — a nickel — cemented the message about the danger of resting on past success through a story about a salesperson's own Kodak moment. At the end of the story she pulled the nickel out of her pocket and showed it to the audience. "This," she said after a dramatic pause, "is what Kodak's stock is worth now." A simple (and inexpensive) prop brought to life a message that made a lasting impact on her audience.

Slides

Yes, your slides are actually a prop. Unfortunately, salespeople have often overused them so that they have lost their novelty and become more an expected part of the presentation. You can make your slides more engaging with a little effort with these tips, but keep in mind as with most slide-related tricks, less is more.

✔ **Annotate your screen.** You can quickly and simply write directly on your slides to call attention to an item or add a note of clarification. This feature is available within PowerPoint or as an app for your iPad. Check out Chapter 21 for ways to draw on screen during your presentation.

✔ **Rely on animation and transitions.** By creating some movement on your slides, you can make your presentation more compelling. Examples of animation include bullet points appearing and disappearing or images bouncing on or off a slide. You can also use *transitions* — the way you move from slide to slide — to engage your audience. Numerous options are available for creating attention-grabbing effects with your slides. Refer to Chapter 9 for a more comprehensive list.

A little goes a long way when using special effects on your slides. Stick with one or two and don't rely on this as your sole means of engagement.

✔ **Use a laser pointer.** Although this tool can be useful to draw your prospect's attention to a point on the slide, few salespeople use a laser point for the purpose it was intended: to point. More often the salesperson seems to have a sparkler in her hand as she traces speedy circles around a spot or quickly darts across the screen before the prospect even knows she is there. To avoid making your prospect feel like a cat chasing that illusive red dot, follow these guidelines when using a laser pointer:

- Find the spot you want to highlight on the screen and point at it.

- Hold it steady for at least a count five. Your audience doesn't know where you're headed, so give them a chance to get oriented before you turn it off or move to another position on your screen.

- Verbally tell your audience where the dot is to orient them on the screen. "You can see that I'm pointed at the upper right corner of your screen on the dashboard."

iPad or tablet

Although your tablet can be your presentation medium, you can also use it as a supplemental prop. Use it as a giant countdown timer for breaks or as a more intimate way to show product samples, recent projects, or highlight a certain feature. Find out more about presenting with a tablet in Chapter 22.

Product model or sample

Sometimes nothing is more powerful than seeing the product itself. See how to demonstrate a product effectively in Chapter 18.

Video

If engagement were a pyramid, video would be up there toward the peak, as in Figure 14-1. Run a video in front of your prospect, stand back, and let it do its magic. Video is prone to problems however, so consider the following when you use video in your presentation:

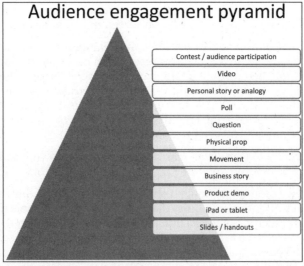

Figure 14-1: Audience engagement pyramid showing the increasing levels of engagement as you move up the pyramid.

Illustration by 24Slides

✔ **Use a speaker.** Computer speakers are notoriously inadequate so bringing your own portable speaker is a must — even if you're sure the venue has one.

✔ **Prepare for connectivity issues.** Don't rely on wireless availability to show a video. Countless presentations have come to a screeching halt because wireless connections are unavailable or spotty. Bring your own hotspot or better yet, embed the video in your presentation or hyperlink to a file on your computer to avoid this problem all together.

✔ **Edit your video.** Make sure your video is set up to start and end precisely where you want it. Making your prospect sit through a bunch of unrelated clips or footage can dilute the effect of your video.

✔ **Compete with video.** In two words: don't try. Saying anything while you're showing a video is wasted effort. Let your prospects focus on the video and wait until it stops and you've regained their attention before speaking.

This figure ranks the various methods of engaging your audience from lowest (least impact) to highest (most impact). Slides and handouts are at the bottom because they're the most overused; at the top are personal stories, analogies, video, contests, and audience participation. The order can vary greatly depending on the quality and interest of the method used.

Handouts

Many people still like to have something tactile that they can write notes on or serve as a reminder after a presentation. Even though handouts do have their place, keep in mind that anytime you put something in front of your prospect, she will read it and possibly jump ahead. You can certainly lose her attention for the amount of time you're handing things out, so follow these guidelines when using handouts:

✔ **Pass out as needed.** Wait until you are ready to discuss the topic before giving your prospect the handout. If you have one handout that covers multiple sections of your presentation, let your prospect know you will be handing it out at the end to ease their mind.

✔ **Use a handout to support data.** Rather than showing complicated slides with difficult to read charts, graphs or rows of data, consider putting the information on paper and walking your prospect through the page, rather than the slide.

✔ **Create an interactive piece.** Since many prospects want to capture important facts and figures during your presentation to help in their decision-making process, don't fight it. Make it an interactive activity by creating a handout that they can fill in as they go. See Chapter 7 for more tips on handouts.

Flipcharts

While decidedly low-tech, flip charts are a surprisingly effective and simple way to re-engage your prospect and underscore or explore key messages. Many have a "sticky" back so you can peel them off and stick them on a wall or hard surface if you want to keep them displayed throughout your presentation. Here are some good uses for a flipchart:

✔ **Tracking benefits:** A flipchart is a great place to list benefits as you cover them because they will then be in front of your prospect's eyes for the remainder of the presentation.

✔ **Tabling questions:** Use a flipchart to keep a list of questions that you want to come back to or research. It's best to put them a few pages back in your pad so that they don't serve as a constant reminder of things you don't know or have yet to do.

✔ **Doing a poll or question:** As a nice variation from slides, you can use a flipchart page to introduce a poll or question. See the later section, "Interacting with Your Prospect."

Here are some tips for using flipcharts effectively in your presentation:

✔ **Use a grid.** Relying on the grid version isn't cheating if you have an option. Don't worry. Your audience won't see the grid, and the grid can keep you from writing like a six-year old.

✔ **Plan your pages in advance.** Rather than taking up valuable time to write out things like polls, agendas, or text as your audience watches, prepare your pages in advance before your audience arrives.

✔ **Use a template.** Take some time at home to write out what you want to put on your flipchart. Bring your template to the venue and place it underneath a blank page on the flipchart and trace over it in light pencil.

✔ **Mark your prepared page.** Use a sticky note to mark your prepared pages so you can quickly turn to them when you're ready.

✔ **Use dark colors.** Draw in colors that your audience can easily see. Green, black, and blue work best. Use others to highlight. Only use red to indicate negatives.

✔ **Buy flipchart markers.** These markers don't bleed through to other pages, and their smell isn't as strong as regular markers.

Consider this example that is prepared ahead on a flipchart, and at the appropriate time the salesperson uncovers it: 1,242 + Tuesday + 38.82605, -104.82519 + 18 + Jen + iPhone6

> Salesperson: "Bob, can you add this up for me? (Bob laughs and shakes his head) "Why not?"

> Bob: Hesitating before finally responding. "Because it's numbers and letters."

Salesperson: "Right. But what if you could add this up? (Rhetorical question followed by pause to give audience time to consider) You see, this is actually very important information for your organization. It's raw data about your customer. She sent 1,242 texts last month, and on Tuesday she posted something about her phone on her Facebook account. 38.82605, -104.82519 are the GPS coordinates of her phone right now, and 18 is the number of apps she downloaded last month. Jen is the name of her best friend who just tweeted about her new iPhone6. Understanding what this information adds up to can help you bring this customer the best possible offers at the most appropriate time, which is what we're going to look at next . . . "

Whiteboards

Attention around the use of whiteboards in the sales process has exploded over the past few years. Although a number of techniques are focused on delivering a collaborative-style presentation entirely on the whiteboard, I concentrate on how to use the whiteboard as a prop in your presentation.

Unlike a flipchart, your whiteboard serves as a more temporary area to illustrate a point, explore an idea, and/or capture audience suggestions in the moment.

Don't be fooled at the seemingly impromptu nature of the whiteboard. To use it well and take advantage of its ability to grab your prospect's attention and create opportunities to interact, it requires some planning and preparation. Similar to a flipchart, don't wait until you actually need to use a whiteboard in your presentation to try it. Here are some tips for using a whiteboard:

- **Practice writing.** All of your life you've been writing on a horizontal surface and suddenly you're going to write on a vertical board legibly and in a straight line? Don't count on it. Writing on a whiteboard takes some practice and requires different motor skills than you're probably used to. Get familiar with the space you have to work with and determine how large your lettering needs to be for visibility. Step back occasionally as you practice and look at your results from where your audience would sit to check its readability.

- **Plan your space.** Unless you want your board to look like an equation that only Stephen Hawking could decipher, have a plan. The board is your real estate so use it wisely.

- **Know your point.** Determine in advance what topics or key messages you want to whiteboard so that you don't blank out or end up whiteboarding everything. Items that make sense include those points that warrant extra reinforcement or require a more visual explanation.

- **Sketch out a concept**. Don't wait to be inspired on the spot. Practice drawing a few ideas that help illustrate your point and choose one to fine-tune.

- ✔ **Leave white space.** Just like a PowerPoint slide, white space helps for readability. Don't bunch things up too closely or what you're trying to make appear simple will seem surprisingly complex.

- ✔ **Choose pens.** Drawing on the whiteboard with a half empty pen is annoying for everyone. Don't count on your prospect to have fresh pens available. Always bring your own. Different colors have different connotations. Use red sparingly and/or only for things that have a negative meaning, such as rising prices, disadvantages, or competitive solutions.

  Always check to make sure you're using dry erase pens on the whiteboard. Lasting memories of your notes on a prospect's whiteboard isn't the last impression you want to make.

- ✔ **Use symbols.** Utilize arrows or the plus and minus sign to indicate relationships or words like "increase, decrease." Use abbreviations where possible as long as you're clear with your audience what they are as you write them. You can lose your audience writing out words like, *logizomechanophobia* (an extreme and irrational fear of technology). Instead opt for FOT and explain it.

- ✔ **Stick to your strengths.** Unless you're an artist, stick to words or very simple shapes. You don't want the presentation to be about your artistic skills (or lack thereof).

- ✔ **Speak to your audience.** Don't explain what you're drawing to the board. Your audience won't be able to hear you. Turn around, make eye contact with your audience, and tell them what you're doing, what it means, and why it's important, before turning back to the board to write.

Books, keys, phones — any object that illustrates a point

Think about what your main message is and what emotion or meaning you want to convey. If it's a story, something obvious in it may call for a prop. It could be something you're drawing a comparison to, like a Swiss army knife as the solution to your prospect's disparate systems (see an example in Chapter 6) or a tablet as an example of embracing new technology (see an example in Chapter 18.) Think creatively and in terms of what you can carry and follow the guidelines of a good prop (which I discuss in the next section): relevancy, customer-appropriateness, and visibility.

Choosing the right prop: The how-to

The right prop can create a memorable moment and re-ignite waning interest. The wrong prop can turn your audience against you faster than a tabasco flavored Jelly Belly. Here are some tips on choosing the right props for your presentation:

✔ **Select a prop that's relevant.** Although a cool video you took may grab attention, if there's not a clear connection to your topic, your audience will feel tricked and your efforts will backfire.

✔ **Consider your audience.** Different types of people respond differently to the same prop. For example, handing out Payday candy bars to reinforce the message that you can get your prospect a faster pay day may work great with a group of product users, but it would probably come across as hokey in a more formal presentation to the C-suite.

Don't throw out the idea of a prop just because you're talking to executives. Engagement knows no boundaries. Just think in terms of relevance.

✔ **Factor in visibility.** Consider your venue and how many people are going to be in your presentation. You want to be sure that the audience member farthest away is able to see your prop. If it's something small, like a dime, hold it up and move around the room slowly so that everyone has a chance to see it — even if they know what a dime looks like, which they do.

Making your prop pop

Just like a magic show, the success of a prop is all about timing and the reveal. Try these suggestions for getting maximum mileage out of your props:

✔ **Reveal your prop.** Don't leave an unusual prop exposed until you're ready to introduce it because that can distract your audience. Likewise, frantically searching in your bag for a prop can make your reveal anticlimactic. Having your prop covered, off to the side, and easily accessible until it's time adds an element of intrigue and expectancy.

✔ **Use dramatic pauses.** A moment of silence before you unveil your prop can build anticipation and add some drama. Similarly, pause after you reveal it and let your audience see it and make the desired association on their own before you jump in with an explanation.

✔ **Handle your prop with care.** How you treat your prop lets your audience know what it's worth. If you're uncomfortable or awkward about it, it will be awkward for your audience. If you treat it like an old shoe, your audience will endow it with the same value.

✔ **Rehearse with your prop.** Adding a prop requires adjustments in the timing and delivery of your presentation, so don't have your presentation serve as your practice run. You can avoid different types of faux pas (illegible chicken scratch on a whiteboard, books displayed upside down, and so on) with a little practice. Rehearse with your prop to avoid embarrassing prop malfunctions.

Don't rely too heavily on your prop. Props are a great way to add interest and attention to your presentation, but they aren't the star of your show. Props should always play a supporting role to your message.

Interacting with Your Prospect

Props are good engagement tools, but sometimes you want to encourage more interaction with your audience. Questions are usually the first thing that comes to mind, but they aren't the only way to interact with your prospect. In order to introduce variety into your presentation, have several methods of interaction in your presentation. In the following sections, I discuss three of them: asking questions, using polls and contests, and giving your prospect a role.

Using questions

Posing a question is a quick and easy way to engage your audience. People are naturally curious, and a good question can stimulate their thinking right away. You may wonder why asking a question often yields such unsatisfactory answers from prospects — or worse, none at all. Throwing a question out to your audience and seeing a bunch of blank faces staring back at you in silence is uncomfortable. If you put some time and thought into what questions you want to ask and what type of response you hope to get, you can improve your results dramatically and eliminate a lot of those empty stares.

Knowing what you want

The biggest problem with the questions salespeople ask is that they're unclear as to whether they expect an answer or not. The following list discusses the two types of questions: Each one has its place and purpose, but if you haven't made it clear to your audience which one you've asked, you won't get the response you're looking for. Here are some ways to use them and help your audience distinguish between the two:

- **Rhetorical questions:** These are best used when you don't expect an answer, when your question doesn't have an obvious answer and you want your audience to ponder it, or if you want your audience to imagine themselves in a particular situation or circumstance.

  For example, "What if you woke up and found that all of your personal data — your health records, your financial records, your passwords — had been compromised?"

Even though you don't expect a verbal response when you ask a rhetorical question, you want your audience to think about the answer so pause for a moment before you move on.

✔ **Literal questions:** Most questions are literal, meaning you expect or want an answer to get your audience verbally engaged. In order to distinguish your question from a rhetorical one and increase the likelihood of getting a response, follow these guidelines:

- **Be intentional:** Be clear in your mind that you want an answer, and your tone and eye contact will naturally convey that to your audience. If your audience is confused as to whether you expect an answer or not, they'll likely remain silent.

- **Avoid filling the silence:** It's a bit uncomfortable at first to have everyone staring at you in silence, but you must give your audience time to process the question before they answer it. Remember that they just heard it and you're laying the ground rules for how your audience should participate. If you answer your own questions in the beginning, your prospect will be even less likely to jump in later.

Developing a questioning strategy

Even though you certainly want to leave time for spontaneous questions within your presentation, having a strategy that includes questions — both planned and unplanned — that incorporates the following points, greatly improves the quality of your responses.

✔ **Preplan questions.** Prepare your questions in advance. Develop a few questions for each topic as well as some extra questions that you can include anywhere within your presentation in case you need to stretch for time while waiting for others to join the group or for technical problems to get resolved.

✔ **Brainstorm answers.** Many people ask great questions but then are stumped by the answers they receive. Brainstorm all the possible answers you might get for your questions and think about how you'll handle them or redirect them to the point you want to make.

✔ **Start easy.** Begin with the easy questions — ones that require a yes or no answer, or even just a show of hands from the audience. Doing so gets your audience used to responding.

✔ **Model behavior.** If you're asking your audience to raise their hands, raise yours up high to show what you expect and encourage participation.

✔ **Use names.** Asking a person by name to answer a question is often more effective than throwing it out to a group. If that person doesn't have an answer, then you can open it up to the group.

Avoiding certain questions

Asking today's savvy prospects the wrong questions can often be worse than not asking them any at all. Here are some questions to avoid asking:

- ✔ **Multipart questions:** Often a question isn't clear because it contains multiple questions or it's too long for your prospect to easily follow.

  For example, "Many of our customers have found that servicing loans is no longer profitable for them, and I wanted to know if that is the case with you and if you could outsource it, what priorities would that free you up to focus on?"

  Make sure your question is singular, clear, and direct to the point. If you have to add any clarification, it isn't a clear question. If you're not getting responses to good questions, it usually comes down to clarity.

- ✔ **Questions that make you go duh!:** These questions are known otherwise as the blatantly obvious question. These types of questions damage your credibility. If your prospect does bother to respond, it's likely to be a grudging agreement after an inward roll of the eyes.

  For example, "How many of you like to save money?" Duh.

- ✔ **Leading questions:** A member of the duh family, leading questions scream early '80s car salesman. Today's prospects are smart, and leading questions insult their intelligence, feel formulaic, and can make them clam up even tighter.

  For example, "If I could show you how this could improve your efficiency more than fifty percent, would that be something that would have value to your organization?"

  Don't lead your prospect down an obvious path. Come up with some thoughtful, provocative questions that inspire conversation.

- ✔ **Discovery questions:** Most of your opportunity discovery should be completed prior to your presentation. Asking too many general questions about a customer's business, goals, or needs makes them doubt — with good reason — that your presentation is uniquely designed for them.

  For example, "Which system do you currently use for generating reports?"

  Questions in a presentation should be used to clarify and connect — not teach you your prospect's business. Even if you aren't able to talk to your prospect beforehand, so much information is available online that you shouldn't be covering the basics in your presentation. Find an insight and turn it into a question to help you get the information you need. See Chapter 2 for how to find the information you need.

For example, "I see you have a new product line. How does that affect your current reporting system?" This question increases your credibility and helps you to get the information you need.

✔ **Questions without expecting an answer:** Too often salespeople ask a question without giving their audience enough time to respond, either due to nerves or impatience. This is a bad habit that discourages participation.

Incorporating a poll or contest

Polls or contests are great ways to make a point and get your prospect actively engaged and thinking about a topic. They can also be a great way to present a startling fact or figure. You can do a poll or contest simply by asking your audience to voice their answers or raise their hands, or you can incorporate an interactive polling feature. Here are your options:

✔ **Basic poll:** If you only have a small group (five or less), you can pose a question to your audience either verbally or on a slide and provide them with three or four options. If the options are complex or require some thought, a slide is best. Then ask for responses to each option and tally the votes to announce the winning choice.

✔ **Live texting poll:** If you have a large group, a question that requires some time for your audience to consider, or if audience members want to keep their identify anonymous, you can ask your audience to use their cellphones to text their answers to a specific number and show the results live on screen. You need to have Internet access and set this up in advance with a polling program that allows for text message polling.

Here's what you need to set up a poll:

✔ Get set up with a polling program that allows for text message polling, like `polleverywhere.com`.

✔ Develop a poll with a number of choices and assign each a unique code.

✔ Create a slide for your poll, clearly displaying the code numbers for each answer and a number to text their response.

✔ Make sure you have web access for your presentation.

✔ Show the poll results in real-time on your screen as your audience responds.

A poll is highly engaging because your audience gets to see how their answer does in comparison to the rest of the group. You can easily make any poll a contest by including some small prizes for the right answer. Gift cards, candy, and company giveaways are especially good for this.

Giving your prospect a role

Asking someone from your audience to participate in your presentation is an excellent way to make the rest of the group sit up and pay closer attention. Think of tasks that an audience member can perform. It doesn't matter how simple it is. The mere act of having someone from your prospect's organization participating in your presentation increases attention dramatically. Here are a couple of roles you can assign to an audience member during your presentation:

- ✔ **Secretary:** Before your presentation ask an audience member to come up and write down notes or ideas from the group during discussion on the whiteboard or flipchart. Make sure you let the person know exactly what you want her to do and how to do it. Show her an example of how you want it written. Don't leave anything to chance or you'll be spending time explaining it to her when you should be talking to your audience.

- ✔ **Prop mistress:** This job isn't as exciting as it sounds. A prop mistress is someone who can help you with your props. Assign a participant to pass out handouts, reveal flipchart pages, and so on at a designated time or signal.

- ✔ **Plant:** Asking someone you trust (a sponsor or internal advocate) to ask you a specific question on a pre-determined cue can help get the ball rolling on a discussion.

Regaining Attention with Movement: Staging

How you use your space, your voice, and your body are also very powerful tools you have at your disposal to gain your prospect's attention. Chapter 11 discusses many ways you can use your voice (volume, pacing, variety, and pausing) and your body (gesturing, movement, and eye contact). This section hones in on how to use movement in particular to reengage your prospect when needed within your presentation.

Movement is something humans respond to on a subconscious level and is an effective and underutilized vehicle to gain your prospect's attention. Purposeful movement is about getting from one point to the next for a reason. Although there's no need to preplan your every move, incorporating some purposeful movement in your engagement plan (check out the next section on how to put together a plan) can keep you from getting stuck in one spot and provide you with some options to move during your presentation.

Here are some places to use movement within your presentation:

- ✔ **Place props.** Place a whiteboard on one side of the room and a flipchart on the other. Tear off a flipchart page and post it on the back wall. This gives you a reason to walk back into the audience to write on it.

- ✔ **Approach your audience.** When you're speaking to your audience, come out from behind your laptop and address them. If you ask someone in the audience a question, walk toward her to hear her answer.

  Be aware of getting too much in someone's space, and take into account cultural preferences when it comes to personal boundaries.

- ✔ **Walk into your audience.** Musicians often walk into a crowd during a song and the crowd goes crazy. Although your audience may not have the exact same reaction, they will certainly pay attention if you walk into their midst if your room setup allows for it.

- ✔ **Stand up or sit down.** Placing a chair or stool nearby that you can sit in when doing Q&A can help you to connect more intimately with your audience, add variety, and — bonus — give your feet a break.

- ✔ **Tell a story.** A story is a great time to come out from behind the safety zone of your laptop and get closer to your audience. Place imaginary objects in your story in specific locations on the stage and cross over or refer to them as you tell your story. Practice adding gestures, physicalizing actions, and using vocal inflection to make your story come to life for your prospect. See Chapter 12 for storytelling tips.

Creating an Audience Engagement Plan

With the wide assortment of tools available to you there's no excuse for not keeping audience engagement high throughout your presentation. The best presenters don't leave this to chance. Using an engagement plan can help you remember when and how to re-ignite your prospect's attention before it's too far gone. See Figure 14-2 for your presentation engagement plan. Here are some best practices for using an engagement plan:

- ✔ **Interact early.** Include some type of simple engagement or interaction (question, story, poll, and so on) in your opening to set your prospect's expectations.

- ✔ **Plan questions ahead of time.** Don't leave it to chance that you will come up with a brilliant question in the moment, unless you like to sweat.

✔ **Leave room for spontaneity.** Just because you are strategically planning to engage your audience every 7 to 10 minutes throughout your presentation doesn't mean you can't interject some spontaneous questions or interaction. But having some set times to engage will make sure you don't let too much time pass between interactions.

✔ **Collect tools.** The longer your presentation the more tools you need to re-engage your audience. Collect them as you go. Watch other presenters and see what works. Don't try them all out at once, but add slowly as you build a toolkit of effective methods.

✔ **Mix it up.** Variety is the key to success here so don't just use the same tool at every re-engagement point. For example, you might start with annotating on a slide, 7 minutes later you ask a question, and 7 minutes after that you show a short video clip.

Use Figure 14-2 to lay out your audience engagement plan. Begin at minute one with the opening and aim for using one form of engagement — emotional, prop, interaction, or staging — every 7 to 10 minutes. Note what presentation element it falls into and develop a relevant engagement technique. For example, if a seven-minute point falls within a topic challenge/impact, consider telling a story, creating some interaction, using a prop, or incorporating movement. Doing so ensures that you maintain your audience's attention throughout your presentation.

Competitive analysis

Prospect:_____
Date:_____

Competitive Factor	Emotional Engagement	Prop	Interaction/Questions	Staging
Opening				
Agenda				
Topic 1				
-challenge/impact				
-resolution				
-proof				
-benefit				
Topic 2				
-challenge/impact				
-resolution				
-proof				
-benefit				
Topic 3				
-challenge/impact				
-resolution				
-proof				
-benefit				
Topic 4				
-challenge/impact				
-resolution				
-proof				
-benefit				
Closing				

Tip: Use at least one engagement technique every seven minutes.

Figure 14-2: An example of a presentation engagement plan.

Managing Your Audience and the Clock

To be an effective presenter, you must manage your audience and your clock. Letting someone in your prospect's company take over the discussion, allowing breaks to run long, or starting or ending late can all derail your presentation and destroy any goodwill you've built up. These sections provide you tips to help keep things on time and keep your audience under control.

Tracking your start time

Starting promptly gives your audience a sense that they're in for a well-planned and executed presentation. It can be a challenge if your audience — especially the decision maker — is running late. One way to handle this is to have two openings: a soft opening and a hard opening.

- ✔ **Soft opening:** Have an engaging opening — a story, an anecdote, a poll — that introduces your topic but doesn't give away the key points you want to bring up in your opening.

- ✔ **Hard opening:** When the decision maker arrives, wrap up wherever you are and do your full opening. If necessary, briefly recap any important points the executive may have missed.

  This way if an executive shows up late, you can still start on time and give both groups a fresh opening without boring the rest of your audience by repeating yourself.

Keeping track of breaks

For presentations lasting longer than 90 minutes, you need to work in some breaks for your audience. Keep in mind that during the break your prospect may get pulled into an intense conversation, receive urgent emails or texts, or simply get distracted. Breaks completely sever your connection with your prospect so you need to do two things:

- ✔ Control the break at the outset to ensure your audience is in their seats ready to go at the designated time.

- ✔ Regain your prospect's focus as quickly as possible when she returns from break.

Here are some ways to accomplish both of these:

✔ **Set up break rules.** Give your audience notice up-front that you will take a break where they'll have a chance to make phone calls and check email. This helps alleviate their need to constantly check their devices.

✔ **Reward promptness.** Before you break, let your audience know precisely what time you expect them back in their seats and that you'll be revealing an insight, playing a video clip, or holding a contest — with a prize — to encourage their prompt return. Your after-break activities should be enough to intrigue your audience but not be a must-know point.

✔ **Use a break timer.** Even though people can see the time on their cellphone, displaying the time left remaining to the end of break with a countdown timer on your screen or your iPad is much more effective. This eliminates excuses about returning late from break. These countdown timers are available in PowerPoint or for purchase online.

✔ **Start on time.** Stay true to your word and resume at the designated time. Don't make a big deal of latecomers — this isn't fourth-grade English — just go on with your post-break activity.

Chapter 19 provides more helpful advice about breaks for multiday presentations.

Handling Q&A

Audience interaction is great, but you have a finite amount of time to make your case. How do you make sure you get through all of your topics in the time allotted, allow for some Q&A, and avoid getting hijacked by audience members with ulterior motives or disruptive behavior? Here are some tips:

✔ **Set a limited Q&A prior to your closing**. A great time to take questions is just before the final recap of your agenda. Saying "Let's take ten minutes for questions before we close," cues your audience that there is a time limit and helps keep questions succinct and your presentation on track. When it's been ten minutes, quickly wrap up the question you're on and move to close. Refer to Chapter 7 for more tips on closing.

✔ **Stick to schedule.** If you've been given an hour, stick to that amount of time. If you only have five minutes left for questions, let your audience know that you plan on ending on time as promised; however, you're willing to stay if someone has questions they want answered.

✔ **Let people go.** Don't let one person make everyone stay — unless it's a superior. In other cases, invite those who can't stay to leave before you start taking questions.

✔ **Schedule more time.** If you need to leave, the questions are too complicated, or you don't know the answer, schedule a follow-up phone call or meeting to discuss with interested parties.

✔ **End early**. Everybody loves extra time. If you've covered all of your material and the Q&A has run its course but there's still time left in your slot, don't just fill it because it's there. Tell your audience you're going to end early and they'll be very appreciative.

Dealing with difficult audience members

Sometimes you have people in your audience who seem to be on a mission to challenge you or throw you off track. Other times you have people who are blissfully unaware that their behavior is disruptive or rude. By recognizing these types and having some proven tools to handle them, you can keep them from stealing the show and sidelining all your hard work.

Here are a few types of disruptors you may have and how you can handle them:

✔ **The enquiring mind:** This person has one question after another. Letting him monopolize your presentation is dangerous and discourteous to the rest of your audience. Don't make him feel bad, but reign him in by tabling his questions with a "Good question, and I want to answer that, but we need to move on to get to everybody's questions here. So with your permission, let me write that down and I'll get back to it after we address some other questions."

✔ **The ADD audience member:** This person is on her phone, on her laptop, and talking to another participant. This audience member seems oblivious that her behavior is noticeable or inappropriate. You can try standing by her. If she is still unaware, put your hand on her shoulder as you address the group. Don't call her out, but make her aware of your presence. This is an effective but nonaggressive way to point out that you notice her inattention.

✔ **The contrarian:** Some people are born to run, and some are born to disagree. This participant disagrees with anything and everything you say and isn't afraid to let you know it. You need to take control of the situation early to avoid having his actions cast a pall on your whole presentation. Try diffusing the contrarian's position by letting him know you value his opinion and that you want to know more about it *outside of the presentation*. If this doesn't appease him, try enlisting help from his manager during a break.

✔ **The comedian:** Humor is great, unless it starts to overshadow your message and steal the show. Assign the comedian a task, whether it's secretary or prop master, to give her something else to think about besides her next joke.

✔ **The latecomer:** It's human nature to turn and watch as someone enters/exits. There's no sense competing with the distraction or trying to make an important point, but don't make a big deal out of it either. Pause as this person enters, acknowledge him, and then jump back in with a compelling question or hook that reengages your group and makes the latecomer anxious to get up to speed.

Chapter 15

Handling Objections Like a Pro

. . . .

In This Chapter

▶ Recognizing the upside to objections

▶ Understanding different types of objections

▶ Anticipating and pre-empting objections in your presentation

▶ Being aware of verbal and nonverbal signals

▶ Making sure you're answering the real objection

▶ Addressing objections on the fly

. . . .

*M*ost people — not just salespeople — dislike objections. They break up the flow of your presentation. They introduce conflict. And they can rattle even the best of salespeople. But the way in which you deal — or don't deal — with objections can make or break the success of your presentation. A variety of different objection-handling techniques are available — some good, some dated, and some just plain silly, but two things are clear:

✔ **You need a process.** Things happen quickly in a presentation. If you don't have a process to fall back on, you can lose your place and your audience.

✔ **You need the right mind-set.** A positive approach to objection handling can dramatically increase your odds of success.

In this chapter you can see objections through a new pair of glasses as you acquire the ability to discern between an objection and a need for more information. I explain how you can recognize verbal and nonverbal objections and find out how your own mind-set may be keeping you from handling objections as successfully as you could. You also explore various types of objections and a method for proactively addressing objections before they arise. Finally, I introduce you to a technique from improvisation for dealing with objections — not if, but when — they come up.

Defining Objections

The word "objection" conjures up a confrontational courtroom scene. Picture two attorneys faced off to determine someone's guilt or innocence. An *objection* actually means a disagreement or opposition. Unfortunately, that term has been adopted wholeheartedly in sales and often that same oppositional stance occurs — a solid, entrenched line with you on one side and your client or prospect on the other. It's not exactly an arrangement conducive to working toward a mutually acceptable outcome. And yet, objections are an important part of the sales process.

According to a well-known study, prospects that buy have 58 percent more objections than those that don't. As uncomfortable as it sounds, having a prospect throw 20 objections at you rather than one "I don't care" is much more promising. Shifting your perspective on objections is vital in order to adopt the right attitude to meet them and navigate through them successfully with your prospect.

In these sections I help you understand why salespeople struggle with objections in their presentations and how seeing them in a new light can improve your ability to handle them effectively.

Grasping why salespeople hate objections

Despite the fact that objections are the sign of an interested — not a disinterested — buyer, you may still not like them any better for one or more of the following reasons:

- ✔ **Disrupting the flow of your presentation:** You had a failproof presentation. If only your prospect would just let you get through it, you could address all of his objections. But sometimes prospects fear that you're not going to get to their issue or that they're going to forget about it before it's too late. Either way, you need to be able to address it without totally losing control of your cool — or your presentation.

- ✔ **Introducing conflict:** Few people enjoy conflict. It's uncomfortable and you've likely learned to associate it with arguing or discord. But that doesn't have to be the case. Conflict can be as simple as wanting two mutually exclusive things: "You want a dog, but you have terrible allergies." "You want to have a family, but you also want to travel around the world." Often people need others to help them make a tough decision and weigh the options. That's where you can help your prospect — by giving him the information he needs to make the best possible decision.

> ✔ **Fearing saying the wrong thing:** You may be putting too much pressure on yourself by expecting to have the perfect response to an objection. Worrying about blowing the deal by saying the wrong thing can leave you paralyzed. But the truth is that you don't need a perfect answer; you simply need a near perfect formula, which I introduce in the later section, "Knowing How to Handle Objections" in this chapter.

Reframing objections as obstacles

In order to develop a more positive attitude toward objections, think of them as an obstacle. *Obstacles* can be merely a temporary roadblock between you and your prospect. Rather than engaging in point and counterpoint with your prospect, which typically only serves to entrench him further in his objection, with an obstacle, you simply consider every possible way across, around, over, or through it. Objections are a natural part of the selling cycle because buyers try to sort through their options, weigh wants and needs, and justify their decisions. By handling objections, you walk away with a better understanding of your prospects' needs, which helps you further target your message to your presentation.

To dread or fear objections and hope they don't come up is akin to expecting the sun to set in the east. If you want to be successful at handling objections discover how to embrace them, or at the very least, shake hands with them in order to keep the sale moving forward.

Identifying the Types of Objections

You can't prepare for every objection, but a significant percentage of the objections you get will probably fall into one of the following common categories — and of course, you probably have a category unique to your industry or product.

Price

This common objection comes in a variety of forms: "You're too expensive," "We don't have room in the budget," or "Your competitor is cheaper." Regardless of the packaging, it all comes down to price. And if you're competing on price, you have made yourself a commodity.

Establishing value is the anecdote to a price objection, but before you leap to respond, you need to find out the true reason for the objection. The reasons for concerns about the cost of your product can vary greatly. What is your prospect basing his expectations on? Make sure that he is comparing apples to apples and that you know what his budget is. You must get to the real root of the objection in order to address a price objection effectively. Refer to Chapter 3 for figuring out how to establish value.

Need

Hearing "I'm not sure we'd really use this" or "I guess it would be nice to have, but I can't really justify it" are signs that you haven't connected your product or service to your prospect's needs yet. Especially for complex products and services, need is a common objection.

For instance, you don't *need* a lot of things, like cellphones, TVs, or cars, but you probably can't imagine your life without them now, right? Handling a needs objection requires stepping back and digging into what the impact on your prospect's life would be as the result of not making a decision. See Chapter 2 for tips on exploring impact.

Status quo

Complacent clients are frustrating. They don't see how much better their current circumstances could be with your product or service. Status quo buyers need to have a powerful reason to change. You must clearly define — and stress — the consequences of no change versus the positive impact of change.

Fear of change

This fear of change often lies underneath the status quo objection, but because it's at the root of so many objections I give it its own category. Fear of change can be paralyzing for many decision makers.

People only walk through their fear of change if they're convinced that the rewards more than outweigh the risks. Prospects who are afraid of change need reassurance that the risk is low and rewards great. An effective way to address this fear is to show through a story that risk can actually be less risky than change. Social proof in the form of comparable businesses making tough decisions and thriving through change can also be a powerful motivator to get this prospect unstuck.

Feature or functionality

Many times prospects get in their heads that a product or service needs to provide a certain feature or capability — one that you don't offer — even though they don't know precisely when or if they would ever use it. Digging deeper and finding out what your prospect thinks this feature will accomplish for him is helpful. If you can establish that the objection isn't a deal breaker, you can often move past this potential sticking point and on to building a case around the features you do provide.

Timing

"This just isn't the right time for us," or "maybe next year" are disappointing things to hear any time during a sale, but particularly in a sales presentation. Timing is typically a stall, which means you need to narrow down what the real objection is. Getting your prospect to acknowledge how you can impact his business can help your prospect see the cost of delay and often turn around this objection.

Overcoming Barriers to Handling Objections

You know an objection when you hear one, right? Don't be so sure. Many times objections are cleverly disguised. Knowing the difference between an objection and a request for clarification or reassurance is important. Many times salespeople jump to respond to what seems like an objection and their reaction turns their presentation sideways.

In the following sections you gain awareness into the behaviors that may be sabotaging your efforts to respond effectively to objections and tips on how to overcome those behaviors. You also get a clear grasp on just what your goal is when you do receive an objection during your presentation.

Changing your reaction to objections

Although you may have every intention of staying cool when you encounter an objection during your presentation, you may find it difficult to do so. Knee-jerk defensive reactions often kick in and make it difficult to change. Here are some common reactions to objections and tips for overcoming them:

- ✔ **Hearing no:** As a salesperson, you may be hyper alert to signs of potential disinterest or problems, which most of the time is very helpful. When you start to hear no in every objection or stalling tactic, it becomes a problem. Statements like, "I'm not sure how this would work for us" or "It would require having everyone on board," *aren't* the type of no that should stop you in your tracks. They're merely roadblocks. Often salespeople hear no in objections that aren't deal breakers and simply are a signal that your prospect needs more information or you haven't addressed his needs yet. Here are some ways to change that:

  - **Explore what no means.** Resist the urge to read no into every objection by exploring what else it could possibly mean. If your prospect says, "We can't afford it," what is he really saying? If he wasn't interested, he would say so. The we-can't-afford-it response actually indicates that your product or service is worth consideration, but the price is a barrier.

  - **Get to the real no.** I worked with one buyer who had a sign over her desk that read: *What part of no don't you understand?* An important question to ask is: What part of no *do* you understand? Continue to probe until you get to a *no* that is understandable. That's the only way you can tell if no really means no — or simply that you have more work to do. See the section on "Clarifying objections" for more on how to probe effectively.

- ✔ **Triggering your fight-or-flight response:** When you sense conflict and think your livelihood is threatened, some real physical reactions take place in your body. Your fight-or-flight reaction kicks in and unproductive behavior ensues, like not asking questions or not probing deeper, getting defensive, conceding too quickly, or simply ignoring signs that there may be conflict at all. Here are some suggestions for calming your fight-or-flight response:

  - **Prepare.** If you prepare and practice your best response to all the potential objections you think may come up, you'll be less likely to feel panic set in when they come up during your actual presentation. See the upcoming section on "Preempting Objections."

  - **Let go of perfectionism.** Disregard the thought that you have to have a perfect response, because there may not be one. Instead, master an objection-handling process so you don't blank out. Refer to the upcoming section, "Knowing How to Handle Objections."

Understanding the objective of handling objections: Move the sale forward

Many salespeople are under the impression that the goal of handling an objection is to change the prospect's mind, convincing him that you're right and he is wrong or misinformed, but that isn't the case. Even though the ultimate goal is to close the deal, the goal of each objection is actually much smaller and thus more manageable. The goal is to move the sale (or the conversation) forward.

If you think it's more than that, you're giving the objection more weight or power than it deserves and putting tremendous pressure on yourself. By pulling back and simply focusing on moving the sale or the conversation forward with each objection you encounter, your next action becomes much clearer, your prospect stays engaged, and you move forward in the sales cycle.

Picking Up on Verbal and Nonverbal Signals

You have so much to focus on when you're giving a presentation: getting your message across, delivering it with impact, remembering what's coming up in your slide deck, and monitoring your audience's responses. You're a regular one woman — or man — show! You can easily lose focus and become so intent on getting through your presentation flawlessly that you ignore some of the less obvious signs that a point isn't resonating with your prospect. Your efforts to give a perfect presentation may cause you to miss the fact that the client is tapping his fingers, glancing at his watch, or changing his facial expression.

Don't let *presenting* take you away from *observing* the constant flow of verbal or nonverbal information that is coming from your prospect. Listening to your prospect is a critical part of your presentation. Don't sacrifice that connection in an effort to get through every slide. Your presentation is there to support you. If you have to go off script for a period to handle an important objection, consider it time well spent.

Objections can be spoken or unspoken. In the next sections you discover how to listen for even subtle objections. You also find out how to identify body language that indicates there may be an objection that needs attending to.

Identifying verbal objections

You're more likely to hear what you expect to hear. If you're only listening for specific objections, you may not notice something out of the norm. The dangers of selective listening are many. What if your prospect doesn't express the objection that you're expecting? What if you aren't paying attention and miss a more subtle objection? Listening to the full meaning and intent of what is being said is critical. If you're just listening for a specific verbal cue, like "it's too expensive" or another glaringly obvious reaction, you're likely to miss your prospect's concern all together.

Listening is a critical part of the sales process, and one in which most salespeople have room to improve. You may be tempted to talk over prospects in your enthusiasm to clarify a point, head off an objection, or disregard the yes that sounded suspiciously like a no. You must be vigilant and listen with an open mind to make sure that you're fully hearing what your prospect is saying and understand his intention for saying it.

Catching nonverbal cues

Have you ever walked out of a presentation where there were no real objections, questions, or obvious negative reactions, thinking, "They were totally onboard!" only to find out later that you didn't win their business? How could your judgment be so off? Odds are that you may have only focused on verbal cues — questions and the stated objections. As a salesperson, you must also be aware of the nonverbal feedback that is coming from your audience.

Although specific body language can have many different meanings, the following can mean you need to stop and check if a point hasn't landed right:

- ✔ **Closed body language:** Arms across chest, turning or looking away, sharing a knowing look with a colleague — all of these can mean your audience isn't in agreement or has some contrary opinion on your topic. Either way, they're a good indication that you should stop and check out what they mean before continuing. Figure 15-1 shows some examples of negative body language so you can identify them when they happen.

- ✔ **Abrupt changes:** People have their own unique body language, which is why broad generalizations about the meaning of body language can be unreliable. What you want to look for instead is any major variation from the body language your prospect has been exhibiting. For example, if a prospect has been sitting quietly with arms folded in front of him on the table and suddenly backs up or starts moving around a lot in his chair, you may have hit a nerve.

Figure 15-1:
Examples
of nega-
tive body
language.

Preempting Objections

The best offense is a good defense. If you can deal with an objection before it arises, you can often keep it from solidifying and building up into something insurmountable by the end of your presentation. But you can't do this without a process.

Here are some steps to make sure you're prepared to preempt as many objections as possible.

> ✔ **Identify potential objections.** Many salespeople are so confident that their presentation addresses all objections that they neglect this critical first step. But there are always possible objections. Review your discovery notes to make sure you have a full list of potential objections. Don't dismiss anything as too trivial or irrelevant. Remember that you have the answers, so an objection may seem rudimentary, but it may be quite valid to your prospect.

Don't let the Curse of Knowledge cloud your thinking and keep you from identifying possible objections. The *Curse of Knowledge* is a phenomenon that makes it difficult for people who have more information to see things from the perspective of a person who has less information. Put yourself in your prospect's shoes and ask, given your circumstances, what would concern your prospect about this proposal. Read more about the Curse of Knowledge in Chapter 7.

✔ **Categorize the objections.** Handling an objection is easier when you know what type of objection it is. Individual objections typically fit into one of several broader categories. For example, "it's too expensive" and "I'm not sure we have the budget" would both fall under the broader umbrella of a price objection.

✔ **Decide when — and whether — to address the objection.** Not all objections should be given a preemptive strike. With each objection, consider if it makes sense to address it within your presentation or save your response for the chance that it comes up. If it's an objection that was brought up in discovery or you think is pretty likely to come up in your presentation, take a proactive approach and include it early in your presentation.

✔ **Consider placement.** If you have decided to address the objection within your presentation, you need to find an appropriate spot for it. If it's a major objection, you may want to consider crafting your opening around it to disarm your audience and shift their perspective right from the start. There's no point in presenting your best case to a close-minded audience. Here are some places within your presentation to proactively address an objection.

  - **Your agenda:** You can treat your objection response as a topic on your agenda, providing context and benefits and giving it the same full treatment you would any other topic in your presentation. The type of objection you're addressing and where it falls in relation to the rest of the topics helps you determine where best to place it. For example, if the objection is likely to come up in your third agenda item, you may want to make it the second agenda item. See Chapter 6 on how to flesh out an agenda item. Figure 15-2 shows an example of using a potential objection as an agenda item.

  - **A story:** A story is an extremely effective way of softening a viewpoint or shifting perspective. See Chapter 12 on how to develop a purposeful story around an objection.

Don't be defensive when responding to an objection. Be open and confident and include good humor if you can. A defensive attitude will only backfire.

Here is an example of how to handle an objection preemptively:

"I heard several of you cough a little when we talked about price, so I want to address price. I realize we're not the cheapest product out there.

But just like you probably don't buy the cheapest car because you value safety, reliability, and comfort, I want to show you that value is more than just the sticker price."

Figure 15-2: Preempting an objection with your agenda.

© John Wiley & Sons, Inc.

Through the use of a story (an analogy to be precise) and a little bit of humor, the salesperson has addressed the objection head-on. Now he can focus on building value in the rest of the presentation.

Knowing How to Handle Objections

After someone has voiced an objection in your presentation, you need to address it, which means that you need to have an objection-handling process in place well before you need it. Dealing with objections on the fly without a consistent process you can count on is stressful for you and it provides inconsistent results.

Here you find out how to uncover the real objection so that you can give the best possible response. You also discover how to keep the conversation moving forward with a great objection-handling technique straight out of improv.

Breaking the objection apart

The first part of the process involves peeling back the onion to discover what's really at the core of the objection before you attempt to answer it. You can do so in the following ways:

- ✔ **Listen.** Listening to your prospect's objection in its entirety takes self-discipline and confidence, but doing so is absolutely necessary with no shortcuts. Interrupting or talking over your prospect is often hard to resist when you assume you know what your prospect is going to say. Tuning out or minimizing your prospect's response can stem from a desire to avoid hearing something uncomfortable. Many salespeople approach listening as the act of waiting to speak, crafting a response to the objection in their heads. Either reaction is a mistake. Instead, focus on actively listening, which takes effort and concentration. Give your prospect the floor and the time he needs to articulate his objection before you rush in with your solution.

- ✔ **Pause.** If you respond to an objection immediately after your prospect utters it, it sounds as if you're parroting back a canned response. Today's buyers have heard all of the tricks, the "feel, felt, found" or the amateur psychologist, "you must have had a bad experience, can you tell me about it?" Take a few seconds to consider what they've said (doing so can help you collect your thoughts and reign in your emotions as well) before jumping in to respond.

- ✔ **Clarify.** After you hear your prospect, continue to ask questions to clarify his objection. Don't assume you understand what his answer is even if it seems self-evident. Your interpretation of what "it's not in our budget" means and your prospect's are very likely two different things. You want to make sure you have the real objection before you start addressing something that is nothing more than a smoke screen. The goal is to get as close to the real objection as possible. If your prospect says, "It's too expensive," that could actually mean a number of things, including:

    - "I'm interested, but I can't afford it right now."

    - "I don't have money in the budget, but I wish I did."

    - "I can't justify this big of an expenditure without involving higher-ups."

    - "I could buy it, but I don't need it."

    - "I can get it for less from another vendor."

    - "I'd sure like to do this, but I need to get a better price by negotiating."

You clearly would have a different response for each of these comments, so before you jump in to answer the price objection, take some time to find out which meaning is accurate. A simple clarifying question, such as "When you say 'It's too expensive,' what exactly do you mean?" or "What are you basing that on?" can help you choose the most appropriate response.

Applying the improvisation rule of "Yes and . . . "

After you get to the root of the objection, you need to know what to do with it. Remember that the goal of handling an objection is to move the conversation forward. One of the best models for moving a conversation forward comes from the world of improvisation. Although improv performers respond to their partners with seemingly random — and often hilarious — results, they aren't operating entirely by the seat of their pants. It may look like improv involves spitting out the first thing that comes to mind, but actually improv performers follow a set of rules that helps them to move past obstacles with ease. Refer to the nearby sidebar for more on using improv.

In the following sections I explore four key elements of the "yes and . . . " technique.

Saying, "Yes and . . . "

The improv rule of "yes and . . . " is at the heart of good improvisation and is ideally suited for working with objections. This rule helps you to address objections in a nonconfrontational, but effective manner, that can get prospects unstuck off an objection. But what if I don't agree with him? I hear you saying. You don't have to agree with your prospect's objection. You don't even have to like it. But as a starting place, you do need to acknowledge your prospect's perception of reality. Arguing with reality isn't a winning tactic. Here's how this technique works for objections:

- ✔ **Say yes to the objection:** Like an improv performer, accept whatever your prospect gives you. In other words, say yes. This first step serves a critical purpose: It gains your prospect's cooperation by making him look good.

- ✔ **Add to it with "and":** In other words, bring something new to the party. As an improviser or a seller, you have to add something — an idea, an opinion, or a solution — in order to keep the scene (or sale, in this case) moving forward. Review your insights for some good ideas to carry in your back pocket. After you have your prospect's cooperation, you can then add your perspective to it and take the conversation in a new, unexpected way. You're basically collaborating on a new solution, which ultimately is what sales is about.

Consider this example of saying "Yes and" to your prospect

Objection: I don't need all of those services.

"Yes and . . ." response: "Yes and that's what a lot of our client's have said before finding out how fully customizable our services are. And what's really interesting is how many have come to realize that they do have additional needs — and we're there for them when they do!"

The prospect's objection has been validated, and he has received social proof that minimizes the objection. Then the focus is shifted off of a potential sticking point and the conversation is taken in a new direction, which opens up additional discussion.

Avoiding blocking

Unfortunately, many salespeople tend to shut down conversational options by responding to objections in a way that invalidates or denies a prospect's reality. This is a no-no in improv called blocking. *Blocking,* or saying no to your prospect, is the quickest way to destroy a collaborative process. Here's an example of blocking.

Objection: I don't need all of those services.

Blocking: "But based on the conversations we had with your team, they said these are exactly the type of services that would help you to be more efficient.

Instead of moving the conversation forward, blocking creates an impasse and effectively shuts down the conversation.

But is simply another form of no. If you've ever had someone apologize to you and then blow the whole thing by adding but . . . you know that they have just negated the apology. Blocking does the same thing by doing at least one of the following to your prospect:

- ✔ **Canceling/denying his reality:** No one likes to be told he's wrong, misinformed, or crazy — least of all someone whom you're trying to convince to spend money with you.

- ✔ **Stopping the conversation:** You've effectively set up a stalemate game of point/counterpoint. You can't move forward from this position unless someone changes his or her stance. Good luck with that.

- ✔ **Putting your prospect on the defensive:** Blocking further entrenches your prospect in his belief — and, puts him in the position of defending his statement — which you never want to do.

You don't have anything to lose and only room to gain by keeping the conversation moving forward, and that's what the rule of "yes and . . ." does.

Redirecting with a follow-up question

After you validate your prospect's objection by saying "yes and . . ." you want to continue to move the conversation forward in that new direction by adding on a good follow-up question. Here are a few pointers on what kind of question to follow-up with:

- ✔ **Experiential question:** This type of question can trigger the imagination and emotion of your listener by asking what his experience is or has been. Some examples include "How would that make you feel to have this resolved?" and "What would happen if two years from now you still hadn't addressed this problem?" A question that invokes feelings and a visualization is a powerful persuasive combo.

- ✔ **Open-ended questions:** Questions that require more than a yes or no answer get your prospect to expand on his thoughts and feelings, often giving him the opportunity to work through his fears and questions without any intervention on your behalf.

Follow-up questions are a critical component of your objection-handling strategy, and you want to make sure you have several planned for each objection. Here is an example of a follow-up question used in the yes and process:

Prospect: "Your competitor offers multiple features on this same product."

You: "Yes and I can understand why that sounds at face value like a desirable thing. More always seems like better to me, too! I'm curious; can you tell me how you see yourself using these additional features over the next year?"

Building on the "yes and . . ." formula allows you to respond on the fly to any type of objection while keeping your presentation and the sales conversation always moving forward. Refer to Figure 15-3.

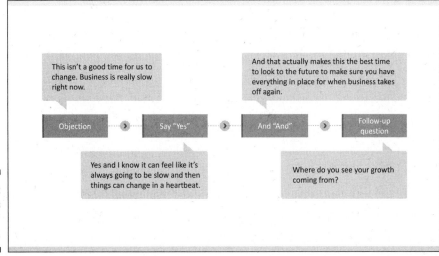

Figure 15-3:
The "Yes and . . ." formula.

Illustration by 24Slides

The rules of improv for sellers

Yes, improvisation has rules. In fact, several of them appear to be custom-made for salespeople:

✔ **Focus on the moment.** Focusing on the moment creates a heightened awareness of yourself, your prospect, and your surroundings. You're actively listening, responding, and adapting to changing circumstances without second guessing yourself.

✔ **Be willing to make a mistake.** In improv, as in sales, making mistakes is part of the process. Because you can't possibly know exactly what's going to come out of your prospect's mouth, you have to be willing to make a mistake. Surprisingly, being willing to fail makes you more willing to take risks and increases your chance of succeeding because you're in the game rather than sitting on the sidelines playing it safe.

✔ **Start anywhere.** All starting points are equally valid, including one's beginning in the middle of a scene. Searching for an ideal way to address an objection or answer a question can often waste time and result in missed opportunities. Of course, do your prep, but eventually you have to jump in the water. Just start where you are, and after you get momentum, it will help you to move forward.

✔ **Say, "Yes and . . . ."** Like improv, sales is a collaborative process. Your prospect's cooperation is vital to move past an objection. With this rule you accept his perspective, make him look good, and introduce a fresh perspective. In other words, you say, "yes and . . . " to your prospect.

Part V
Focusing on Special Types of Presentations

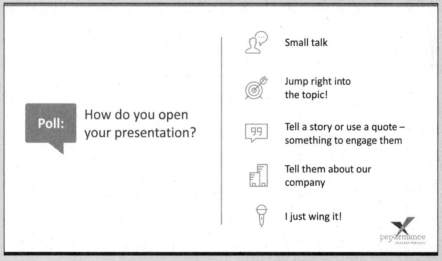

Illustration by 24Slides

Many types of presentations rely on a script. Whether you prefer to memorize your script, simply wing it, or rely on presenter notes, discover best practices and the pros and cons for each at www.dummies.com/extras/salespresentations.

In this part . . .

✔ Present a unified front during team presentations through proper planning, practice, and collaboration.

✔ Discover how to combine content, delivery, and technology for an engaging online presentation.

✔ Know when to demonstrate your solution and how to tailor it for your prospect.

✔ Address the challenges of presenting a complex solution, dealing with a request for proposal (RFP) and multiday presentations.

✔ Prepare for an interview-style presentation by developing cues and building on team member's answers.

✔ Adapt your presentation quickly and easily to changing circumstances by knowing three simple options.

Chapter 16

Presenting as a Team Sport

. . . .

In This Chapter

▶ Building a winning team

▶ Determining roles and responsibilities

▶ Rehearsing as an ensemble — not a soloist

▶ Presenting a united front when handling Q&A and objections

. . . .

The way you work as a team gives your prospect a good indication of what working with your company will be like. Sloppy transitions, disjointed delivery, and discord among team members can feel more like working with a dysfunctional family than a valued business partner! Presenting a united front with consistent messaging, seamless interaction, and good chemistry delivers a vote of confidence to your prospect. It can be a real differentiator in a competitive selling situation.

If you're involved in a complex or high stakes sale, more than likely you'll present as part of a team — competing against other sales teams for a major piece of business. Big dollars are often at stake during these road shows, making it critical that everyone involved be on the same page. In an ideal team-selling world, roles, expectations, and deadlines combined with ongoing communication are clearly assigned to eliminate gaps as well as adequate time for team rehearsal. But you don't sell in an ideal world. Team members are often spread across the map, involved in additional projects, and have varying levels of knowledge, skill, and motivation. How do you communicate effectively as a cohesive group? How do you support each other in the presentation during discussion, Q&A, or objections? Presenting is a team sport, and you need to make sure that you know the rules so you can score points with your prospect.

This chapter explains what constitutes a team-selling opportunity and how you can ensure that your company's investment of time and resources is well spent. You find out how to build a winning team, delegate and assign tasks, and keep your presentation on time and on track. You discover how to effectively rehearse as a team and how to read each other and the audience like a true ensemble cast. I also show you how to prepare for potentially rattling Q&A sessions and objections.

Bringing in the Team

Big opportunities or major accounts often require more than an individual salesperson to pull them off successfully. Prospects often want to meet the people who they'll be working with after they purchase your product or service, get a feel for the management team, or receive more detailed information than you, the salesperson, can provide.

Because team presentations can involve a significant commitment of time and resources, it's important to determine when a team effort is really called for and, when it's deemed necessary, how to make sure you make the most of everyone's time and effort. In the following sections you see what conditions typically require a team presentation and how to set your presentation up for success.

Knowing when you need a team

Although you may be perfectly capable of handling a sales presentation on your own, certain situations — especially in more strategic B2B sales — call for a team presentation, which can be more effective and even expected. Here are conditions that typically warrant a team effort:

- ✔ **You require subject matter experts.** Often complex sales effect several departments within an organization, each one requiring specialized knowledge. Or you may be responding to a request for proposal (RFP) that requires product demonstrations or a deep dive on a specific topic or area that you aren't proficient in. To handle these situations yourself is inviting trouble and could slow down the progress of the sale. Having a specialist on hand to properly cover and answer any direct questions related to that topic is critical, particularly if the prospect is going to have her own experts or stakeholders in these areas on hand to ask the questions.

- ✔ **You're a small fish selling to a big company.** Big companies may have concerns about whether your company has the bandwidth to handle their business. Having more than one person from your company at the presentation can help create a bigger presence for your company and lessen those fears.

- ✔ **Your presentation is lengthy.** Presentations for complex sales or major purchases can go on for a full day or even several days, which is a long time for your prospects to listen to one person. Bringing in additional team members to break up the day and address different topics is a great way to inject some new energy into your presentation and your audience.

✔ **You need to show respect.** Every prospect, especially large accounts, wants to feel important. Bringing in additional team members, members of your executive team, or subject experts, can make a prospect feel like her business is valued.

Taking your show on the road

Having a group of people from your company travel to your prospect's location to give a presentation isn't cheap in terms of time and money. These *road shows,* as they're often called, can turn into an expensive sales call when you start factoring in the time of executives, sales team members, and subject matter experts.

Keep these tips in mind to make certain that a team presentation is called for to avoid any misunderstanding or disappointment.

✔ **Qualify, qualify, qualify.** Ensure that the opportunity is sound and the potential warrants the cost of resources invested. Get all the facts together and discuss them with your manager. The last thing you want is to show up with a team of seven for a prospect who is only in the early stages of identifying a need. Chapter 2 discusses what you need to do to qualify.

✔ **Confirm expectations.** Don't surprise your prospect by showing up with a team. Make sure she knows that you're bringing in additional resources. If you get any sort of hesitancy, go back to qualifying.

✔ **Guarantee the meeting.** Get a commitment in writing from your prospect as to who will be attending from the prospect's company, how much time you have, and where the presentation will be held.

✔ **Send an agenda.** Include a list of attendees from your company, their titles, and what they'll cover. Providing this information gives your prospect a sense of whom to invite on her end.

✔ **Stay in communication.** Especially when lead times are long, stay in touch so the presentation is on your prospect's mind. Communicate any changes in the prospect's situation — attendee dropouts, topic requests, budget or timing changes — to your manager so you can decide whether to scale back or make any other adjustments on your end.

Preparing For a Team Presentation

As a salesperson you may be used to doing things on your own. Bringing in additional team members can feel a bit like taking your hands off the wheel. The key is to take control of the planning process early. Having a structure in place allows you to focus on what you do best, which is moving the sale forward!

You want to take a leadership role in putting your team together and determining what each team member's contribution will be. In the following sections you discover how to build a winning team and how to establish clearly defined roles to make sure you maximize your team's involvement.

Building your team

You want the best people on your team, and you want them to bring their A game. But just like prospects, team members have differing goals and interests. Discovering what motivates team members to give their best effort is one consideration you need to think about as you start putting your team together.

Following are some tips for determining who you need on your team and how to get the most out of them:

- ✔ **Match your audience.** Find out who will be at your presentation on the prospect's side and make sure you have an appropriate counterpart on-site from your team. For example, if your prospect's VP of operations will be there, so should your company's VP of operations, or equivalent.

- ✔ **Bring in the big guns.** Clients like to see management supporting a project. If it's a deal of significant value, either in terms of money or prestige, you may want someone from your executive or management team involved. Make sure that the executive's time is warranted. To do so, provide a clear role for the executive in the presentation beyond just shaking hands. Refer to the next section for more information about assigning roles.

- ✔ **Enlist in-house support.** If you're part of a large organization, you may have sales engineers or consultants, marketing, service, or technical experts who support sales efforts. Keep in mind that these people probably work with other salespeople as well and have additional responsibilities, so make sure that you communicate clearly what the expectations are in terms of their contribution and commitment. Give them as much advance notice as possible so they can carve out the necessary time on their schedule.

- ✔ **Recruit subject matter experts.** Product or subject matter experts are critical when the prospect wants more detail than you as a salesperson can provide. You may have subject matter experts within your organization, or you may need to bring in outside consultants, subcontractors, or other vendors. Keep in mind that these experts typically aren't salespeople; therefore, they may not have as strong a motivation to attend. Understanding what motivates them and enlisting the aid of management to get them on board may be necessary. They need to understand that their job isn't to just work in a silo, show up, and deliver information, but also to take an active role in the preparation and practice necessary to present their subject as part of a unified team.

Assigning roles

All team members should have a clearly defined role, a timeframe for completing it, and an expected outcome. The lead salesperson is typically responsible for assigning tasks based on strengths, expertise, and availability. For example, Bob may be the best for demonstrating how your product works. If he is unavailable for any of the presentation prep, you're better off selecting Gina, who has the time available.

Here are some of the key team member roles that you want to assign to help in the preparation of your presentation:

- ✔ **Team leader:** Having one person as the point person can keep information from getting lost or balls from being dropped. Most likely the team leader is the lead salesperson or account executive; however, some occasions make more sense to give that position to someone who has the time available to devote to the presentation or a better knowledge of the prospect or topic. Part of being a leader is knowing how to delegate and match the right person with the right task.

- ✔ **Logistics coordinator:** Assign one person to schedule all team meetings and rehearsals, including locations (physical or virtual), communicate this information to the team, and keep everyone updated on any changes. This person may also be the logistics coordinator for the presentation venue as well, making sure that the room is set up accordingly, projectors and whiteboards are available, and so forth.

- ✔ **Presentation coordinator/designer:** This person is in charge of getting the presentation materials from the team members and putting the materials into a single presentation format. Assigning one person to build the presentation ensures that all elements of your design are consistent. A bunch of different fonts, graphics, and styles makes the presentation look amateurish, like it was thrown together at the last minute. The coordinator can be the designer, or you may wish to assign that duty to someone who has a good eye for design and the time to devote to it.

Planning Your Presentation

In many ways you approach planning the team presentation as you would an individual presentation: doing discovery, mapping out a strategy, and considering value. But because you want your presentation to come across as a unified effort — not several disparate parts strung together — include your team members in these planning tasks as early as possible so that they have a good understanding of the objectives, responsibilities, and goals and can provide valuable input.

Here are the tasks where it makes sense to get your team involved early in the planning process:

- ✓ **Determine the objective.** In most cases everyone should be involved in agreeing on the presentation's objective and key messages so that you have buy in. As the lead salesperson, guide the conversation and aim for selecting a specific definable outcome from the presentation. Of course, the overall objective is to win the business, but you need to know what that next step is you want your prospect to take so that each team member's section contributes to the same goal. See how to develop an actionable goal in Chapter 2.

- ✓ **Define your intention.** To make sure your presentation has a consistent tone across presenters, decide *how* you are going to move your prospect to take action. Having each presenter come up and simply deliver her information isn't going to do it. Think more actively in terms of what effect you want to have on your prospect. Do you want to excite your prospect? Reassure her? Prove something to her? By establishing a clear intention up-front you create a seamless bridge between presenters that drives toward a specific outcome. See Chapter 10 for more on intentions.

- ✓ **Identify information needed.** Like an individual presentation you need to do discovery on the opportunity to find out the challenge you're addressing, the impact it's having on the organization, the key players, and the competition. In addition, find out how the room is set up so you know where you'll be sitting, standing, and exiting and entering from. Chapter 2 has more about discovery.

- ✓ **Gather the information.** Assign people on your team to gather the research and information necessary to prepare the presentation. Because the discovery process is partly establishing a relationship with the prospect in addition to identifying needs and gaps, as the salesperson you may want take the lead or be involved with any direct conversations with key decision makers. A product or technical specialist may need to speak to people in different capacities within your prospect's organization to get a better understanding of her issues to tailor that section of the presentation. Be sure to get the names of these people from your key contact and encourage everyone to follow good discovery practices when talking to prospects. Make sure all findings go back to the team leader to be distributed to the group.

- ✓ **Determine the content.** Figure out how much time you have as a group and how much time each person has for her section. You may need to negotiate with team members who think they need more time versus how much time is actually available. Don't forget to factor in introductions, transitions, opening, closings, and questions when figuring out timing.

✔ **Organize and outline.** After you gather all the necessary information, you need to organize and structure it into a presentation. Assuming each team member is playing a role in the presentation, this effort should be collaborative with one point person in charge. Technology allows you to do this task online through collaborative presentation programs, like Google docs or SlideRocket.

✔ **Establish a timeline.** Work backward from your presentation date and schedule the following:

- **Discovery deadlines:** Determine when team members need to have their research done and submitted to the team leader.

- **Travel deadlines:** If the presentation requires travel, provide travel guidelines and requirements as soon as possible and a deadline for completing travel reservations to avoid any issues.

- **Material deadlines:** Assign a date for team members to have any presentation materials or documents to the presentation coordinator.

- **Rehearsals:** Schedule at least two rehearsals early in the process so that team members can reserve time on their calendars. Have the logistics coordinator send out reminders and meeting details.

- **Drop-dead changes:** Establish a final date for any changes in content that allows enough time for the team leader to review and the designer to incorporate into the deck.

✔ **Prepare the presentation.** The team should decide on a style and theme, if applicable. Make these decisions before you start building your slides. Check out Chapter 4 for how to create a theme for the presentation.

✔ **Assign presentation roles.** Determine who will present which part and how the team will handle questions or objections. The later section in this chapter, "Handling the Q&A session" provides more concrete advice. Everyone attending the presentation should have a speaking role during the presentation, even if it's short. That way it doesn't look like some of your team members are just there to bulk up your presence or satisfy a weight requirement. Here are some suggested ways to assign roles in the presentation:

- **Salesperson:** In a *bookend-style* presentation the salesperson opens and closes the presentation and subject matter experts or product specialists deliver the interior content. See Chapter 19 for more on this type of presentation. Alternately, the salesperson may do the opening and closing as well as an interior section of the presentation, depending on her level of expertise. Even if the other team members cover the bulk of the presentation, the salesperson should have an active role and maintain a strong central presence throughout the presentation to keep things on track and show support for the team.

- **Managers or executives:** They may do the presentation opening, which should include all the elements for an effective opening as discussed in Chapter 5. Or executives may do a kickoff prior to the opening to show the company's executive support for the project. For a *kickoff opening,* also called a *pre-opening statement,* executives should keep it brief — 30 to 45 seconds — to avoid adding too much length to the presentation opening, which immediately follows. The kickoff should set the tone and create anticipation without stealing the thunder from other presenters by going into great detail.

- **Sales support or subject matter experts:** They present a section on their area of expertise. They're also involved in the Q&A.

Practicing Your Presentation like an Ensemble

Not rehearsing together as a team is like being cast in a show, practicing your part on your own, and not performing with the rest of the cast until opening night. The timing is off, the chemistry is nonexistent, and the audience is uncomfortable. It's a sure way to lose a deal. Until you rehearse together you have no sense of timings or flow to your presentation. Your transitions will be rough and awkward, and your Q&A will be a chaotic mess.

A well-rehearsed team can be a big differentiator in a competitive situation. Here are some tips for rehearsing for a successful team presentation:

- ✔ **Schedule team rehearsals.** Depending on how much advance time you have, the ideal number is three rehearsals. Although they should be in person, sometimes team members are out of town or conflicts arise. In this case, have the unavailable party log in via Skype or Google+ Hangouts to participate in the presentation.

- ✔ **Maximize team rehearsals.** Ask individual team members to practice their part on their own — aloud — before you gather as a team. Team rehearsal isn't the place to hear yourself saying your part for the first time or familiarizing yourself with your content. Respect your team members and show up prepared.

- ✔ **Set up your practice area.** Try to reflect your actual presentation environment: mark off your stage area with tape, and note where the audience, the screen, the whiteboard, and other key items are you may be using or referring to. Figure out where your team will sit when they're not presenting and practice taking the stage from that position.

- ✔ **Do a full rehearsal.** This means everything from the bottom to the top, including introductions, openings, closings, and Q&A. Interact with props, demonstrate your product, and show slides and any videos.

✔ **Use good delivery skills.** Don't let any team member just go through the motions. Set the expectation that full vocal, physical, and emotional connection with the audience is expected. See Chapter 11 to brush up on your delivery skills.

✔ **Practice transitions.** Do the actual transitions and handoffs in real time so you can avoid doing that awkward dance when transferring control of the presentation during showtime.

✔ **Time it.** Appoint someone to time the entire presentation as well as note the timing of each element so that if the presentation as a whole or one part is too long, you can see where you need to cut.

✔ **Record your rehearsal.** Video is a great tool not just for studying individual presenters, but also for seeing how the whole presentation flows and looks from an audience member's eyes. Look out for major disparity between presentation styles, awkward transitions, or glaringly different content than anticipated.

✔ **Stage a mock Q&A session.** Have someone play the role of an audience member and throw out planned and unplanned questions to see how you respond as a team. Read the later section, "Handling the Q&A session" for specific advice.

✔ **Deliver feedback.** Use a checklist or ask each team member to take notes as other members present on a few key areas, such as content, presentation skills, engagement, and presence. The team leader should keep the comments specific and constructive. Comments like "I didn't believe him" aren't as helpful as "Because you kept looking down, you didn't come across as credible as I know you are." See Chapter 11 for tips on how to practice.

Delivering Your Presentation as a Team

Rather than looking like five separate presentations, the best team presentations look like one seamless event. Make sure that each section of your presentation leads naturally into the next by following these guidelines.

Opening

The opening of a team presentation should be no different than that of an individual presentation. Your objective is the same: to gain your audience's attention and quickly give them something of value and a reason to stay tuned. Check out Chapter 5 for tips on opening.

Many team presentations fail by starting off with a long list of who's who, who does what, and what each team member will talk about. That company-centric focus needs to go. Your prospects aren't nearly as interested in "what a great guy Jim is" or how long you've worked together as you may think they are. Start your presentation as you would if you were on your own.

Making introductions

As you go through the agenda, you can also give a brief overview of your team — *brief* being the key word. Save the slightly more detailed introductions for just before each presenter takes the stage. For example: "Ava Morgan is our architect, and she'll be presenting the design strategy. Jake Daniels is our project manager and will be taking you through our master plan . . . "

When the first presenter wraps up, she should introduce the next presenter. Still striving for brevity, provide just enough context to give the audience an understanding of the value the next presenter brings to the table. Keep your introduction focused on the prospect and how each team member's role relates to your prospect. For tips on how to smoothly introduce another person, flip to Chapter 8.

Transitioning to new presenters

Handing over the reigns to each new presenter is where many teams stumble and lose valuable points in their prospect's eyes. It should be a smoothly planned transition that accomplishes the following:

- ✔ **Prompt the next presenter.** Don't count on team members to remember other presenter's sections. Have each presenter go back to the agenda slide to introduce the next topic. Otherwise Presenter B may be distracted and not realize that Presenter A is wrapping up and he's on deck. If Presenter A introduces him too abruptly, there may be an awkward pause and wasted time as Presenter B makes his way up to the stage. See Chapter 8 for tips on building an agenda.

- ✔ **Transition smoothly into the next topic.** Like in the previous bullet, you want to very quickly — one sentence or two — connect the dots between each presenter's sections. Doing so gives a consistent thread to the presentation.

- ✔ **Give thanks and move on.** The second presenter quickly thanks the previous presenter and uses a transition sentence or two to connect to his topic.

This isn't the Emmy Awards. It's tedious for your audience to hear team members thank each other repeatedly. They expect you to be polite, but not obsequious.

Consider this example of how to make a smooth transition between presenters:

> **Presenter 1:** "Now that we've shown you what our vision is for the site, you're probably wondering how we're going to get you there. Jake Daniels is a project manager who will work closely with you to keep you informed on progress and make sure the project is on time and on track. Jake has worked in the industry for more than 25 years and overseen the development of some major projects like Stoney Brook Center and the Cherry Grove Plaza."

> **Presenter 2:** "Thanks Ava. She's right. How do we get from here to there? It's not unlike how you start any journey. First, you have to figure out where you are and what you have to work with. Then you have to look at what you need to fill those gaps. Over the next 30 minutes I'm going to cover some of the more important areas we'll be focusing on."

Reading your audience

When presenting to a big group, nerves and distractions can keep you from reading the room as well as you would when presenting on your own. The good news is that you don't have to do it alone. Team members who aren't presenting should be on the lookout for signs that indicate an audience member isn't getting the point, growing frustrated, or zoning out. When she sees that, she needs to get the presenter's attention. The easiest way to do this is to use a cue.

Creating a cue

A *cue* is a predetermined body or eye movement that sends a signal to your teammate. It's similar to a guitar or drum solo in a musical group. Often the band doesn't know at what precise moment the soloist is going to finish up, so the other band members watch the soloist for a signal alerting them as to when they should jump back in. It may be a certain musical phrase or section, a hand signal, a raised drum stick, or simply catching the leader's eye for an extended moment. Either way, it's determined ahead of time that "When I do B, it means C."

Think ahead to what types of reactions you want to be sure to pick up from your audience and develop a cue. The subtlety of your cues depends on whether your team members are sitting up-front or within the audience. Here are some suggestions based on team members being seated in the audience:

- ✔ Raising a finger to the nose: You have a minute left. Start to wrap it up.
- ✔ Standing up: Time to introduce the next speaker.
- ✔ Lowering a hand in front of your face: Slow down.
- ✔ Touching an ear: Louder. We can't hear you.

- ✔ Raising one finger: There's a question in the audience.
- ✔ Placing hand on chest: I have something to add.

Don't have more than five signals or your team members may confuse their meanings, resulting in some mixed signals.

Acting on the cue

After the presenter sees the cue from a team member, she can respond accordingly. If the cue indicates that the audience is lost or that she's going too fast, she can ask a question, restate a point, or offer a better explanation. If the cue indicates the audience is restless or bored, she can quickly pick up the pace or move to the next topic. If the cue indicates that a team member wants to say something, she can wait until she comes to a natural stopping point before asking him if he has something to add.

The audience is always watching

Everything you do reflects on your team as a whole, whether you're sitting in the back checking your messages or sitting up front fidgeting or gazing out the window. You're communicating to your prospect that this part of the presentation isn't that important.

As a result, any time that you're sitting where the audience can see you, you must look at the presenter and stay engaged, occasionally checking the audience to see how they're responding. Sit with your feet firmly planted on the floor and avoid any distracting movements, gestures, or sounds. Occasionally nodding in agreement or reacting to the presenter is fine, but avoid stealing the spotlight when it's not your turn.

Catching a cue with The Roots

The Tonight Show band, The Roots, is an extremely talented group of musicians. But their talents at improvisation are almost as legendary. During host Jimmy Fallon's popular segment called "Freestylin' with The Roots" Fallon goes into the crowd to get various pieces of information from audience members. The Roots then create a song on the spot based on this information — without any words or notes passed between the group members. How do they do it? They're following the rules of improvisation:

- ✔ **Someone is designated as leader.** Everyone cues off the leader and others follow suit.

Imagine if everyone in the band had a different idea as to how the song should go and all started at once. It would be a cacophony.

- ✔ **They use a cue.** A certain beat or a shared look from the leader lets the rest of the band members know that they're changing pace, going to a bridge, or approaching the final licks. Next time you watch, look for those secret cues being passed between band members.

Handling the Q&A session

More than likely you have some time set aside at the end of your presentation for questions, especially if it's a panel format. You must have a plan for handling questions both during the presentation and at the end during the Q&A.

As the final impression with your audience, you want to make sure it's a positive one. Without a question-handling strategy, team members can talk over each other, step on toes, and look more like a quarreling family than a potential corporate partner.

Preparing for questions

Planning ahead for questions should be done as part of your preparation process and incorporated into your team rehearsal. Here are some ways to prepare for and handle those Q&A sessions.

- ✔ **Brainstorm potential questions and objections.** Go through each section of your presentation as a team and think about what questions or concerns might arise. Major questions typically fall into certain categories, like budget, timing, and resources. See Chapter 15 for more on handling objections.

- ✔ **Decide on a response and a responder.** Get agreement from your team on a response to the major questions and decide who is best qualified to handle each type of question.

- ✔ **Appoint a moderator.** Unless the questions are addressed to a specific person, have one person handle the question and then pitch it to the appropriate team member.

- ✔ **Read your teammates.** Just like reading the audience, you need to read each other to see if someone wants to answer a question. Throwing a question at someone like a hot potato when they aren't prepared to answer it puts them on the spot and makes everyone look bad. Eye contact or a simple hand motion can serve as a signal that someone is prepared to address a question.

Dealing with questions

When a question does arise during your presentation, use good listening skills, show respect for your teammates, and build on each other's responses. Here are some tips for handling questions effectively as a team:

- ✔ **Be a good listener.** Allow the prospect to get her entire question out. Never interrupt or assume you know where she is going.

- ✔ **Clarify the questions.** If you're not sure what the question is, ask for clarification. Don't guess.

✔ **Repeat the question.** To make sure you have it right and for the benefit of yourself and others, state the question again.

✔ **Keep it brief.** Summarize quickly what the answer is. Resist the urge to overexplain, which is often where Q&A goes south. After you answer the question to the best of your ability, stop. If the prospect looks confused or unappeased, you can ask "Does that answer your question?" or "Was that helpful?"

✔ **Maintain your cool.** If an audience member gets on edge, don't rise to the occasion or get defensive. Keep a calm and steady presence.

✔ **Have a note taker.** You may want to do some research later or incorporate questions into future presentations or communication. Designate someone to take notes so that you can follow-up.

✔ **Admit that you don't know it all.** Even if you brought a dozen experts with you, your audience may ask a question that your team doesn't know. Have your note taker write it down and let your prospect know you'll find out and get back to her.

✔ **Use the rule of "Yes, and . . ."** When you're working as a team, this improv rule is a good one to keep in mind. Always build on your teammates' responses and then add your own. It keeps things connected and makes you sound like an experienced team. For example, "Yes, and to Mark's point, we're also able to improve the user experience in three other ways . . . " See Chapter 15 for more information.

Using other good team practices

One of the things many prospects look for in a team is good chemistry and collaboration. Follow these guidelines to make sure you show your prospect what a high-performing team looks like.

✔ **Don't interrupt.** When a team member is clearly connecting with the audience, don't interject just because you have something to add. Wait it out and if it's still relevant, then add your comments.

✔ **Don't contradict.** Unless something is blatantly incorrect, don't show discord among your team. If you must correct, do it in a non-inflammatory way. "I think what Bob meant was the figures from 2012, not 2002, right Bob?"

✔ **Avoid inside jokes.** Yes, your prospect wants to see that you all get along, but not at the expense of being left out of the conversation.

✔ **Allow team members to shine.** As a salesperson, you can easily feel like you need to comment on each topic or fill every silence, but resist the urge to take over. Let each team member own his or her section. Add your comments only if it's necessary or helps bridge the subject back to the prospect's business.

Chapter 17

Mastering Web Presentations

*H*ello . . . is this thing on?

Delivering an online presentation is a lonely experience for most salespeople. It's hard to tell if your prospect is engaged, confused, or even in the room. After you're done, you may wonder if you've made any impact. If you're simply repeating what you do in a live presentation in a virtual world, chances are good, you haven't.

Although prospects and salespeople don't always agree on a solution, a price, or timing, they can usually agree on one thing: Online presentations have all the excitement of a visit to the motor vehicle department. Heralded as the wave of the future, with all their challenges, remote presentations can feel like a trip back to the past. Not being able to read your audience, to fill awkward silences, to avoid technical gaffes — the best you can hope for is often not to lose the sale.

As companies and employees get more scattered and travel budgets tighten, opportunities to deliver sales presentations over the web will continue to increase. Fortunately, an engaging and persuasive online presentation isn't simply a lofty but unreachable goal for those salespeople who acknowledge the different requirements between a live and a web presentation and embrace a set of proven techniques to bridge the gap.

In this chapter, you understand why a successful live presentation doesn't always translate to a successful web presentation. You discover how to get started presenting on the web, including what type of platform to use and how to adjust your message to fit the medium. You find out how to create a personal connection with your prospects, increase visibility on both sides of the computer, and keep your audience engaged throughout your presentation. Lastly, I introduce a variety of techniques and tools that allow you to be a more effective online presenter.

Understanding the Differences between Live and Virtual Presentations

In the 2012 Oscar winning movie, *The Artist,* a silent film star refuses to adapt to new technology by trying to force an old style into a new medium. It didn't work for him — and it won't work for you. Simply doing the same thing you're doing in a live presentation fails in a web presentation because delivering a presentation to a remote audience has some inherent differences than presenting to a live audience, which are as follows:

- **Your prospect is invisible.** You can't see your audience so gauging their interest or comprehension is difficult. More importantly, your audience *knows* that you can't see them, which makes it easy for them to lose focus. What do you do when you're an audience member and the web presenter wanders off track or takes too long to get to the point? Text, check email, freshen your coffee? Temptations abound in a virtual world, and that's exactly what your prospects are doing if you've failed to keep them engaged and focused on your message.

- **You're invisible.** Another challenge you must contend with when you present virtually is that your audience can't see you. Your physicality — presence, movement, eye contact — plays a huge role in your ability to connect with and affect your prospect. Eliminate that physical piece entirely and you have lost one of your most powerful communication tools. You do need to do something to compensate for that fact.

- **Lack of movement.** All day long things are moving at a fast pace for your prospect. Everywhere he goes things are in motion. He sees video on the plane, on the elevator, and in the lobby. Then he enters your web presentation and suddenly everything . . . slows . . . to . . . a . . . crawl. Today people are quickly bored with a static visual. Not taking that into account when planning your web presentation is a common mistake that you can avoid.

- **The setting is passive.** The average American spends 34 hours per week in front of the television. When a screen comes up, people prepare to sit back and be entertained or informed. They don't typically talk back to the television (unless it's politics or sports) or answer questions posed by the host (unless it's a game show.) A web presentation places your audience in that familiar environment — minus the popcorn. Your prospect isn't going to be inclined to jump in and participate without some planning and encouragement on your part.

✔ **Your energy is lower.** Often web presentations are delivered from your home or your desk where you may be just a little bit too comfy. Although you don't have to be uncomfortable to give a good virtual presentation, you do need to work at elevating your energy because your energy level affects your voice, your meaning, and your pace.

✔ **Technology isn't your friend.** Login problems, connectivity issues, frozen screens, the list goes on. How many times have you been on a web session where the first five to ten minutes were spent working out the bugs or waiting for others to join the meeting? Although sometimes preventable, these engagement killers always require alternate plans to reduce their sometimes-disastrous effects.

✔ **Multitasking is a myth**. You're both the host and the producer during your presentation. You must deliver your message and interact with your audience, all while managing your screen, fielding questions, conducting polls, and tracking people coming in and out of the room. Although keeping all the balls in the air may feel like a major victory, the primary goal of inspiring your prospect to take action often gets dropped in the confusion.

Getting Started with Web Presentations

The ability to deliver your presentation to prospects from all over the world from the convenience of your own desk is a pretty remarkable achievement that most business people have come to take for granted. But all that magic doesn't just happen automatically. You need to do a number of things ahead of time, which the following sections examine, to make sure that your presentation comes off without a hitch. Don't wait until the day before to do them.

Choosing a platform

Three basic options for delivering a web presentation are available:

✔ **Screen sharing:** Just like it sounds, this option involves sharing your screen with your audience in real time via a web application. Screen sharing is included as an option on most web conferencing platforms, but it can also be a stand-alone application like `Mikogo.com`. The downside is that all participants can see all open applications on your computer and your desktop (so close your email and clear your browser). Even though it displays your presentation, screen sharing doesn't offer as much in the way of interactive tools unlike most web conferencing services. Here are a couple services that provide screen sharing:

- **Google+ Hangouts:** This service is worth noting because if you have a Google account you have access to Hangouts and can give a presentation to up to nine other participants at this time for free. It's simple and has a webcam feature built in. It's a little clunky, but for a more casual presentation, it's certainly worth considering. Refer to the nearby sidebar for more information.

- **Skype:** In addition to a video conferencing service, Skype enables you to share your screen with any users with which you're on a Skype call when you have a premium account. The downside is if your prospect isn't on Skype, he has to go go through an extra step to set up his own account. Furthermore, the call quality can be inconsistent, which can come across as unprofessional. It's suited for a more casual presentation. Check out the nearby sidebar for additional help.

✔ **Web conferencing:** This option is a more full service platform and includes names you're probably familiar with, like Webex, Adobe Connect, or Go to Meeting. It involves using an application through a website that hosts the service that both you and your prospect log into. Depending on the host, web conferencing services typically offer a variety of advanced and interactive features, like polling, chat, video, recording, and so on, that screen sharing doesn't. It's usually billed on a month-to-month or per-user basis and is scalable as your company or needs grow.

✔ **Webinars:** A *webinar* is less collaborative than web conferencing or screen sharing and more often used as a marketing vehicle, but it may make sense to do a webinar if you're presenting to a large group or using your presentation to sell your product or service to the general public. Webinars require participants to register and allow you to collect names and information for follow-up sales efforts. Many of the same companies that offer web conferencing, like Webex, Adobe Connect, and Go to Webinar, also allow you to host webinars.

The lines between screen sharing, web conferencing, and webinars continue to blur as new technology and new players are introduced. Be sure to check out each platform carefully to make sure you are selecting the best match for your purposes.

Using Google+ Hangouts for your presentation

Google has entered the world of web presenting by introducing the ability to give a presentation to up to ten participants (including yourself) for free. You may need to install a plug-in, so be sure to test it out a few days before your presentation. To use Google+ Hangouts, stick to these steps:

1. Log in to your Google+ profile.

2. Click Hangout options.

3. Make sure your PowerPoint or slide deck is on your desktop.

4. Use the Invite option to invite your prospects to join.

5. Click Screenshare on Google+ Hangouts.

6. Start your PowerPoint in slideshare mode, being sure to click the option to show your slides in full screen.

7. To stop the presentation, click Screenshare.

Selecting a provider

After you decide on which option is right for you, you need to choose a provider. Your company may have one already; however if not, many good applications are available from which you can choose. Some, like Google+ Hangouts, are even free; however, you want to consider certain things as you compare your choices:

- ✔ **Maximum number of attendees:** How many people do you expect to attend? Most free sites, like Google + Hangouts, limit attendance to 10 or less.

- ✔ **Per use or monthly pricing:** Many options are free, but if you're going to be a regular user or need more tools, you may want to check out some of the paid ones to see what you're missing. Paid web conferencing programs generally run from $30–50 per month.

- ✔ **Presenter tools:** Most platforms allow you to do the basics — share your screen, annotate, chat — but if you're looking for more advanced tools, like the ability to upload files, pass control to another user, or record your session, be sure to check the features before you sign up.

- ✔ **Participant tools:** Look for features that make it easier for your audience to participate like the ability to annotate or log on with social media.

- ✔ **Mobile-friendly options:** If you or your prospects are on the go a lot, be sure to choose a platform that lets you present and your prospect's attend from a mobile device.

Skyping your presentation

Skype isn't just for video chatting with your friends across the pond. Skype also offers a screenshare option so you can show a presentation from your computer to participants on a Skype call. You need to do some work ahead of time, including making sure you have the right version of Skype and that your prospects are connections, so don't wait until the day of your presentation to try it out. Here's how to launch a Skype presentation:

1. **Make sure you have a Skype premium membership to access screen sharing.**

2. **Add your prospects to your Skype contacts.**

You can search by their full name, Skype user name, or email.

3. **The day before your presentation, confirm that you're accepted as a contact.**

4. **Place a Skype call to your prospect.**

5. **Click the small plus-sign icon in the call.**

6. **From the pop-up box, select Show My Desktop to begin sharing your screen.**

7. **Open your Presentation and start sharing in slideshow mode.**

Getting familiar with your platform

Each option is different and you want to be very comfortable with whatever you choose well before you deliver your first presentation. Go through the tutorials, set up your account and your slide deck or demo so you have easy access after you're in it, and practice it in real time a few times. The last thing you want to be thinking about during a presentation is how to use your service. Refer to the later section on "Preparing For Your Web Presentation" for more guidance.

Improving Prospect Attention

Hands down, the number one problem with online presentations is the frustrating lack of attention. Although more attention seems like an easy fix — faster, bigger, louder! — you can't just crank up the pace and the volume and expect results. You need to start by looking at what you need to adjust in your content and your delivery style to fit the needs of a virtual audience. Then you need to get familiar with the different web tools that are available to you. Understanding when and where you're at high risk for audience tune-out and making some adjustments in those areas to prevent it can take your presentation from "Is anybody out there?" to "Are we done already?"

The following sections look at how to adapt your content and your delivery from a live presentation to a virtual one to improve your prospect's attention and interest.

Adjusting your content

Although the basic structure of an online presentation is the same as a live presentation with an opening, body, and closing, some areas need to be adjusted in order to maintain the attention of a remote audience. These sections take a closer look at those areas.

Have two openings

If you've been on time for a web presentation, you know how frustrating it can be to have to wait for others to join the meeting. As the host apologizes and makes lame attempts at small talk, your frustration merely grows. The unfair truth is that some of your audience will be late, which affects the first impression other audience members have of you. You have a dilemma: you don't want to frustrate the audience members who are on time by starting late, but you also don't want latecomers to miss your opening with its important points.

To resolve this issue, you can have two openings. The first opening is a false opening designed to get your audience engaged without revealing your big hook. The second opening is your real opening, reserved for when everyone is in attendance so you can start on the same page.

Here's how to employ a false opening:

1. **At the designated start time, give an abbreviated introduction of yourself.**

2. **Introduce a pre-opening poll.**

   A *poll* is essentially a multiple choice questionnaire. It's a great way to get your audience interacting from the start, as well as buy a little time to allow for latecomers to arrive. Use a poll question that is relevant to your presentation topic and frames your presentation. For example, if you're presenting to an HR team, you may ask "How much time do you spend a week evaluating employee performance?" Then list three to four options. Refer to the later section on "Interacting with your prospect" for more tips on how to run a poll within your presentation.

3. **Give your audience a specific amount of time to complete the poll.**

   The questions shouldn't be SAT level, so give them just a minute or so. You don't want to drag the poll on too long or you risk losing what audience you do have.

4. **Discuss the poll results until the rest of your audience joins you.**

    Use names and draw individual participants into a conversation based on their answers. For example, "Sarah, I see here that you spend about ten hours a week doing this. What frustrates you the most about that activity?" If the latecomers join while the poll is in progress, invite them to take the poll. If they are quite late, tell them about the poll and let them know you'll share the results with them later.

5. **When all are in attendance (or you have exhausted your poll), deliver your real opening.**

Utilize your agenda

Regularly letting your prospect know where you are in your presentation is even more critical in a web presentation than in a live one. Refer back to your agenda after you cover each item and before you introduce the next one. Make your agenda interactive by checking off items as you cover them and writing in points you want them to remember using the annotation tools in your web conferencing platform. Check out Chapter 8 for tips on creating and using an agenda in your presentation.

Visually reinforce key points

You can get away with using fewer slides during a live presentation because you can easily gauge how well your audience understands a particular point by their body language or facial expressions. They're also more likely to speak up in a live presentation. In a web presentation, silence doesn't equal understanding. Rather than asking your audience "Does that make sense?" every five seconds, give your key points some reinforcement by putting them on a very clear, simple slide.

Create word pictures

In a virtual presentation your words have to work even harder than in a live presentation. Think about creating pictures with your words. For example, when describing something, be specific and avoid broad generalities (for example, "It weighs 510 pounds" as opposed to "It's really big.") Use personal stories or interesting comparisons.

Listen to your favorite podcasts and radio shows, and notice how they use their voices, dramatic pauses, and descriptive words to keep you engaged. Try some of these techniques out in your next web presentation.

Simplify your slides

Have you ever decided not to watch a movie on that little airplane screen because it wouldn't do it justice? The same holds true for a web presentation. What works on the big screen doesn't necessarily translate to the small screen. Keep your graphics simple and crisp and instantly recognizable. See Figure 17-1a and 17-1b to see the difference between a busy slide and a simplified slide.

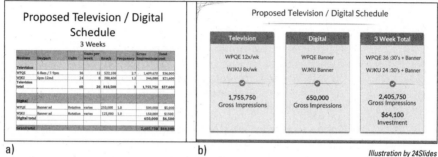

Figure 17-1: An example of a busy slide (a) and a simple slide (b).

a)

b)

Illustration by 24Slides

Limit special effects

You worked hard on those cool animations and transitions, and now I'm telling you to get rid of them! Don't shoot the messenger. Web conferencing services can delay or lose all of your hard work so just avoid using them. Having to explain to someone what they should be seeing is like having to explain the punch line of a joke. Stick to simple movement and transitions between slides and save the special effects for your message.

End the party on time

Although ending the presentation on time applies to live presentations as well, it plays even greater importance in web presentations where people can easily check out if the presentation goes on longer than they had committed. Make it clear that you're going to stop at a specific time up-front, which means you have to build in time for potential questions. Do an official close at the designated time — or earlier (your audience loves this), and if anyone has additional questions either take them off-line or schedule another call. Never let one person hijack the rest of your audience. Find more tips on how to manage your audience in Chapter 14.

Revising your delivery

Not only do you need to adjust your content for a web presentation, but you need to make some changes in the way you deliver it as well. For an audience that's used to a steady stream of visual input, the sudden lack of movement can feel like stepping off of a moving sidewalk. Lack of movement is a big problem in web presentations and you must compensate for that fact or risk losing your audience.

If your audience gets ahead of you at any point, they're going to drift. Fortunately you can give your prospect a sense of movement through the way you use your voice and your screen. Here are some tips for keeping things moving online:

- **Tighten up transitions:** Those in-between sections — your introduction, agenda, company overview — are prime checkout time for your prospect. Don't rush through them, but keep your presentation moving at a good pace and eliminate any unnecessary text or talking points in order to keep your audience from jumping ship.

- **Keep your slides moving:** To give your presentation a sense of movement, don't stay too long on any one slide or visual. In a live presentation you don't have to change your slides as frequently as a web presentation because you're able to balance attention with your physical presence. In a web presentation your audience has nothing else to look at. Don't linger on any one slide for more than two to three minutes — the average length of a YouTube video — or your prospect's eyes may be tempted to wander to his cellphone or the to-do list on his desk.

- **Follow that mouse:** In a live presentation you can easily point to a specific area on a slide and tell whether your audience sees it. In a web presentation being able to ascertain whether they see it's unclear. Unfortunately, as the presenter, falling into the curse of familiarity is easy, so don't assume that your prospect can locate something on your screen, when in fact, he can't. If it's something worth pointing out, take the time to confirm that your prospect sees it by following these steps:

    1. **Tell your prospect where to focus on the screen.**

        For example, "Take a look in the very top right hand corner of your screen under the bright green square . . . "

    2. **Move your mouse to that spot.**

        Give your audience a brief moment to get oriented.

        Don't jiggle your mouse around or move it too fast when pointing. Making quick, jerky movements can be very distracting on a small screen.

    3. **Read the point while holding your mouse in place.**

    4. **Remove your mouse when done and go to the next point, or simply move on to the next screen.**

Increasing your presence

Presence, that ability to grab and hold on to your audience's attention, is more challenging without your physical body. Here are a few tools that you can call on to create a larger presence with your prospect and thus help them stay engaged with your message. Find out more tips on expanding your presence in Chapter 10.

Create virtual energy

Energy is contagious. Just as a stage actor feeds off his audience's energy, so do you gain energy from a live audience. In a web presentation, you can't rely on your prospect's energy to boost yours so you have to create your own. Here are some ways to do that:

- ✔ **Focus on your intention.** A strong *intention* (a determination to act in a certain way or achieve a specific goal) like "I'm going to excite my prospect" or "I'm going to challenge them" focuses your energy and creates momentum to start your presentation. You can read more about intentions in Chapter 10.

- ✔ **Warm up.** Before you begin, quickly warm up your voice and body so you're ready. Read more about some exercises you can do in Chapter 11.

- ✔ **Stand up.** Sitting can instantly lower your energy. Unless you're using a webcam, try standing up when you present so that you can gesture freely. Standing up boosts your energy and your vocal power. If you're going to move around, be sure not to stray out of wireless range, introduce any outside noises, or affect your connection in any way.

Leverage your voice

Your voice takes on more than its fair share of responsibility in the virtual world. By eliminating your physical presence, your voice carries the full weight of your presentation — multiplying the positive effect of a clear, pleasant voice as well as the negative impact of a monotone, unclear, or hard-to-hear voice.

As your primary communication tool, you need to make sure that your voice is at its best. Following are some specific ways to improve the effectiveness of your voice in your presentation:

- ✔ **Reduce outside noise.** Turn off anything that beeps, buzzes, or rings. The only sounds you want your audience to hear are those that you have planned.

✔ **Be clear.** Your voice doesn't go directly into your prospect's ears. Your voice now has to travel through filters on both your end and your prospect's end, before finally arriving at its destination. Hence, anything that is hard to understand in person is doubly hard to understand remotely. Make sure you employ the following good vocal skills:

- Articulate clearly.

- Keep your volume strong.

- Don't drop your sentences off at the end.

- Keep a brisk pace (moderate — not too fast, not too slow).

✔ **Use vocal variety.** A monotone delivery is deadly on a web presentation. That same steady pace over thirty minutes or an hour can work like a metronome on your audience, lulling them into a trance-like state. Try varying your pace during key sections of your presentation. For example, when you get to a benefit, slow down or speed up. When you tell a story, get quieter, get louder, or change your tone. Your voice has many colors, and you need to find as many shades as possible to keep your audience engaged. You can find more vocal tips and exercises in Chapter 11.

✔ **Embrace the pause.** Salespeople are often afraid if they stop talking that they're going to lose their prospect, especially during a web presentation. But the opposite is often true. A web presentation isn't a filibuster, and non-stop talking just to fill space can cause an audience to tune out just as easily as too much dead air. A well-timed pause, however, can be a great attention-grabber. For example, use a pause before revealing an important point to build anticipation. Pause at the end of a key message to give your audience a chance to take in and process what you've said. Used with purpose and discretion, the pause is an important tool in your virtual tool kit.

Increasing your visibility

The more visible you make yourself to your prospect and the greater your presence, the more engaged he will be. If you doubt this, think about how easy it is to say "no" to a salesperson on the phone as opposed to one who is standing right in front of you. When you make the transition from live to virtual presenting, you need to make up for that loss of physical presence and visibility. If only there were a tool that could help people see you and feel like there's a real person behind the screen . . . oh wait, there is!

Webcams are the most underutilized sales tool in the world, yet they are hands down the easiest and quickest way to increase your visibility. Discover in the following sections how much webcams can add to your presentation and how to use them like a pro.

Knowing what a webcam can do for your presentation

Webcams give you instant visibility that leads to greater audience attention and engagement. Here are more good reasons why you should be using a webcam in your presentation:

- ✔ **Draw attention.** Human beings respond to faces. Research shows that even babies stare at faces longer than any other image. Giving your audience a face to anchor your presentation, your company, and your solution to is a smart move.

- ✔ **Stand out from your competition.** Although not adverse to the infamous selfie, most salespeople have yet to get on board with webcams. Take the leap and you can give yourself the easiest differentiator money can buy.

- ✔ **Wear flipflops.** Basically wear anything you want from the waist down. Salespeople who have no problem standing in their most uncomfortable shoes for two hours cringe at the idea of being on camera from the comfort of their own chair. The reality is that a webcam is a headshot that's less than two inches wide. Unless he uses a magnifying glass, your prospect isn't going to notice your blemish, unironed clothes, or even that stain on your shirt.

- ✔ **Use it strategically.** You don't have to have the webcam on during your entire presentation. In fact, you don't want to use it when you're showing slides, data, your product, or any other visual that you want your prospect focused on. Use the webcam at those points during your presentation when you want to interact directly with your prospect. For example, using it during your opening, closing, and Q&A sessions makes more sense.

Using a webcam effectively

Talking to a camera isn't natural. Actors and television personalities make it look easy because they've practiced it many times and discovered a few tricks. You can look like a pro on camera too by applying these tips:

- ✔ **Set the stage.** Your background is the co-star in your presentation so make sure it is clean, uncluttered, and free of distractions. Because the screen is tiny, look for anything (pictures, lamps, art) that may appear to be growing out of your head on camera. Avoid placing yourself in front of anything that moves, (such as TV screens or monitors) or looks unprofessional (laundry, posters, or pets). If you're doing your presentation from home, make sure that you've alerted family members or roommates beforehand so they don't inadvertently make a guest appearance on their way to the kitchen. You can also use your background to introduce product placement — a mug or screensaver with your company's logo — but aim for subtlety with your branding efforts so your prospect doesn't feel like they're being hit over the head.

✔ **Know your frame.** You really have two choices:

- **Head and shoulders:** If you opt for just the head and shoulders, limit your gestures because they'll appear on screen as random, odd apparitions, which means, keep your hands off your face and hair.

- **Full torso:** If it's a torso shot, keep your gestures within the frame to avoid the jerky appearance and disappearance of body parts.

✔ **Check your lighting.** Make sure that you're well lit with the light shining on your face (not just from behind you, which will give you a halo effect). Experiment with various lights to get the ideal placement and avoid dim or inconsistent lighting. See Figure 17-2 for suggestions on proper lighting.

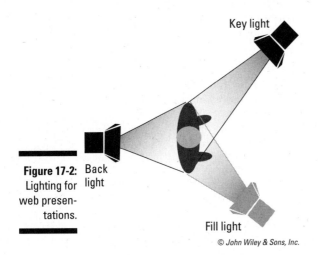

Key light

Figure 17-2: Back
Lighting for light
web presen-
tations.

Fill light

© John Wiley & Sons, Inc.

Use a simple three-point lighting set up for web presentations: one behind and over you, and two in front of you angled on either side of the camera.

✔ **Make eye contact with the camera.** Just like in a live presentation, you need to make eye contact with your prospect. The trick is that your prospect's eyes are actually the little camera staring at you. In your mind's eye you need to think of the camera as your prospect's eyes. That doesn't mean that you constantly have to stare at that little red dot, but you do need to make an effort to talk to it on a consistent basis, especially when asking or listening to questions.

✔ **Talk to one person.** This is the secret to how great artists, musicians, and actors can mesmerize a crowd of thousands, making each person think they're talking just to them. Have one specific person in mind when you speak, and it can come across as much more intimate and conversational than if you think of talking to a group. And while you're at it, make that one person you're talking to a friendly prospect who is eager to hear what you have to say, which will affect your tone and your confidence as well.

✔ **Slow down your movement.** Fast, jerky moves on a two-inch screen look cartoonish. Gesture freely, but keep your movements slow and deliberate.

✔ **Lean in.** If you lean forward in your chair about 15 percent, you'll look more engaged and approachable to your prospect. Just be careful not to tip over.

✔ **Smile.** Just like a live presentation, find moments to express yourself. When your prospects arrive, when you introduce yourself, when you're listening to a question are all great places to break out your million-dollar smile.

✔ **Coordinate your clothes.** Check your background before you get dressed. You don't want to blend in with it or inadvertently create a distraction (stripes on checks or red on green.) Think contrast and as a general rule, stick with simple styles and colors and stay away from stripes or any overly busy patterns.

✔ **Be natural.** The truth is that the web cam is just a way for your audience to connect with the real you. If you act like a one-dimensional talking head, the camera isn't going to help them do that. Acting natural on camera only comes with practice, so before you try it live, have a few dress rehearsals so that you become friends with your camera and it becomes second nature so that you can place your focus on connecting with your prospect during your presentation. For some tips on rehearsing with a webcam, refer to the section "Preparing For Your Web Presentation" later in this chapter.

Interacting with Your Prospect

Web presentations have a huge potential to move the dial on your business, but they can also be a complete waste of time if you don't effectively engage your audience. In a live presentation, you can get feedback by looking at the prospect's face and body language. They may nod to agree with a point, furrow their brow when puzzled, or cross their arms when in disagreement.

Being able to decipher what your prospect is thinking in a web presentation, especially when you can't see or hear them, isn't as easy. Because you lose the opportunity to gauge physical feedback from your audience, you must work harder to read and engage them. Following are some tools to interact with your audience in a web presentation.

Using polls

Polls are fairly easy to set up and use in most web conferencing software and a good way to get an audience engaged early in a presentation. Here are some tips for maximizing their value:

✔ **Create a poll slide.** Although you can create a poll directly in most web presentation platforms, the poll interface isn't always inviting or obvious to your audience. To draw more interest and attention to your poll, create a PowerPoint slide in your deck to introduce the poll question and talk your audience through it before you bring up the actual interactive poll. Figure 17-3 shows a PowerPoint slide that introduces the audience to a poll.

Figure 17-3: Example of a poll slide.

Illustration by 24Slides

✔ **Ask relevant questions.** Questioning your audience about what movie they liked better or what sport they prefer may seem like a great way to create interaction, but the questions will feel forced if they aren't related to your topic. Because you likely use a poll at the beginning of your presentation, think of a question that springs your audience into the conversation. For example, if you're making a case for how much free time your solution is going to provide, you could ask: "How much free time do you currently have: 1) Free time? What free time! 2) Not nearly enough. 3) Just about right. 4) Too much."

When asking a question, have a good sense of what the answer will be so that it leads into your point. If you ask the previous question and everybody says they have just enough time, you'll have to do some pretty quick re-focusing of your message.

✔ **Give specific directions.** Don't assume that your audience knows what they're supposed to do. Tell them exactly how and when to vote in the poll. For example, "Read through the answers and then click that little button on the left next to the answer that best describes how you shop for a lender."

✔ **Give a time limit.** You don't want the pace to slow down too much, so when you see about half of your audience has responded give them a 30-second warning that you're going to shut the poll.

✔ **Share results in real time.** Keeping your audience abreast of the results as they come in is a great opportunity to interact with your audience so don't let the time pass in silence. For example, "I see fifty percent of our respondents say they don't have enough free time. In fact, Bob added that 'He wouldn't know what to do with it if he got it!' Thank you Bob."

Employing the chat feature

Inviting people to share during your presentation with a chat feature is a good way to monitor engagement or comprehension. Just be sure if you use it, that you check it regularly. Keeping an eye on all your tools can get tricky, and it's one of the many reasons you want to really have your presentation down cold so you can handle impromptu questions as you juggle technology.

Questioning your prospects

Don't expect to come up with questions on the fly; you have way too many things to think about. Plan some good questions ahead of time that both check in with your audience members to gauge their understanding ("So Pat, does that make sense to you?") or uncover any resistance ("Beth, do you have any concerns about what we've just discussed?).

Using names

Using audience member's names is especially important in a web presentation. As soon as attendees realize that you're going to be calling out people's names, they'll be sure to pay greater attention.

Print a list of attendees' names and have it in front of you during your web presentation. As you call on people, check off their names so that you spread your attention across the group and don't end up picking on the same person every time.

Prepping an audience member

To avoid that awkward silence when you ask for questions, enlist your internal advocate or someone on your prospect's team ahead of time to ask a pre-planned question or two. Most prospects will be glad to help, and it gets the ball rolling and encourages others to jump in.

Mastering Your Technology

As technology continues to improve, the expectations of your audience grow, and your competitors step up their efforts, you need to employ every tool possible to be a more effective online presenter. Poor production or a lack of planning can cause a lack of attention and confusion. Even worse, your web presentation is your first impression, and your audience may associate an unprofessional web presentation with you, your company, or product.

Here are some ways you can start to master your technology, as opposed to letting it master you:

- ✔ **Use a headset.** The quality of most computer speakers is notoriously poor. They pick up sounds from anywhere within the room and can produce feedback. To reduce the background noise and feedback, always use a good quality headset to project your voice clearly and avoid making your audience struggle to hear you.

- ✔ **Project to a second screen.** Having a second computer set up allows you to see what the audience is seeing. There is often a delay between when you change slides and your audience sees the new slide. This delay may be only a matter of seconds, but talking about a slide that your audience can't yet see can be confusing. A second computer is also valuable because it serves as a handy backup. Here are some tips on using a second screen:

- Sign on as participant on a second screen using a slightly different log-on.

- Set the screen where you can easily see it.

- Use the second screen to give you the same view that your audience sees as well as to observe your audience participation — raised hands, chat questions, and so forth.

- When you advance your slides, check the second screen to make sure the slide is up before you start to talk about it. That way, your words will be in synch with the visuals that your participants are seeing.

✔ **Pick a standard resolution.** Although you may have a wide screen or high resolution monitor, reduce your screen resolution to a standard 1024 x 768. If you use a higher resolution, your slides may take longer to load and they may appear distorted to your non HD audience members.

✔ **Use your annotation tools.** In a web presentation where movement consists of going from one slide to the next, the simple act of circling or highlighting text or adding your own text can be surprisingly engaging. It's an easy way to draw your audience's attention and give your delivery some real-time presence. Most web conferencing services offer annotations, including the ability to point, write, or highlight text, draw rectangles or circles, change colors, and erase. To avoid your slides looking like your child's first art project, spend some time familiarizing yourself with your tools and use them sparingly and precisely. Here are some best practices for using annotations in your presentation:

- **Keep it simple.** Don't take on too much. Attempting to draw anything too complicated or that takes longer than a few seconds will test your audience's attention and likely shift focus from your point to your poor drawing skills. Stick with simple shapes and figures. Use pre-determined shapes, like rectangles and ovals, as opposed to using the draw-your-own feature.

- **Preplan annotations.** Don't rely on spontaneity for creating annotations during your presentation. Instead, have some slides in mind where you may use them. For example, if you have a slide that shows four silos that represent your client's business processes, you can use the annotation tool to draw a line or arrow between them to show the relationship or a process flow.

- **Smooth it out.** Keep your movements and drawing as smooth as possible to avoid having your audience think something is wrong with their connection.

- **Zoom in moderation.** Zooming in and out is a feature available on some service providers and is handy for focusing on a particular detail in a slide or screenshot. Don't get drunk on your zoom power because moving in and out too rapidly or too often can make your audience queasy.

- **Use a whiteboard for variety.** Most conferencing services offer a whiteboard feature where you can capture thoughts and brainstorm ideas in real time for your audience. This is a great way to engage your audience and use as an idea collective. Avoid using it as a place to capture questions or anything that may be construed as a negative because you'll be referring back to it throughout your presentation.

- **Consider hyperlinks.** Slides aren't the only thing you can show during a presentation. Perhaps you want to show your product or a website. You can create a hyperlink on PowerPoint to quickly and easily link to other programs without fumbling around on your computer. Refer to Chapter 8 for directions on adding hyperlinks to your PowerPoint.

✔ **Create a backup.** Having a backup that you can quickly access should anything go wrong is even more important in a web presentation than a live presentation. Your backup can be your second computer or a team member ready to take over controls in the wings. You can also have a video of your presentation ready to run as a last resort. Whatever you do, don't count on everything going smoothly and get caught off guard. Those precious moments where you search for a solution are precisely when your audience starts checking out — often for good.

Preparing For Your Web Presentation

Although you may not have to leave the comfort of your own home or office, a web presentation requires just as much planning and preparation as a live presentation — with the added layer of technical considerations. In order to make sure your web presentation is a success, be sure to set aside plenty of time to practice and create a presentation checklist to make sure you stay on track.

Practicing your web presentation

Both the technical aspect and the content aspect of your presentation are equally important and provide their own unique challenges, so it's best to run through each separately first. Following are some guidelines to help you prepare like a web presentation jedi:

✔ **Content run-through.** Your content is a vital piece of your presentation but can sometimes get lost with all the technical details of preparing for a web presentation. Do several content rehearsals to make sure you have your messaging down. Don't make the mistake of assuming that you can rely solely on your notes just because you're presenting virtually. Even if your audience can't see you, they will hear it in your voice if you're reading from notes. Besides, with all the balls you have to juggle during a web presentation, you don't want to be unsure of your message.

Employ all the same preparation and practice skills you would as if you were preparing for a live presentation. Pay extra care to warming up your voice.

✔ **Technical run-through.** Every good production does a tech run to find the potential problem areas and limit the odds of spoiling the show. Although you don't have to run through your entire presentation, focus on the transition spots during the technical practice, such as going over the opening, moving from slide to slide, and testing the webcam and annotation features you're using like polling and chats. See the following section, for specific things to look for.

✔ **Dress rehearsal.** Doing content and technology separately is one thing, but putting them together can be a bit like scratching your head and patting your stomach; it takes practice. Do at least two full rehearsals logged into your platform and using live timings. If you have it in your conferencing platform, use your record feature and then review how you did and note areas for improvement. Ask a teammate to participate as an audience member so you can test the sound and video quality as well as practice tools like chatting and polling.

Creating a web presentation checklist

You have a number of important items and duties to do to ensure that you have a successful web presentation, so don't wait until the last minute or you'll be pulling your hair out. To avoid missing any, follow these checklists.

A week prior to your presentation,

✔ Send invitations to your prospect with clear and easy-to-follow login instructions.

✔ Include a contact link in your email where prospects can go to resolve any problems they may experience while attending the presentation

✔ Prepare all your content, making necessary adjustments from a live presentation. Refer to the "Adjusting your content" section earlier for more details.

Two to three days prior to your presentation,

✔ Do your content and tech rehearsal.

✔ Record yourself and make any necessary adjustments.

✔ Check that you have downloaded any software necessary for your presentation.

✔ Prepare your backup.

Two to three hours before your presentation,

✔ Print out the list of final attendees' names and titles and place near your computer.

✔ Make sure your screensaver is audience ready.

✔ Assure your phone connection is clear and working.

✔ Test your speakers, your mic, and your webcam.

✔ If you're using a webcam, check your frame, lighting, and wardrobe. Check out the earlier section, "Knowing what a webcam can do for your presentation" for how a webcam can help your virtual presentation.

✔ Have your materials spread out and accessible so you don't have to shuffle around or go off camera to find them.

Right before your presentation,

✔ Close out all windows on your desktop that you won't be using.

✔ Turn off your messenger, email, social media organizers, like Tweetdeck or Hootsuite, and any other programs that may be distracting.

✔ Turn off anything in your immediate area that beeps, buzzes, or plays music.

Keep your phone on vibrate or put it somewhere that you can see it so that audience or team members can call or text you if they're experiencing access or connectivity issues.

✔ If you're presenting from home, close windows and doors, and put a sign on the door instructing visitors not to knock or ring the doorbell.

✔ Do a pre-presentation warmup to get energized and put a smile in your voice. See Chapter 11 for some tips on ready for showtime.

Chapter 18

Delivering a Product Demonstration That Drives Sales

For medical devices, equipment, software, and technology, a product demonstration is a key part of the sales process. A demonstration can prove that your product can do what you say it can, that it's a good fit for your prospect or her organization, or that it's easy to use. A widely held belief is that a demo can't win a deal, but it can lose one. However, a good demo can do more than just keep you from losing ground; it can move your sale forward, shorten your sales cycle, and increase your closing ratio. Unfortunately many demos are poorly executed, delivered too soon in the sales cycle, not tailored to the prospect, or a loosely strung together list of features.

Many salespeople forget that the same best practices for a presentation apply to a demonstration: a solid structure, a compelling message, strong engagement skills, and a clear call to action. Taking shortcuts or ignoring these elements during a product demo is a major reason many of them fail to drive the sale forward — and can even bring it to a screeching halt.

This chapter explains how you can plan and adapt the key structural elements of a presentation to your demonstration. You can see how to tailor it to your prospect, focus on features that resonate, and highlight benefits in a memorable way. You discover the secrets to delivering a demo that differentiates you from your competition, keeps your prospect engaged, and delivers a strong call-to-action. When you're finally ready to deliver your presentation, you can use some best practices and do's and don'ts for giving a consistently great product demonstration.

Planning a Successful Demonstration

The difference between a good demo and a poor demo starts with the planning. Poor demos are based on the misguided notion that "one demo fits all," which couldn't be further from the truth. Your demo will vary based on not just who you are showing it to, but also why you're showing it, when you're showing it, and what you hope to accomplish from showing it. All of this begins with a plan.

The following sections help you understand why defining a clear and specific outcome for your demo is important and how and when you deliver your demo can significantly affect your results.

Clarifying the purpose of your demo

Just like a presentation, your demonstration must have an actionable goal. You need to know why you're giving a demo and what you want your prospect to do as a result of seeing it. Doing a demo just because you think it will make your prospect realize she needs or wants your product, or because she has simply asked to see how your product works isn't a goal; it's a reflex. The more clear and specific you can be about the goal of your demo, the more on-point your demo will be and the greater your chances for success.

Here are some examples of clear and specific goals:

✔ To prove that your product is easy to use and won't involve a heavy investment in training or additional services or products.

✔ To reassure your prospect that you can handle all of their requirements.

✔ To convince your prospect that your product can help her company remain competitive in her industry.

All three of these goals are clear and actionable and result in a different demo. In the later section, "Finding out key information," you discover how to use research to bring the goal of your demo into greater focus.

Eyeing your desired outcome

If you finish your demo, shake hands with your prospects, and part ways, you have missed a golden opportunity. When a demo goes well, it's the ideal time to make a *call to action,* asking your prospect to take the next step in the sales process. A call to action should be specific and measurable, like "Let's schedule a deep dive with your operations team within the next two weeks."

Most demos end with a statement like, "I hope you can see the value of our solution," which is neither measurable nor specific.

Here are some well-defined, actionable outcomes you may ask for after a successful demo:

- ✔ **Signed contract:** Obviously this is the best-case scenario and the logical next step for products like smaller equipment or technology solutions and many in-home products. But for larger products or strategic sales where the demo is part of a multistep sales process, your goal may be to advance the sale to the next step.

- ✔ **A meeting or demo with key decision makers or stakeholders:** Perhaps your demo was given to one or two people within your prospect's organization so that they could validate that your product is a good fit before bringing you in to demo for executives.

- ✔ **Deeper-dive demonstration:** If your initial demo was an overview of your capabilities, the next step may be to focus in on specific areas or capabilities for the prospect's technical team or product users.

- ✔ **Recommendation to financial decision maker:** If the demo is the final step in the sales process, you may just be a signature away from closing the deal. Ask for the recommendation within a specific timeframe. Don't be afraid to ask how the decision-making process works and what you can do to help expedite it.

- ✔ **Product evaluation or trial:** In some cases your prospect may want to try the product out in her own everyday working environment. If this is something your company accommodates, ask for a commitment from your prospect that if your product does perform according to predetermined goals, she is willing and capable of making a purchase. Be sure to establish clear guidelines around usage, timing, and liability, and get everything in writing.

Always know what you want to happen and don't be afraid to ask for it. See Chapter 7 for tips on closing with a strong call to action.

Knowing when to demo

The cardinal rule of comedy holds true in product demonstrations: Timing is everything. Many salespeople commonly give a product demonstration too early in the sales process. Salespeople that rush to do a demo at the first sign of interest are often surprised when the prospect isn't bowled over and stalls the sale. But the stalled sale actually isn't surprising at all.

Here's what happens when you demonstrate too soon:

- **Making assumptions:** If you give a product demo prior to doing adequate discovery, you're either doing a general overview or making assumptions about what your prospect is or isn't interested in based on some very preliminary conversations. This can result in a demo that fails to connect with your prospect or address her unique challenges or interests. In fact, she may see something that she doesn't need or want, which creates another set of issues that you're not prepared to handle.

- **Looking for disconnects:** Early in the sales process, buyers look for reasons to disqualify vendors. They see something that they don't like or need, and boom! They have little invested in you, so they can easily cross you off the list. Conversely, later in the process after they've spent some time getting to know you and your company, they're more likely to look for reasons to qualify you.

- **Showing too much:** This is the number one cause of death by demo. Odds are that your product can do a lot of cool things. Showing as many of those cool features as possible in the time that you have allotted is tempting. Unfortunately, more isn't better in this case. Prospects get overwhelmed by too much information and shut down.

- **Demonstrating the wrong things:** It's like a travel agent showing you diving destinations all over the world without realizing that you're afraid of the water. Presenting things that don't matter — or worse — things that set off alarms or cause your prospect to question whether you really understand her needs and goals can lead to instant disqualification.

- **Appearing complicated:** When you show too many features — or features that aren't relevant to the prospect's needs — your product appears complicated, which can trigger fear and shut down the buying process completely.

You must take control of the timing of your demonstration. Don't jump in too soon simply because your prospect asks. Take the time to get the information you need so you can tailor your demo to your prospect. Doing so benefits not just you, but your prospect as well.

Tailoring Your Demo to Your Prospect

A demo should make the prospect feel like the product was created especially with her in mind. Everything in it should be planned and purposeful. Although you certainly want to include room for questions and conversation, ensure that you have a well thought-out framework in advance.

In order to align your demo with your prospect's needs and goals, you need certain pieces of information, just like you would for any presentation. It's particularly important to find out who will be in your demo, what their level of expertise is, and how they would use the product in their business in order to develop a demo that resonates with your audience.

Finding out key information

Although you may have uncovered much about your prospect's challenges and goals in your initial discovery, a demo most likely requires additional conversations with key stakeholders within your prospect's organization to fully understand what features are important and how they'll be using your product in their business. That way you can put your product within a context that is familiar to your audience. For example, if you're selling an HR solution, you would certainly want to talk to HR managers, HR employees, and even non HR employees who use the program occasionally, to get a full picture of how it impacts their jobs and any challenges or changes they want to see.

Here are some key areas you want to explore before you put together your demo. A more detailed checklist of items to address in discovery is available in Chapter 2.

- ✔ **Who will be in the demo?** Some new faces may be present in the room that weren't at your initial presentation or meeting. Find out how each audience member interacts with the product or is affected by it. Performing a detailed process for an audience of executives will cause tune-out faster than you can say "click here," just as delivering a surface-level overview may frustrate product users. Find out who will attend the demo, their role, and their contact information so that you can include them in your discovery and tailor your message to their unique needs and expectations.

- ✔ **What's the opportunity?** Be specific when defining the problem or opportunity. For example, "They want to reduce the amount of manual reports and duplicated efforts for their sales team" provides a clearly defined scenario that guides you as you start to build your demo. "They want to see what our product can do," doesn't.

- ✔ **How is your prospect currently dealing with the problem?** Discovering how your prospect is coping with the problem can help you define the status quo, which may turn out to be your biggest competitor. For example, if you find out that your prospect is currently using an older, outdated product, this information gives you a point of comparison and an understanding of what you may be up against.

- ✔ **What's the impact?** Determine what and who the problem affects. For example, does your prospect' current product cause any errors or inefficiencies? What is the cost to maintain it? Figure out the extent and the cost of the impact in terms of time, cost, and lost opportunities. This information can help you establish value.

✔ **Who is your competition?** What else are they considering to resolve the problem? Who you're competing with can tell you a lot about the scope of the problem and the financial resources available to solve it. For example, if you're selling a solution that specifically focuses on inventory management, but your prospect is talking to enterprise solutions as well, you know the budget is there but the problem may be more far-reaching and you need to prepare to address any product limitations.

✔ **What would keep your prospect from buying?** This question is important to consider as you plan your demo. Are you competing against the current vendor or the status quo? Is your prospect concerned about the difficulty of implementation or gaining employee buy-in if she does buy? Addressing potential roadblocks early in your demo can diffuse your prospect's concerns before they turn into solid reasons not to buy.

✔ **What is your prospect expecting to see?** Are there specific processes or features that your prospect wants to see demonstrated? Perhaps she has a script she wants you to follow so she can check off the box on various features as she compares vendors. Assess whether you need to show everything on the script or if there is a specific order you must adhere to. Keep in mind that scripts are often put together by consultants or infrequent buyers of your product. If the script seems ill-suited for addressing your prospect's needs, you may want to take a proactive stance and suggest a different order or question the need to show certain features. See Chapter 16 for tips on how to fight back on a scripted demo in a complex sale.

Focusing your message to your audience

Your message must speak directly to the prospects who are in the room, whether they're product users, stakeholders, managers, or executives. Many times demos miss because salespeople fail to connect the dots between what their product does and how it benefits the people who are at the demo — not just the ultimate decision maker or people in the C-suite (the senior executives).

You're likely to have two types of prospects in your demo and therefore, two types of messages to tailor for them:

✔ **Product users:** Very often you're demonstrating to people who are going to be using your product. In smaller sales, the user and the decision maker may be one and the same, but in many larger sales, the decision maker may not be a user and may not even be at the demo. For example, with a medical device you may be demonstrating your product to physicians and nurses. The decision maker, the CFO, isn't in the demo but will rely on input from physicians and nurses to make the decision.

Product users want to know how your product is going to help them do their job better or faster. Telling a nurse how the device is going to improve the hospital's bottom line is likely to fall on deaf ears.

 ✔ **Decision makers:** These may be managers who oversee the product users or, depending on the investment, C-level executives. For example, if it's an IT solution, the decision maker could be the CIO or a head of the department most effected by the issue.

 The decision maker wants to know that the product is going to address the product user's needs and be readily adopted, as well as how it is going to affect the overall goals of the organization. For more on establishing value check out Chapter 3.

Building Your Demo around Your Prospect

A good demo is structured around your prospect's priorities and needs and how she would use it in her life as opposed to what your product does or the order that it does it in. Put yourself in your prospect's shoes when building your demo to make sure that you're telling your product story in a way that makes the most sense for your prospect.

Most demos show the product in an order that is logical from a company's perspective or based on how the product works or the way it's designed. That's why most demos are boring and don't connect with their intended audience.

For example, say you were shopping for a car and really just interested in something that could get to a high speed, fast. If I demonstrated that car in the way that most demos are, it would go something like this: "First, I'm going to put the key in the ignition, like this. Now, I'm going to place my foot on the gas pedal here as I turn the key to the right, which will engage the engine. The pressure of my foot on the pedal will open the throttle, which will allow air into the engine, creating a vacuum that will mix with more fuel and cause acceleration . . ." You may have died of boredom before you found out what you really cared about — that the car could go 120 miles per hour in 5.8 seconds!

Following are some ways you can ensure that you build your demo around your prospect:

 ✔ **Framing as a day in the life:** In this scenario you take the prospect through the product in the way that she would actually use it based on her own work flow by creating a *persona* — a hypothetical member of their organization. For example, if you're demonstrating CRM software to a room that includes salespeople, you would create a salesperson persona and structure your demo based on how this persona would interact with the product throughout the day.

 For example, "When our salesperson Carol turns on her computer in the morning, she is presented with a list of opportunities and tasks to be completed. So Carol looks at the first task here, which is to schedule a meeting with a new prospect. If she clicks on the task bar . . ."

✔ **Shifting perspectives:** If your product has an application for different users, for instance, a manager and a salesperson, you can show the same feature through a different persona, in this case, a manager.

For example, "As a manager, Ben can now see that Carol has set up a meeting with the prospect. She's also changed the lead potential from 20 percent to 40 percent, and if Ben clicks on her notes here on the right of your screen, he can see why. This helps improve the accuracy of management forecasts . . ."

✔ **Impact areas:** This option organizes your demo around like features that achieve a certain impact on the organization.

For example, "With these two features, the salesperson can update leads and research potential opportunities all while in the system, which means that she is much more efficient and can qualify and close deals faster, which greatly improves your bottom line."

Applying a Proven Structure

You may be tempted to jump right into your demo after the briefest of introductions, especially if your demo is just one of multiple presentations. After all, that's what the audience came to see. But in order for your demo to really make an impact on your audience and drive toward a sale, you need to stick to a proven structure just as you would in any presentation.

A powerful opening can influence the outcome of your entire demo by focusing your audience's attention and framing your solution. A clear agenda provides your audience with confidence that you're going to address their interests. A strong closing with a clear call to action ensures that your demo is remembered and acted upon. I discuss all of these parts of your presentation in the following sections.

Opening your demo

Your opening needs to gain attention, provide value, and set the stage for what's to come. Here's an example of an opening that accomplishes all three goals:

"My mom isn't what you'd ever call a 'techy' person. Mention the word *computer* or *smartphone*, and she just starts tuning you out. It seemed like too big of a change for her. But a year ago my brother and his wife had twins and something changed. My brother started sending photos and videos. But my mom had no way to see them until we got together.

Soon, she was asking me to come over almost daily. Finally I said, 'Mom, we're getting you an iPad.' For the first time she was willing to consider it. I took her to the store, and the salesperson showed her how easy it was to access pictures and videos. Now she's even watching movies and playing games on it. The change was much easier and better than she could have imagined.

"In the same way your company has an opportunity to change. You're working with systems you've had in place for many years — and you could probably continue to do that — but the question is, what are you missing out on? Today, I'm going to show you how our solution can help you improve your processes, reduce duplicated effort, and set you up for a better future."

Chapter 5 discusses how you can create a powerful opening for your demo.

Providing an agenda

Give your prospect a quick preview of what you're going to show them and why it matters with a brief agenda of topics to be covered. You don't want to give away too much, but you do want to reassure your audience that you're going to address features and processes that they want to see. The agenda is also a good spot to check in with your audience and confirm that you're hitting their primary interests and haven't left anything out. See Chapter 8 for developing an agenda.

Differentiating with features

The bulk of your demo may be showing specific features or processes, so getting them right is important. If you think about it, features are neutral. Many of your competitors probably have similar features, which means that you're on a level playing field with them right out of the gate. Proving that you have certain features or can perform specific processes puts you in the game, but it won't win you the deal. It's the way that you show those features and processes that sets you apart from your competitors.

Here are some ways to differentiate your product with features:

- ✔ **Determine what features you need to show.** You want to show just enough to prove your point. No more, no less. Although it may seem logical that if you show a prospect enough bells and whistles she will be sold, this couldn't be further from the truth. In a product demonstration, simplicity is your friend. The more features you show, the more likely you are to show something that disqualifies you ("we don't need that"), opens the door for discounting ("we won't use that so we shouldn't have to pay for it"), or makes your product appear complicated ("Our people will never do all of that!").

✔ **Test for relevancy.** Everything you show must be tied to an interest or need that the prospect has. If it's something you think would be relevant to your prospect . . . some day . . . under the right circumstances, let it go. Just because you can do it doesn't mean that you should show it. Pick a few key things to show and make each one shine.

✔ **Tell a story.** Don't just rush from feature to feature or process to process. Give your prospect some backstory first. Under what circumstances would your prospect use this feature? How is your prospect currently performing this process? Creating a quick scenario and providing context can help your prospect more readily see herself using your product.

✔ **Make it easy to follow.** You're familiar with your product, but your prospect isn't. Although you want to keep a good pace, find places to pause so your prospect can absorb what you're showing her. Check in occasionally to see if she has any questions. If you race through the demo, your prospect is going to be more confused than impressed.

Highlighting benefits

The most important part of your product is not what it does, but the results your prospect can get from using your product. In other words, the benefits are key. However, focusing on benefits when you're demonstrating a product can be a challenge. You're showing how your product works, so directing most of your dialogue toward what you're doing is natural. These sections show why you need to be vigilant about including benefits.

Empower the influencer

If you're involved in a complex sale, the ultimate decision maker may not even be in the demonstration. For example, if you're selling a drilling rig to a large oil company, you may be demonstrating to a group of engineers and managers, but the ultimate decision maker is likely a financial executive or even a purchasing group. Your *influencer* is your internal advocate who will be at your demonstration. She is the key to making the connection between your product and the decision maker.

Your goal is to give your influencer the tools she needs to support your product internally. That's why you want to be very clear about highlighting the benefits. If your influencer tells the CFO, "I think we should buy this because it's going to cut down on costly downtime in the field and improve our efficiency by 30 percent," he is apt to understand your product's value and render a favorable decision. If your influencer tells the decision maker that your rig has rack and pinion steering and a drill rating of 300 to 800 feet, he's not likely to be interested — or to know if those features are good or bad.

Assuming is dangerous

As the salesperson, you can easily assume that the benefits are obvious because you're familiar with your product. But that isn't necessarily the case for your prospect. Your product may be something your prospect purchases only once in her lifetime. So although the benefits are obvious to you, your prospect isn't going to work as hard to make that connection. Make it easy for your prospect by highlighting the benefits every time you discuss a feature.

Every feature needs a benefit. Focus on the benefits that your prospect may receive by using the feature you're showing — saving time, gaining visibility, or eliminating redundancies. That's what prospects want to hear!

Closing with purpose

After you finish the demo, it's time to close. Return to your original purpose — what you set out to achieve and what action you want your prospect to take. Here are some tips to a good demo close:

- ✔ **Summarize what you showed your prospect.** Quickly recap the major topics you covered in your demo and the benefits your prospect can expect to experience. You just covered this in greater detail so don't belabor it.

- ✔ **State the value.** Summarize value based on who is in your room and when possible, use facts and figures to quantify the value of your solution. For example, "You've seen how we can reduce downtime in the field by an average of 20 percent. Based on your volume, that could save you approximately $600,000 a year." See Chapter 3 for tips on identifying and customizing value.

- ✔ **Call back to your opening hook.** You've covered a lot of information, now it's time to revisit your opening *hook* — a relevant attention-grabbing device, like a story, a question, or an insight — to make sure your message is remembered. See Chapter 5 for more on opening hooks.

- ✔ **Ask for the next steps.** After a good demonstration, you have earned the right to ask for something, and in fact, your prospect will expect it. If you don't ask for the next step, you have just wasted your time.

Delivering Your Demo

Delivering a demo is the process of explaining or showing your prospect the capabilities of your product. Whether this means walking your prospect through a process in your software or the capabilities of your equipment, following the literal definition of demonstrating — to explain or show — results in a dull demo that does little to advance the sale.

Avoiding demo crimes

Demo Crime is a term coined by Bob Riefstahl, author of *Demonstrating TO WIN!* and founder of 2WIN!Global, a leader in the professional development of high-tech sales and pre-salespeople. According to Riefstahl, Demo Crimes are the poor practices you can fall in to when you demonstrate your solution. Eliminating them can give you a distinct advantage in a competitive selling situation. Here are just three of the 28 Demo Crimes explored in Bob's book, how they impact your prospect, and how to avoid them.

✔ **The Blind Leading the Blind:** Going through three or more clicks or screens as you try to find a feature or function or setting in your product while the prospect watches. This crime encourages your prospect to offer suggestions, makes your product appear complex or difficult to use, and reduces your credibility.

The fix: Block the display and do your research privately. Switch the projection to your workstation only or put something in front of the projector lens. If after three attempts you can't locate it, write the question down and move on. Do your research during a break.

✔ **The Field by Fielder:** Demonstrating software by going menu item by item, tab by tab, or field by field through a window or screen with no real purpose or context puts your prospect to sleep and may also cause you to hit a roadblock that's impossible to overcome.

The fix: Plan your demonstration around a process flow or task steps. Always show the software from the perspective of how someone will use it, not from how it works.

✔ **I Love this Part of My Solution:** Showing the prospect processes or capabilities in your product that are very powerful and interesting, but don't relate to the prospect's situation or environment wastes time and also risks alienating the prospect or raising issues that you then must address. This often happens if you have extra time at the end of a demo.

The fix: Trust what you uncovered during discovery and stick with it, or do some on-the-spot discovery to find out if it's relevant.

Although a demo does include some elements of explanation, your prospect doesn't need to walk out with the ability to operate your product; she only needs the knowledge of how your product is going to improve her life. Your job is to make that connection for her. Not to show your prospect as many features as possible, which is a common mistake when demonstrating products. If showing features sold products, buyers could just watch a video or read a manual. As you deliver your demo, never forget that you're selling.

You have many things to consider when delivering your demo: do you sit or stand? How and when should you interact with your audience? How do you make sure something doesn't go wrong? I explore answers to all of these questions and more in the following sections.

Comparing standing versus sitting

Although sitting when showing your product seems more natural in some cases — especially when you're demonstrating software — you're actually doing yourself and your prospect a disservice. Your voice and your energy naturally drop when you're seated. The connection between you and your prospect all but disappears. You become simply the man — or woman — behind the curtains. To avoid this problem, keep your energy and your connection high by standing during your demonstration.

If you're using a laptop and find bending over it awkward, use a wireless mouse to help you while you're in PowerPoint. You can also elevate your laptop by setting up a base for it by propping up a box or other items underneath your laptop. (Be sure and cover your base with a cloth or something that hides a messy structure.) Or better, invest in a portable, adjustable laptop table and have one with you wherever you go. The one I use is available at www.pctabletote.com.

Interacting with your audience

Doing everything that you need to do — demonstrating your product, highlighting benefits, and interacting with your audience — isn't easy. Make it easier on yourself by pinpointing some times to get out from behind your laptop or product and connect with your prospects.

You can do this in several spots within your demo: the opening and the closing and when you're introducing or wrapping up a new topic or feature. You also want to be sure to check in with your audience throughout the demo. Although you're not training your audience how to use your product, you do want to make sure that they're following along and you haven't lost them along the way. Do this by periodically asking questions like, "Can everybody see how I arrived here?" gives your audience a chance to catch up if they've fallen behind. Be sure to mix up your choice of words. "Does that make sense?" can get repetitive and insulting after the third or fourth time.

For more tips on using interaction within your demo, check out Chapter 14.

Sticking to some demo do's and don'ts

You want to keep in mind some unique aspects of doing a product demonstration. The following do's and don'ts can help you avoid common pitfalls and elevate your presentation above your competition.

✔ **Do stick to your plan.** It's tempting to think, "I'll just show them this while we're here. They might use it some day." This seemingly well-intentioned thought can take you down a rabbit hole you may not return from. Save yourself the trouble and stick to the plan.

✔ **Do rehearse.** Giving a demonstration without rehearsing is courting disaster. Practice at least three times and recreate the demonstration environment as closely as possible. With so much to pay attention to during a demo, you want to have as much of the mechanics down as possible. Proper rehearsal gives you greater confidence and allows you to place the focus on the real star of your demo — the prospect.

✔ **Do test your equipment.** A nonworking demo is every salesperson's nightmare, but it doesn't have to be yours. Test it before you go and when you get to the venue. Check with the IT team at your venue in advance and make sure you have the right equipment on hand (projector screen, adapters, speakers, internet connection, and so on) and bring whatever you need to fill the gaps.

✔ **Do have a back-up plan.** Having screenshots or printed reports of what your product does can be a lifesaver when equipment fails you. If you're part of a team, work together with team members to appoint someone from your team to take over while you try to fix the situation. See Chapter 20 for more tips on recovering from presentation disasters.

✔ **Don't use unfamiliar language.** You can easily forget that your prospect isn't familiar with your product's special lingo, buzzwords, or acronyms. You aren't there to teach your prospect new terminology. Put things in your prospect's language whenever possible. You want her to focus her brainpower on what your product can do for her.

✔ **Don't split your prospect's attention.** Save your key messages for when you aren't demonstrating your product. The brain only pays attention to one thing at a time so if you want to make sure your key message is heard, wait until you're done showing the feature and you have regained your prospect's attention.

✔ **Do step away from your product.** Whether it's a laptop, a piece of equipment, or a desk where you have your products spread out, don't get stuck in demonstration mode. You're not handing out samples at a warehouse store. Come out front and center and interact with your prospect as much as possible.

✔ **Don't forget to turn off messages and reminders.** Unless that important reminder to get your tickets to the beer festival is something you want to share with your audience, make it a habit to disable or turn off all those notices and pop-ups before you leave your house.

Chapter 19

Adjusting for Specialty Presentations and Audiences

A strategic sales presentation that lasts one or more days, an interview presentation designed to test your teamwork, a listing presentation that takes place in a prospect's home. Although many best practices in presentation planning, discovery, and principles remain the same, there are many types of sales presentations, each with its unique characteristics and challenges. How you adapt to your individual circumstances and environment is often key to your success.

Adapting is nothing new for salespeople who must be quick on their feet to deal with ever-changing conditions. A one-on-one presentation you prepared for morphs into a more formal group of ten. A live presentation opportunity moves to the virtual stage. Being able to adjust is an important skill to master to make the most of every presentation opportunity. Different types of presentations call for special considerations, whether it's in timing, content, structure, or engagement.

In this chapter, I explore some different types of presentation opportunities from full day or multiday presentations to strategic sales, in-home, interview style, and large group presentations. I look at the most effective strategies and tools for each and how you can easily adapt the principles of building value and audience engagement to fit the circumstances and address the challenges. I also show you how to flex your improv muscles to adjust your presentation effectively when things quickly change.

Delivering Full Day and Multiday Presentations

The ultra-marathon of giving full day and multiple day presentations aren't uncommon as part of a complex sale. They do present some unique challenges — not the least of which is the need for an unlimited supply of energy drinks.

These sections identify some of the primary challenges that you may encounter when making longer presentations and some effective strategies to overcome them and deliver a consistent message that keeps your audience engaged.

Pinpointing some issues

While a full day presentation might seem as simple as stringing together several one-hour presentations, there are some inherent differences in giving a day or more presentation that require special planning and consideration:

- ✔ **Covering more material:** More time means more topics, more presenters, and exponentially more features and benefits. But of equal importance, it means extra work for your prospect's brain and additional work for you to ensure that your prospect remembers the key points.

- ✔ **Testing attention spans:** As anyone who's delivered a shorter presentation knows, keeping today's busy, attention-challenged audiences engaged is no easy task. Doing it for a full day or a multiple number of days is a daunting task that seemingly calls for the versatile entertainment skills of a Neil Patrick Harris or Hugh Jackman.

- ✔ **Working in breaks:** Naturally your audience — and you — are going to need breaks throughout the day, which means you're going to lose the attention of your audience. Repeatedly. And you have to regain their attention. Repeatedly.

Using some effective strategies

Presentations of a full day or more don't have to be a slow death march for you and your audience if you use the following strategies to keep engagement, interest, and variety high.

✔ **Create a theme.** You don't want your audience to feel like they're in the movie *Groundhog Day,* showing up for more of the same, hour after hour, day after day. To keep your presentation fresh, especially during a multiday presentation, structure each day around a new theme, or a sub-theme of your overall theme, that sets each section or day apart to help your prospect anchor it in their minds. For example, if the overall theme for your presentation is "Join the Winning Team," day one's subtheme may be team commitment, day two's subtheme team strategy, and day three's subtheme team execution. See Chapter 4 for more about developing a theme.

✔ **Introduce activity.** Sitting for a full day can be nearly as tiring for your audience as standing. Keep the energy flowing by including some activities or interaction that requires physical movement. Examples can be breaking out into small groups or table discussion on a topic that you just covered or one you're going to address, or inviting audience members to come up and write on the whiteboard.

✔ **Keep them engaged.** Engagement is crucial during long presentations so don't leave it to chance. Create and stick to a *prospect engagement plan,* which maps out how and when you plan to keep your audience engaged throughout your presentation. Incorporate a lot of variety, for example you might open one section with a story and start the next with a video. Keep your audience on their toes by periodically introducing something unexpected in your presentation, like a story, a prop, or a video. See Chapter 14 for tips on developing a prospect engagement plan.

✔ **Plan breaks.** Your audience can't sit still for hours at a time. You need to plan breaks throughout the day to keep them comfortable. Here are some tips for breaks:

- **Schedule more breaks in the afternoon.** Energy and attention spans hit their lowest points then so don't fight it; take a break to keep energy up.

- **Put your audience's minds at rest.** Let your audience members know at the outset that there will be breaks where they will have time to get coffee or snacks, make phone calls, and check email.

- **Use a break timer.** Having the time remaining in a break count down on the screen eliminates excuses about returning late from break. These countdown timers are available in PowerPoint or for purchase online.

    Here's how to access the countdown timer in PowerPoint:

    1. **In PowerPoint, select File, then New.**

    2. **In the Search Bar, type in Countdown Timer.**

    3. **Download one of the templates and paste it into your deck and edit accordingly.**

- **Plan a post-break activity.** It takes people a few minutes to settle back down and refocus after a break, so don't deliver your most important message of the day. You do want to quickly grab their attention, however. Reward those who are back on time with a story or video that ties to your previous topic or leads into the next one. You can even give a quiz with points that add up to a prize for the most right answers at the end of the day.

The minute you say "break" your audience will be thinking of little else. Don't announce the break (other than to introduce the concept) until you're actually ready to take the break or you'll have a mass exodus of attention.

Presenting for the Strategic Sale

Strategic sales, including technology, infrastructure, and large-scale development projects, require special attention and often involve a series of presentations and/or demonstrations. Most often strategic sales are a B2B (business to business) sale that impacts the prospect's company in a major way. A B2C (business to consumer) sale can also be strategic if it involves a major investment, multiple decision makers, and steps.

With more at stake and more people typically involved in the process, make sure you understand the unique aspects of a strategic sale as well as develop some winning strategies for ensuring a successful outcome.

Noting some challenges

Here are some of the primary challenges you're faced with when doing a presentation as part of a strategic sale:

- **Winning over multiple decision makers:** Products like enterprise software, infrastructure, or large construction projects have a major impact on the organization as a whole, a large price tag, and perceived risk. Because of these factors, typically more than one decision maker and multiple stakeholders are involved in the process. Hence, you must convince the majority of these decision makers to buy your product — even though you may not get a chance to speak — or even present — to them all.

- **Selling as a team:** If you're involved in a strategic sale, you're very likely doing it as a team. A team member drops the ball, doesn't communicate well, or fails to show up prepared, and the whole team's performance goes down a notch in the prospect's eyes. Communication, planning, and delegation are critical to your team's success. (Chapter 16 discusses presenting as a team.)

✔ **Extending the sales cycle:** In a strategic sale the time from identifying the opportunity to closing the deal can be anywhere from five months to five years. As you make your way through the process, many changes can occur in the prospect's situation, personnel, and objectives, all of which can threaten to derail the sale.

✔ **Responding to an RFP:** Often in a purchase of this magnitude the prospect's organization will have identified and vetted (pre-qualified) you and some of your competitors as potential vendor partners. It also likely has established its buying criteria and outlined what it expects to see in a presentation and/or demonstration through a request for proposal (RFP). This scripted presentation or demo likely doesn't show your product or service in its best light, and more likely is an easy way for the prospect to check off features on a list or score you on those features and compare you to your competition to arrive at a decision.

✔ **Competing with status quo:** Doing nothing is often your greatest competitor in a strategic sale. Large, whole scale change can be frightening for a more risk-adverse organization to embark on. Many salespeople are caught off guard when no one wins the deal because they have built their entire presentation around the question of "Why buy us?" instead of the more accurate "Why buy?"

Examining some strategies

Although the hurdles may seem immense with a strategic sale, with the proper planning and preparation you can set yourself up for an effective and persuasive presentation that advances the sale in the following ways:

✔ **Find an advocate.** You need someone within the organization — ideally a decision maker — who can either help you understand or gain access to other decision makers. A good advocate helps you get the information you need to further your cause and carry your message internally if you give him the right tools. Find out more about internal advocates in Chapter 18.

✔ **Do a thorough discovery.** An RFP isn't sufficient to prepare your presentation. With so much at stake, doing your research and speaking to key members of the prospect's organization are particularly important in a strategic sale. You need to find out what and who are driving the change, what the impact is on the business and each decision maker, what the key metrics (KPIs) are, and so on. See Chapter 2 for more tips on conducting a thorough discovery session.

✔ **Avoid teaching.** Often in a strategic sale your prospect has little or no experience with the product or service. You can easily get pulled into teaching your prospect how your product works, but don't do it. Even when demonstrating the product, you need to stay focused on your goal: showing the prospect how your solution is going to impact his organization and help him achieve his goals.

✔ **Fight back on bad scripts.** An RFP may give you a script to follow that isn't structured in a way that advances your prospect's understanding of your product. It may have a misplaced focus: too much attention on things that don't really matter and too little on things that deserve more weight. As your prospect may have little experience buying your product, you may be in a position to educate him in this regard. You can make him aware that the script isn't designed to most effectively achieve his goals and provide him with a proposed script and a rationale for each change. Yes, it's a bit more work, but having a structure that not only shows your product or solution in its best light, but more importantly, also makes it easier for your prospect to make a more informed decision based on relevant criteria is worth it.

✔ **Address the status quo.** Don't get too distracted by the lineup of competitors pitching your prospect. Focusing exclusively on how you can outsell the competition without addressing the more dominant competitor in the room — the status quo — can leave you high and dry. What you find in your discovery affects how you address this concern. Determine whether your prospect is fearful of change or has had a bad experience. Keying in on the underlying issue that is blocking him from moving forward and addressing it in your presentation can save you a lot of investment in time and resources as well as disappointment later on when no one wins.

Making In-Home Presentations

Real estate, water purifying systems, roofing, or skincare are just a few examples of the types of products and services where presentations in the home are the norm. Giving a presentation or demonstration in someone's home is very different than standing in a board room or sitting across from a prospect in his office, but the basics of good presentation development and skills remain the same — doing discovery, planning and outlining your presentation, understanding the impact, and preparing for objections.

In the following sections you find out what makes an in-home presentation different and how to adjust your presentation and your delivery accordingly.

Considering the differences

In order to deliver an effective in-home presentation, you need to factor in some special considerations that make it unique:

✔ **Throwing out structure:** Because products and services sold in-home are often sold to your network, and your network consists of people who you know or have been recommended by — friends, family, neighbors, and acquaintances — you may be tempted to throw aside protocol and the presentation all together. In fact, your prospect may feel very comfortable jumping from small talk to the bottom line: "So how much is this going to cost?" or "What do you think you can get for my house?" Even though this may seem harmless, skipping steps in your presentation can be dangerous because it gets you into a discussion on price before you've had a chance to establish value.

✔ **Reading body language:** If you've never met your prospect before, coming into his home can be fraught with potential missteps. If you don't pay good attention to body language or keep appropriate boundaries, you can unwittingly create an uncomfortable atmosphere that leads to a lost deal.

✔ **Getting off track:** An in-home presentation lends itself to a more free-flowing conversational format. Too many slides and one-sided monologues are as out of place in an in-home presentation as wheat bread on a gluten-free menu. But more conversation means less time to deliver key points and build your case. Before you know it, it's time to wrap up and no decisions have been made.

✔ **Increasing interruptions:** When you're in someone's home, plenty of distractions — family members coming in and out, barking dogs, crying children, ringing phones, and so on — can pull your prospect's focus and sidetrack and stall your presentation.

✔ **Closing pressure:** The expectation for many in-home sales is to close the deal and get a signed contract at the end of the presentation. For many products and services sold in-home, statistics show that if you don't close the deal during your first visit, the odds of ever closing can decrease as much as 75 percent.

Eyeing in-home presentation strategies

Applying the following strategies during an in-home presentation can increase your likelihood of walking out with a signed contract.

✔ **Take cues from your prospect.** Let your prospect be the guide as to what is appropriate in terms of space, seating, and formality level in his home. Don't take anything for granted. Ask before sitting in a cherished, antique chair. Watch your prospect's body language as carefully as you listen to his words.

✔ **Keep to a structure.** Having a structure is important, even if it's loose, to give your subject the attention it deserves. Don't get trapped into jumping ahead in your presentation when you're not ready. Without having set up your case and established value and credibility, you're in for trouble if you respond to his questions about pricing, marketing, or terms. Get the discussion back on track with a statement like the following:

"I know this is a big decision and I want you to be sure that I did all my homework to come up with the best solution for you, so what I'd like to do first is just walk you through the process before we address your question. Does that make sense?"

✔ **Build rapport.** When building your presentation, you need to keep in mind that there will likely be more conversation both before and during your presentation. Building rapport plays a much larger role in an in-home presentation than a B2B one, and you can appear rude if you jump too quickly into business. In order to accommodate a more conversational style, use the minimum number of slides or handouts you need to keep things moving while still addressing key points.

✔ **Have a clear call to action.** With so much riding on getting a contract signed while you're there, you need to show up prepared to deliver a strong closing and call to action. Many salespeople think closing will happen naturally, but it doesn't always work that way. Being prepared with a strong closing and call to action helps you feel confident as you approach the end of your presentation. Be sure your call to action is specific and concrete. See Chapter 7 for more tips on closing.

✔ **Choose a visual aid.** Handouts have been the vehicle of choice for in-home sales for years, but that is starting to change for good reason. They get buried in other papers and don't have the visual impact of slides. Although you certainly won't bring a projector to a prospect's house, slides are still an option. A tablet is a great medium for showing your work or your products. For example, a real estate agent can use it to show listing photos or comparable properties. A roofing or security salesperson can use it to identify other homes in the area that use their services. You may still want to provide printouts of more detailed information, like pricing or market comparisons for leave behinds.

Don't get drawn into using your tablet as an on-site research tool during your presentation. If you're a real estate agent, searching for properties on the fly with your prospect can drag you off course and you may never get back. Wait until after your presentation and you have a signed contract to do additional research.

Shining as a Team in Interview-Style Presentations

In industries like architecture and construction, instead of a linear presentation, your team may be asked to go before a panel where you're judged on answering questions and how you work together as a team. These interview style presentations typically take place after you've been *shortlisted* — competition narrowed down to two or three firms — and you can't afford any missteps. Although you use the same preparation strategy, discovery, and planning for interview-style presentations (also called *panels*) as you would for a more traditional presentation, you have the added challenges of figuring out how to naturally work your key messages, like competitive differentiators, value proposition, and benefits into your answer, as well as display great chemistry as a team and with the audience.

The following sections look at some of the common difficulties when delivering an interview-style presentation and offer some creative and practical solutions for addressing them.

Looking at unique challenges

Interview-style presentations are by nature less scripted and involve teams. This change in the dynamics of the presentation can present numerous challenges, including:

- ✔ **Lacking control:** You may not be sure of the questions that you'll be asked or the order in which your prospect may ask them. This type of spontaneity is a challenge even for professional improvisers, much less people who have perhaps only worked together on the occasional project basis.

- ✔ **Judging team interaction:** Not only are your prospects listening for your response to their questions, they're also looking to see how you interact as a team. Do you get along? Is there discord? Are there any power struggles? If it looks like your team just met for the first time in the lobby that morning, you're not going to score many points.

- ✔ **Managing time:** Unlike in a linear presentation when you have the floor for an extended period of time, you often get a set time to answer a specific question in an interview-style presentation. And for most people, especially technical people prone to long explanations, that set time is rarely long enough.

Strategizing for interview-style presentations

By applying the following skills as you prepare for an interview-style presentation, you can demonstrate the knowledge, teamwork, and chemistry necessary to make your team the one to beat:

✔ **Brainstorm questions.** Have a clear idea of your prospect's questions. Meet together as a team and consider the types of questions that may arise and categorize them, for example, financing, project management, design, and so forth.

✔ **Develop compelling answers.** Simply answering the question is boring and doesn't differentiate you from your peers. Here are some steps to help you respond in a more memorable way:

  • Decide as a group on the answer to the question.

  • Make sure the answer includes the full arc of an agenda item: challenge, impact, and solution. See Chapter 6 for building out your agenda items.

  • Don't just answer the question. Frame your answer with an opening hook — a story, a quote, or a prop — to make it more memorable for your audience. Chapter 5 offers more opening hook ideas.

  • Wrap up your answer by highlighting the benefit for your audience.

✔ **Decide who will answer.** Assign team members by type of question, as opposed to specific questions to avoid team members talking over each other or awkward silences.

✔ **Show interaction.** Your prospect wants to see how you work together so find some opportunities to play off each other. Here are some good ways to do that:

  • **Predetermine topics.** Select a few topics where two or more people can tag team each other with each one giving a part of the full answer. Doing so shows strong collaboration and like thinking.

  • **Create cues.** Develop some physical cues to indicate when a team member wants to take a question or, alternatively, when a team member needs assistance when answering a particular question.

  • **Build on each other's answers.** To show solidarity, expand on each other's answer by using the improv rule of "Yes and . . . " In other words, agree with what your team mate said and add something new.

  Make it a dialogue by really listening and responding to the question in a conversational tone. See Chapter 16 for more tips on using "Yes and . . . " and working together as a team.

Presenting for Large Groups

At times you may be called upon to present in front of a large group (20 or more people). It may be a user group, a conference, or a project that requires company wide support.

Even salespeople who are fearless presenting to top executives can feel intimidated when speaking to a large group. From the varying acoustics to the challenge of connecting with your audience, group presentations present their own unique set of dynamics that you must address in order for you to move your audience to take action. The following sections can ease your anxiety.

Dealing with group dynamics

All you have to do is think back to a large presentation where you were an audience member to recognize that people behave differently in large groups. Were you in the back of the room texting? Did you zone out because you didn't feel like the presenter was talking to you? The following list introduces some additional considerations when giving a presentation to a large group, not the least of which is how you handle that extra boost of nerves:

- **Staying connected:** You can easily lose that one-on-one connection with a large group if you don't work at it. Talking over people's heads or to the room in general is a sure way to create more distance.

- **Losing visibility:** If you're up on a stage or the audience is quite spread out, they won't be able to see the small text or bullet points on your slides or less obvious movements or facial expressions that can bring a presentation to life for an audience.

- **Losing the message:** The larger the room, the more challenging the acoustics. Making sure everyone can hear you and any media you may be using in your presentation is crucial.

- **Keeping your audience engaged:** Like in a virtual presentation, your audience can easily feel invisible, which means that they're much more likely to check out and go right to their smartphones if they don't find you or your subject engaging.

Tackling large groups

There's more to presenting to a large group than simply speaking louder. You need to take control of your environment, your stage, and your technology. Following are some strategies for making sure your message resonates with your audience.

Simplify slides

Use simple graphics and large easy-to-read type. Get rid of bullet points; you're not giving a lecture. If you do use them, you'll be tempted to turn around and read them, which makes you look amateurish and annoys your audience. Instead of bullets, choose bold images and simple statements.

Set up the room

You want to find out well in advance how the room is configured and what type of equipment is available so you can be prepared with the necessary adapters, speakers, or projector. On the day of your presentation, arrive early and get familiar with the room before you present. Know your space and test your equipment before anyone comes in. Walk the stage and see what options you have in terms of movement. Check the lighting to make sure that it's dark enough for the audience to see your slides clearly, but not so dark that they're tempted to curl up and take a nap.

Check sightlines

Make sure that your audience can see you with ease and vice versa. You want the opportunity to make eye contact with everybody at some point. Many times venues have blind spots. Know where those blind spots are and make a point to include the people in them by creating a reason — stashing a flip-chart or accessing a prop — to walk over to one of these sections during your presentation. Doing so goes a long way toward making everyone feel included.

Greet people as they arrive

Connecting with a large audience is difficult from the stage or across the room. To combat that problem, make a point to introduce yourself and shake hands with as many people as possible as they arrive. Doing so is a great way to bridge the gap and forge stronger relationships. It also helps calm your nerves to have a few friendly faces to look out at from the stage.

Be introduced

With a large group of people in one space it often takes everyone longer to get settled. To avoid having your first words be the much maligned, "Can I have your attention please?" ask your key contact or highest-level executive in the room to introduce you. Besides giving you an instant boost of credibility, doing so settles down and focuses the audience before you begin. Make sure that you're seated nearby so there's not a long pause as they wait for you to get to the stage. See Chapter 8 for tips on using an introduction.

Make yourself bigger

Small gestures and subtle movements don't read well from the back row. You need to be bigger than you would in a smaller group in order to look energized and animated, and maintain the attention of your audience. Make large gestures away from your torso. Use big, slow movements as opposed to small, rapid movements. By the way, large gestures will feel very odd if you don't practice them before hand. See Chapter 11 on gesturing.

Interact with your audience

Just because you have a large group doesn't mean you can't interact, but it does require some preplanning. You can get everyone involved by doing a live text poll — asking your audience to weigh in on a specific topic or quiz by texting their answers to a specific number and showing the results live on screen. You need to have Internet access; set up in advance a polling program that allows for text message polling. Refer to Chapter 14 for more on setting up a poll and other ways to interact with your audience.

Amplify your voice

Soft voices can easily get lost in a big space or even a smaller space with lots of bodies. Think about trying to project to the back of the room. If you're a naturally soft talker, prepare by doing vocal exercises designed to increase your power and connect your voice to your breath. Depending on the room's acoustics, you may need to use a microphone to be heard evenly. Here are some tips for using a mic:

✔ **Use your normal voice.** Most mics amplify your speaking voice quite well so you don't need to shout or talk extremely loudly. If you do, you may blow away the front row.

✔ **Do a sound check prior to people arriving.** Have someone move around the room and let you know if he can hear you and then make necessary adjustments.

  • **For podium mics, position yourself so that you're speaking just over the microphone, not directly into it.** Make sure it's not blocking your face for most of the audience, although some people will be unlucky. Don't get too close to the mic because every sound and breath you make will be amplified.

  • **For handheld mics, keep it a consistent distance from your mouth.** Limit rapid movements and resist swinging the mic from side to side as the sound will vary radically.

  • **For lavaliere mics, place it eight to ten inches below your mouth.** A lavaliere mic attaches to your collar or lapel and is usually wireless. Hook the transmitter on your belt or waistband (dress accordingly). Don't turn your head too far to either side to avoid having your voice fade in and out. Think about a V extending up from your mike and try to keep your head movements in that range.

TIP

For all mics, be sure to turn them off when you're not presenting to avoid the audience hearing anything that you don't intend them to hear.

✔ **Know how to handle questions with the mic.** If you anticipate a lot of questions from the audience, have a secondary mic or a traveling mic placed in the audience. Prior to your presentation, enlist the help of someone in the audience to look for people who have questions and hand them the traveling mike or monitor the mic stand. Doing so avoids that sloppy and time-consuming back-and-forth handoff between presenter and questioner that can occur. Always repeat back the question for the rest of the audience, which also gives you some time to formulate a response.

See Chapter 11 for more tips to keep you in your best voice and work the stage purposefully.

Talk to one person at a time

By trying to talk to a group, you end up talking to no one. Focus on directing your message to one person at a time. Doing so makes you come across more conversational and makes the person you're talking to feel connected as well as the rest of your audience.

Channel your nerves

Big groups can multiply those butterflies in your stomach until you feel like you might fly away with them. Although expecting your nerves to completely disappear is unrealistic, you don't have to let those nerves undo you. Knowing your material inside and out can help give you confidence, as will being prepared for any type of presentation mishap with a good backup plan. Preparing your body and your voice helps ensure you're in good form, energized, and free of tension as you present. Ultimately you have to make peace with nerves and put them to good use by channeling that nervous energy into delivering an energized presentation. Chapter 13 has more tips on dealing with stage fright.

Adjusting Your Message on the Fly

"I've only got 20 minutes." Disappointing to say the least to hear this from a prospect when you've been preparing for weeks for a two-hour presentation. Regardless of the reason — the prospect is running late or short on time — the tendency is to acquiesce and race through your presentation like an auctioneer, rushing through your deck, dismissing slides right and left. But don't do it. Hurrying through your presentation with no plan has no upside. In fact, it often does more damage than good. It makes your product or service sound complicated because your prospect is only picking up bits and pieces of what you're saying, and your nonstop monologue as you race to the finish line doesn't invite interaction with your prospect.

As a salesperson, you need to be able to successfully maneuver these types of changes because they can all happen with little or no notice. You need a strategy that helps you adjust your presentation quickly and seamlessly on the spot without breaking into a sweat. The following sections provide a three-option strategy. If you prepare for each option, you'll be in good shape no matter what is thrown at you. Besides the odd rotten tomato.

Never speed through your presentation. Decide among these three options: Reschedule, do discovery, or deliver an abbreviated preview version of your presentation.

Rescheduling the meeting

In most cases, rescheduling the meeting is the preferred option if you can't give the full arc of your presentation — situation, complication, resolution — in the time available. Rescheduling gives you time to deliver your presentation at the pace you need to a fully attentive audience. If your prospect insists by suggesting that you just "Run through the main points," or "Get to the bottom line," hold steady unless it's your only opportunity with this decision maker. In which case, the third strategy — delivering an abbreviated presentation — is necessary. Otherwise, offer a compelling explanation as to why your prospect should reschedule your presentation by intriguing him with an insight and showing value. For example:

> "I don't want to do you a disservice and rush through your proposal. I've uncovered some interesting things about your current efforts to increase your social presence — including how you can increase your campaign open rates by as much as 30 percent — and I want to be sure and give you the full picture. What does next week at this time look like for you?"

Letting a prospect know that you've done your homework and have something of value to offer can usually get him to reschedule the meeting, especially if he's at fault for cutting it short.

Turning it into a discovery meeting

You can always use what time you have to find out more about your prospect to help you further tailor your presentation. Discover if anything has changed in the prospect's situation since you last spoke that you need to address in your presentation, such as a change in priorities, personnel, or strategy. Use this opportunity to find out all you can. Sometimes prospects are more willing to open up in an impromptu discovery setting.

Delivering an abbreviated presentation

If this is your only chance to present, you need to deliver an abbreviated version of your presentation. What you leave in and what you omit in your presentation depends on your objective — to close your prospect during this presentation, to convince him to give you another opportunity to give a full presentation (if your initial attempt fails), or to move to the next step in the sales process. Here are tactics for either attempting to close or moving the sales process to the next step.

Attempting to close

If you need to make a strong case in a short period of time that motivates your prospect to take action, prioritize your message and stick to the agenda items that are most critical to the prospect, and provide a clear call-to-action. Here's how to do so:

1. **Deliver your opening hook.**

2. **Pick the one or two (depending on time) agenda items most important to your prospect.**

3. **Deliver the full arc of each agenda item — challenge, impact, resolution.**

    See Chapter 6 for addressing a topic.

4. **Finish with your value proposition and a clear and specific call to action.**

Previewing your presentation

If you're hoping to get your prospect to give you an opportunity to do a full presentation, think of this abbreviated version as a movie preview designed to get your prospect to buy a ticket to the movie. Previews don't typically give away the ending or reveal the entire plot. They provide just enough of the story to hook the viewer. In the same way, you want to reveal just enough of your story to hook your prospect so that he wants to see the entire presentation. Here's how:

1. **Deliver your opening hook.**

2. **Pick two agenda items that are a priority to your prospect.**

3. **For the first agenda item, cover the entire scope of the topic — challenge, impact, resolution.**

4. **For the second agenda item, cover only the challenge and impact.**

    By leaving out the resolution, your second agenda item becomes a cliffhanger.

5. **Deliver your value proposition.**

6. **Close with a call to action to schedule a full presentation to show your prospect how you resolve the second agenda item as well as the additional topics you'll address.**

Part VI
The Part of Tens

So many presentation tips and so little time? Get ten quick tips for a winning presentation at www.dummies.com/extras/salespresentations.

In this part . . .

- ✔ Know how to remain calm when something goes wrong during your presentation.

- ✔ Find out how to overcome technology problems and maintain your audience's attention.

- ✔ Discover secrets for using PowerPoint to direct your audience's focus and create a seamless presentation experience.

- ✔ Understand how and when to use your tablet in a presentation.

- ✔ Discover best practices and killer apps for iPad presentations.

Chapter 20

Ten Ways to Recover from Presentation Disaster

In This Chapter

▶ Keeping cool when disaster strikes

▶ Improvising when technology fails

▶ Maintaining your prospect's attention when problems arise

Despite all your best efforts, the ugly truth is that if you do enough presentations, at some point, something will go wrong. Your presentation material will malfunction or disappear. Projectors will refuse to communicate with your laptop. Your demo will freeze. Vital team members will miss a flight. The way in which you handle unforeseen circumstances or mistakes can make or break your presentation. Just like an actor who misses a cue during a live performance, you too have to be prepared and ready to adapt without losing your audience in the process.

Without a game plan it's easy to panic and lose focus when things go south. The following tips can help you handle any challenge that comes your way.

Staying Cool under Pressure

You're standing in front of an audience and suddenly some unanticipated event throws all your careful plans out the window. The most important thing you must do is remain calm. Keeping your composure helps you manage the situation and keeps you prospect calm as well. If you suddenly look like you've just witnessed a crime, your prospect will be understandably alarmed as well. Here are some ways to avoid a meltdown:

> ✔ **Pause.** Most of the time your audience doesn't notice the problem or it's quickly resolved, so give yourself a moment to collect yourself. What seems like an eternity of silence to you is a fraction to your audience.

✔ **Breathe.** When you get anxious, resist the urge of your body tightening and constricting. Staying loose and taking deep breaths relaxes you and sends needed oxygen to your brain so you can think more clearly.

✔ **Keep perspective.** Unless the mysteries of the universe are on those slides, most presentation problems have an acceptable workaround. It may not be ideal, but it won't be a total loss either.

✔ **Raise your expectations.** Your mind-set and expectations can impact your results. If you expect this presentation to be a disaster, it will. Expect to have a successful presentation regardless of the obstacles, and you're much more likely to find a way to pull it off.

Using It, Losing It, or Laughing at It

So you've skipped an entire section of your presentation, you can't pull up a video, or the projector up and died. Put it through the use-it-lose-it-or-laugh-at-it test. This handy rule of improvisation can help you determine which, if any, action to take to get you back on track.

✔ **Use it.** Many mistakes are recyclable. Flub a line? Forget a name? Use it as an ongoing joke that your audience is in on or see where the moment takes you. Spontaneity often spices things up and adds for some interesting impromptu moments and opportunities.

For example, "You know what? I just jumped ahead because I was so excited to show you what this capability means for your company. I'll leave it up to you guys. Would you like to see how this works?"

✔ **Lose it.** If the problem or mistake doesn't affect the basic premise of your presentation and your audience is none the wiser, just drop it. If they notice, apologize once and quickly move on. You don't need to draw undue attention to it.

✔ **Laugh at it.** If there's no hiding the problem (you forgot your deck, your laptop, or your mind), laugh at it. Prospects typically respond positively to a salesperson who can admit making a mistake and carry on with good humor. Besides, if your deck is so important that you can't go on without it, it's time to rethink your presentation.

Enlisting Help

No one expects you to be superman — or woman. Asking for help is okay if the problem is out of your control. When the problem is technology related, ask your prospect if an IT person is available who can help. If yes, then you have two options:

✔ **Delay the start.** If you recognize the problem before you begin, ask your audience members if they can use 15 minutes to take phone calls or check email before you start. If that doesn't work, go to the next option.

✔ **Carry on sans slides.** While waiting for assistance to arrive, forge ahead with your presentation as if computers had yet to be invented. Resist saying "I had a really awesome slide I would be showing you here . . . "

When help arrives, let the person work on it in the background while you continue delivering your presentation until she gives you the thumbs up that the problem is resolved. Quickly and professionally dive in without giving more attention to the delay.

Blocking the Projector

Attempting to resolve the technology issue yourself? Block the projector by either unplugging it or placing something in front of the light source — you don't want your audience to see what's behind the curtains. Half the audience doesn't want to watch you try and fix it, and the other half will be only too happy to give you their opinion. Avoid both and keep the screen black.

Allow no more than two to three minutes to identify the problem; otherwise you'll lose your audience before you even begin. After that time, enlist help, take a break, or use one of the other strategies in this chapter to keep your prospect engaged while you fix the problem.

Taking a Break

Depending on where your gaffe occurs, giving your audience a break may be natural. Doing so allows you some breathing room to focus on finding a solution without a room full of people staring at you. Set the break for no more than 15 minutes to avoid people getting too involved in any particular task. Be very clear on the time you plan to reconvene. See Chapter 14 for more tips on how to manage a break.

Having Handouts

Prepare handouts of key slides in advance so that when you refer to a graph, diagram, or chart that you're unable to show, your prospect has something to review. Avoid handing out copies of your entire presentation; otherwise your audience will be reading instead of focusing on what you're saying. See more tips on handouts — including how to make them interactive — in Chapter 7.

Save your slides as a PDF so if your PowerPoint or slide program fails, you can simply show your PDF on the screen.

Engaging with Your Audience

Use this time as an opportunity to talk to your audience members. Get their thoughts on the topics covered so far, ask them questions about their experience, or start a round-robin discussion. Doing so may actually prove more valuable than any slides you were going to show.

Telling a Story

Telling a story — especially a personal one — is a great way to both buy time and establish a connection with your audience. As you may be understandably rattled, make sure that your story is well rehearsed and polished and that you're confident with the details — especially the ending — before you launch into it. Chapter 12 discusses the power of storytelling in greater depth.

Doing an Activity

Take the pressure off yourself by giving your audience an activity to do while you're trying to recover. Having an activity requires a little improvisation because it depends on where you are within your presentation. If you are

- **Near the beginning:** Ask your audience to list topics that they want to see discussed or the major challenges they're experiencing.
- **Near the end:** Ask your audience to write down the top three things they've gotten out of your presentation so far or any questions they may still have.

Whiteboarding Your Presentation

People have been selling for thousands of years without PowerPoint or computers. That may seem a small comfort when your technology goes kerplunk, but keeping it in mind can help you maintain perspective. Most companies have whiteboards and markers available. Using them is the simplest stand-in for a slide deck if your technology fails. In fact, research shows that presenting via whiteboards even offers some significant advantages over traditional PowerPoint presentations in terms of recall and interaction. For tips on how to use whiteboarding to finish out your presentation on the fly, check out Chapter 14.

Chapter 21

Ten PowerPoint Tips You Must Know

- -

In This Chapter

▶ Using PowerPoint tools to direct your audience's focus

▶ Navigating PowerPoint during your presentation with ease

▶ Leveraging PowerPoint features to take your presentation to the next level

- -

*Y*ou know enough about PowerPoint to get by . . . or do you? As prospects and technology continue to get more sophisticated, making sure that you don't lag behind is important. You don't need to be a design professional or a tech wiz to create or deliver a great presentation, but you do need to make sure your skill level lives up to your content. Although running a smooth, professional PowerPoint presentation may not win you a standing ovation, searching for slides, making awkward transitions, or showing off your desktop can give you some bad reviews.

A wealth of information on how to create effective PowerPoint slides is available online and in bookstores; however, decidedly less is available on how to interact and deliver PowerPoint presentations. In this chapter you can fill in the gaps in your knowledge base with some practical PowerPoint tips and tricks that will make you look like a seasoned pro.

Going to Black

Talking about one thing while something entirely different is on a slide is a common and costly mistake that salespeople make. Your prospect can only focus on one thing at a time. If you have two conflicting messages, your prospect's attention likely isn't where you want it to be. Using the B key on your keyboard when you're in PowerPoint — or the blackout button on the preferable wireless mouse — makes the screen go black.

Use this button whenever you aren't talking about what is on the screen and want to pull your prospect's focus to you and your message. When you're ready to go to the next slide, simply hit the B key again and your slide will come back up. This technique makes you look professional and keeps your prospect focused on the topic. Although going to black sounds very simple, it's easy to forget after you get in to your presentation, so be sure to practice going to black and back several times.

Transitioning to Another Program or File

At times in your presentation you may need to temporarily leave PowerPoint in order to show another program or file. Typically presenters exit their presentation to find the task bar, and then search for the desired program or file — in the meantime giving their audience an unexpected glimpse of their pristine (or even worse, cluttered) desktop. Follow these steps for an easier and better way to navigate between a program and PowerPoint on a PC:

1. **Before your presentation, make sure that any file or program you want to access is open.**

2. **In presentation mode, hit ALT TAB.**

   Doing so displays all of your open windows.

3. **Keep clicking on the TAB key until you land on the window that you want to use and then let up on it.**

   The window will open, and you can go right into the program or file.

4. **When you're ready to go back to your presentation, hit ALT TAB again.**

The ALT TAB key continues to switch back and forth between the last two files opened, so if you've opened more than one, you have to tab through until you get to the appropriate window.

Jumping to a Slide

Say your prospect asks you a question and you have the perfect slide to address it somewhere later in the deck. Too many presenters make the mistake of advancing through their slides — with the audience watching — until they find it. Not only is doing so distracting, but you also lose an element of surprise by letting your prospect see future slides. No need to do that when you can easily jump back and forth between slides while in presentation mode. Here's how:

The day before your presentation:

1. **Go to Outline View and collapse the details.**
2. **Print View to have a list of all slide numbers and titles.**

During your presentation,

1. **Bring your printed slide list.**
2. **Go to Slide Show mode and using your keyboard type in the number of the slide you want to jump to.**
3. **Click Enter to go to that requested slide.**

This technique is useful for moving to a prepared Q&A slide or for skipping parts of your presentation if time becomes an issue.

Turning Off the Pointer

That little pointer arrow looks pretty harmless on your 13-inch laptop screen. However displayed across the screen at your prospect's office, it takes on major proportions and can prove distracting to your audience — especially when it moves whenever you use your mouse. Make this simple adjustment before your presentation to prevent that arrow from displaying or moving across your screen:

1. **In Slide Show mode, press Ctrl-H to disable the pointer.**
2. **When you want to use it again, press the A key to re-enable the pointer.**

Drawing on Screen during Your Presentation

Using a pen to write, highlight, or underline something on a slide during your presentation can really draw an audience's attention. Though this feature has been available for a few years, it still has a wow factor because not a lot of people use it. Luckily, you don't need one of those special pens that come with some tablets or laptops because this feature is available within PowerPoint. Simply follow these steps to circle, highlight, write, or draw on your presentation:

1. **Press Ctrl-P to display a pen on the screen.**

2. **Hold down the left button of your mouse as you draw on the screen.**

3. **Right click your mouse to bring up more drawing options, including changing the color of the ink and using a highlighter.**

4. **To erase what you've drawn, press the E key.**

5. **To get rid of the pen, press A or Ctrl-H.**

Preparing Final Slides

Many salespeople get to the end of their presentation and accidentally advance, which throws them out of presentation mode, leaving your audience a nice shot of your program and desktop. Remember, last impressions matter. If you want yours to be professional, avoid this snafu by creating two copies of your last slide and placing them at the end of your deck. That way if you accidentally click your mouse, your audience won't know because the slide looks exactly the same. Have a blank slide as your final slide.

Stopping a Video

Video is great for engaging an audience, but because of time or relevancy, you may need to cut it off before it finishes. Rather than try to jump to the next slide (which often ends up in clicking too much and jumping out of the program), all you need to do is click Alt Q to stop playback of the video.

Removing Picture Backgrounds

Sometimes you find the perfect image for a slide, but the background is distracting or irrelevant. You can actually remove the background in PowerPoint by sticking to these steps:

1. **While in PowerPoint, select the photo and click on it to go into Picture Tools.**

2. **Select Remove Background.**

   Your selected image will be a nice shade of purple. Everything in this purple area is what PowerPoint will remove, unless you tell it differently.

3. **Choose either Mark Areas to Keep or Mark Areas to Remove.**

   The minus sign indicates that it will be deleted.

4. **Adjust the area you want to keep or remove by clicking and dragging the lines.**

5. **When you have the area that you want to keep or remove isolated, click Keep Changes.**

Adjusting Your Slides for the Projector

Remember when videos came in widescreen? If your television wasn't wide screen, it would cut off some of the film. That's not unlike what happens when you have slides that aren't in synch with the projector being used for the presentation. You have two choices when designing your slides:

- 4:3, known as standard aspect ratio
- 16:9, known as widescreen aspect ratio

Almost all new projectors today are 16:9; however, plenty of old projectors are floating around. Unless you carry your own projector with you, find out what your prospect's projector is before you design your slides, because even though you can switch a deck from one size to the other, you still need to go back and manually check and adjust the placement of a lot of the content on your slides.

Using Presenter Mode

Presenter View allows you to see your notes and your upcoming slides on your computer while the audience sees only the current slide on their screen or monitor. Here's how to set up Presenter mode:

1. **In PowerPoint, click Slide Show.**

2. **In Monitors group, click Use Presenter View.**

   The Display Settings dialog box will appear.

3. **Click the monitor that you want to use to view your presenter notes and select, "This is my main monitor" checkbox.**

   (If that isn't an option, then your computer is already designated as the primary monitor.)

4. **Click the monitor icon and select the second monitor that the audience will be viewing.**

5. **Select Extend my Windows Desktop onto this monitor check box and then click OK.**

6. **Click on End Slide Show or ESC to exit presentation.**

Even though there are notes on Presenter Mode, use it as a quick reference for what is upcoming. Everyone will know if you read from your notes and quickly become disengaged.

Chapter 22

Ten Things You Need to Know When Presenting with Your Tablet

*T*hough more than 40 percent of the American adult population owns a tablet, you still can ride on a certain novelty wave if you use your tablet to give a presentation or demonstration. Tablets are lightweight, fast, and flexible, and they set a less formal tone for smaller or more casual presentations. And by allowing you to walk around, switch between applications, use a whiteboard, and do other cool options, they can create a more interactive presentation.

For a growing number of salespeople, tablets are rapidly replacing a lot of the old printed brochures and flip books of yesterday and are on their way to becoming the presentation vehicle of choice. This chapter discusses ten must-know tips to help you get the most out of your tablet in your presentation.

Using a Stand

When using your tablet to present directly to one or two people, you need a stand. Holding a tablet perfectly still for the length of a presentation is physically impossible. Every time you interact with your prospect, you'll find yourself in a new position and your prospect in turn will have to readjust to see the screen. Folding screens are too flimsy. You need something sturdier that you can count on. Here are some good options:

> ✔ **Belkin's FlipBlade Adjust:** A good value ($30), this aluminum stand folds down into 3.75 x 5.5, and opens in four different angles. Good for all tablets but it's larger size makes it ideal for older, bulkier tablets.

✔ **CoolerMaster's JAS mini:** Also aluminum and the same price, it's a little smaller than the FlipBlade at 4.4 x 2.4. It's available in five colors, if that kind of thing is important to you.

Keeping It Clean

At the risk of sounding like your mother, "clean your tablet before your presentation!" I've been at presentations where the salesperson pulled out a tablet and it looked like someone had used it to serve pizza on. Even if your presentation is more informal in nature, your prospect doesn't want to look at your fingerprints from your last meal. Carry some pocket cleaners in your case or car and give it a thorough wipe before you start your presentation.

Disabling Notifications

After cleaning your tablet, the next thing you should do is disable notifications. You certainly don't want a push notification from your Facebook account to interrupt your presentation. Although some older model tablets may require you to disable notifications on an app-by-app basis, newer Android tablets and iPads allow you to activate a Do Not Disturb feature.

To activate Do Not Disturb on your Android tablet, follow these steps:

1. **Go to device Settings.**
2. **Go to Sounds & Notifications.**
3. **Turn Do Not Disturb on or schedule a time to turn it on and off.**

To enable Do Not Disturb on your iPad, follow these easy steps:

1. **Go to Settings.**
2. **Find Do Not Disturb.**
3. **Switch the manual slider to ON.**

Connecting to a Projector

If you're presenting to more than two people, you're going to need a projector. More than two people and you have your audience members jockeying around to see the tablet or the disruption of passing it around. You can connect your tablet to a projector in one of two ways:

- ✔ **VGA or HDMI:** You can connect your tablet directly to the projector by using the appropriate cable and the video port on your tablet. Most newer projectors use HDMI but video and input ports vary widely so find out the requirements of the projector you'll be using and purchase the appropriate adapter or cable to fit both your tablet and the projector.

  If you're connecting to a projector with VGA and your presentation has sound or music, you need to connect your tablet to an external speaker to hear the audio.

- ✔ **Bluetooth wireless:** If your tablet is Bluetooth capable (which most newer models are), you can connect to a projector that is also Bluetooth ready. Here's how to connect to a projector via Bluetooth on a tablet:

  1. **Activate the Bluetooth feature on the projector by pressing the button or making a selection on the screen.**

     In the case of older projectors, you may need to insert a Bluetooth USB adapter into the projector's USB port.

  2. **On your tablet, choose Settings from your menu.**

  3. **Select Wireless Networks.**

  4. **Select Bluetooth Settings and turn On.**

  5. **Choose the projector from the list of devices.**

  If you have an iPad, you need to access wireless through AirPlay — a feature included on your iPad that allows you to wirelessly stream media to an AirPlay-capable device, such as an Apple TV or a Mac or PC with AirServer.

  Here are the steps to connect your iPad to an AirPlay-capable device:

  1. **Make sure you have an AirPlay-capable device plugged into the screen that you'll be presenting on.**

  2. **Turn on your AirPlay device.**

  3. **Connect your iPad to the same wireless network that the AirPlay device is connected to.**

  4. **Open the Control Center on your iPad.**

  5. **Select your AirPlay device.**

     Enable mirroring if you have an iPad 2 or later if you want to have the same display on your iPad screen as on the display screen.

Choosing Your Presentation Platform

There are a few familiar faces but fewer choices when it comes to creating and sharing slide decks on your tablet. Here are the main players and some things to consider when choosing your platform:

- ✔ **PowerPoint:** If you have PowerPoint on your computer, you can find the app version for your tablet or iPad very similar and fairly easy to use. The basic PowerPoint app is free, which allows you to create and edit slides on your tablet or iPad, but to access more advanced features, like the ability to view Presenter Notes, you need a qualifying subscription to Microsoft Office 365.

- ✔ **Keynote IOS:** Keynote is the default program for iPad. Keynote also works with iCloud, so your presentations are saved and automatically updated on all of your Apple devices. You need to get the Keynote IOS app ($10), which can import presentations made in PowerPoint or Keynote.

If you create your presentation in Keynote or PowerPoint on your computer, you're likely to lose many of your fonts, transitions, builds, and audio in the import because they're not available on the tablet. You can avoid this by creating your presentation directly on your tablet, or using the SlideShark app, which I discuss later in this chapter.

- ✔ **Google Slides:** A free app available for tablets and iPads. You can create, edit, and share new presentations as well as open, edit, and save PowerPoint presentations. It automatically saves your work as you go.

Controlling Your Presentation with PowerPoint or Keynote

Even though there are many similarities between using PowerPoint or Keynote on a computer and a tablet, you want to familiarize yourself with a few differences before you give a presentation. The last thing you want to do is to struggle with the basic mechanics in front of your audience.

Here are some tips for using PowerPoint on your tablet:

- ✔ To start the slide show, tap Slide Show, and then tap From Beginning.

- ✔ Swipe from right to left to go forward. Swipe left to right to go backward. You can also use the arrow buttons in the lower left corner of your screen.

- ✔ To use Presenter View, tap the screen to show the Presentation Menu Bar, click the Circle, and select Show Presenter View. (It's only available with an Office 365 subscription.)

- ✔ To end the show, swipe down in the middle of the slide. Then tap, End Show.

Here are some tips for using Keynote to present on your iPad:

- ✔ Select the slide you want to begin with and tap Play.
- ✔ To view Presenter Notes, tap Layout and choose either Current and Notes or Next and Notes.
- ✔ To advance to the next slide, tap once anywhere on the screen or swipe left.
- ✔ To go back, swipe right.
- ✔ To hide the slide navigator, tap anywhere on the slide.
- ✔ To end the presentation, pinch anywhere on the screen or tap the Close icon.

Showing Your Presentation with SlideShark

SlideShark, which is the leading app for showing PowerPoint presentations on your tablet, preserves all your fonts and images. You can also share an online version of your presentation that others can view on-demand from any device, and you can track and view the results. It's free and simple to get and to use. Here's how:

- ✔ Go to www.slideshark.com and set up a free account.
- ✔ Upload a PowerPoint file to your online account. The slides are then automatically converted to a mobile-optimized format.
- ✔ Use the SlideShark app on your tablet or iPad to download your converted presentation and show by hitting the green Play button.

Using Your Tablet as a Whiteboard

With the right app your tablet can turn into a portable whiteboard that you can either use straight from the tablet or project onto a screen. Great for brainstorming and capturing ideas and feedback, the whiteboard feature gives you a quick and easy way to make your presentation super interactive.

Several apps are available, depending on how creative you want to get:

- ✔ **Whiteboard: Collaborative Draw (Android) and Whiteboard: Collaborative Drawing (iPad)** This is a free whiteboard app that allows you to open any image or photo on your device and choose from a full-spectrum of colors and marker transparency levels. And, you can save and share your work.

✔ **Splashtop Whiteboard:** This app ($35) has a lot of power and a version for your Android or iPad. You can annotate anything, use gestures to draw, highlight, or write, take snapshots on the screen, save them and then email them to your prospect. You can use a wide variety of colored and sized pens, stamps, highlighters, shapes, and text tools over existing content or on one of the flipchart backgrounds. This app is highly collaborative and worth the investment if you're a creative type.

Planning for Blackouts

The ability to black out your screen during a presentation is an important functionality to have to direct your prospect's focus. The computer option of hitting the B key or the blackout key on your remote isn't currently available on tablets but you can still create the same effect with a little pre-planning:

✔ **Creating a black slide:** Insert black slides in your deck wherever you're planning to engage in a discussion or need to have all eyes on you. If you need more flexibility, create one black slide and jump to it by entering the slide number each time.

✔ **Blocking the projector:** Place something in front of the projector lens — a book or file — until you're ready to go back to your slides.

Getting the Right Slide Aspect

If you've ever watched a movie made for the widescreen on an older television, you have an idea of what the slide aspect can do to your images. Android tablets have a ratio of 16:1 — close to the standard widescreen aspect of 16:9 and well-suited for widescreen. However the iPad and many other tablets have a 4:3 aspect ratio so if you create your slide deck in another ratio, your images may be distorted when you convert to PowerPoint or Keynote. Here is what you need to know to avoid image distortion:

✔ **Standard slides (4:3 aspect ratio):** Your slides will fill the screen on your iPad or other 4:3 aspect tablet. However, if you're using an Android tablet, presenting on your iPad to an Apple TV, or using a newer projector with a 16:9 aspect, your slides will fill the height of the display but not the entire width, giving it a less professional look.

✔ **Widescreen slides (16:9 aspect ratio):** These slides fit the full screen of an Android tablet but on the iPad or tablets with a 4:3 ratio they'll fill the width of the screen but not the full height. Use 16:9 aspect slides when you're presenting on an Android tablet, to a 16:9 video projector, or using AirPlay to project your iPad on an Apple TV.

Index

• B •

• C •

• Y •

• Z •

About the Author

Julie Hansen, sales trainer, speaker, and actor, specializes in training sales teams to craft and deliver winning presentations by applying best practices and proven tactics from acting, storytelling, and improvisation. She has worked with sales teams from Fortune 500 companies across the globe. She is the president of Performance Sales and Training (www.performancesales-sandtraining.com) and a frequent speaker at sales conferences, annual meetings, and corporate events.

In addition to *Sales Presentations For Dummies*, Julie is the author of *ACT Like a Sales Pro! How to Command the Business Stage and Dramatically Increase Your Sales with Proven Acting Techniques* (CareerPress) a finalist for Top Sales and Marketing Book of 2011 by Top Sales World.

Prior to launching Performance Sales and Training, Julie was a sales leader in a variety of competitive industries, including technology, media, and real estate and served as Director of Sales for *The National Enquirer and Star Magazine*.

As a professional actor Julie has appeared in more than 75 plays, television shows, including HBO's *Sex and the City*, and commercials. She trained at the American Academy of Dramatic Arts and HB Studios in New York City.

A recognized thought-leader on sales presentations and the use of performance skills and storytelling in sales, Julie's methodology has been featured on NBC and the cover of Ken Blanchard and Stephen Covey's *Sales and Service Excellence.* Her articles have appeared in numerous magazines including *Selling Power, Sales Management Digest, SOLD Magazine,* and *Entrepreneur.* Julie's blog, Acting for Sales, was named Best Innovative Sales Blog by Il Commerciale/The Salesman, 2013–2014, and she was named a Top 50 Sales Blogger by Top Sales World, 2014–2015.

Julie is also a senior facilitator and master coach with 2WIN!Global, a provider of presentation and demonstration training, specializing in companies that sell complex solutions. Julie resides in Denver.

Dedication

To all the sales professionals I've worked with — from Hong Kong to Copenhagen — your willingness to embrace new ideas and to challenge the status quo serves as my ongoing inspiration. And to all the salespeople who read my blogs, subscribe to my newsletter, and watch my videos, thank you for sharing this journey with me.

Author's Acknowledgments

Many talented, dedicated people helped shape this book. Thanks to Stacy Kennedy, acquisitions editor at John Wiley & Sons for her guidance and patience while I wrote my way around the globe. To Chad Sievers my project manager, development editor, and copy editor for keeping me on track and pulling this all together so masterfully, and to the rest of the Wiley production crew for working their magic. Thanks also to David Lutton for reaching out to me to write this title.

A big thank you to Tobias Schelle and Raditya Zayadi from the fabulous 24Slides who created all of the "good" slide examples in this book. I may never design my own slides again.

I want to acknowledge Jill Konrath, Lori Richardson, Colleen Stanley, Kendra Lee and all my friends and colleagues at Women Sales Pros for their inspiration and encouragement, as well as Jonathan Farrington and Marco Rasi for championing my work. Special thanks goes to Ross Jacobsen, Bob Riefstahl, Dan Conway, Ron Kendig, Chad Wilson, and the rest of the crew at 2WIN!Global who set the bar for great presentation skills and continue to raise it. Thank you to Molly Gibson for her copyediting and research assistance. Finally, much gratitude to friends and family, especially Jean Hansen, Shelly Burnett, Dan Hansen, Beau Lundy, Liz Wendling, and Becky Laschanzky for their enthusiastic support.

Publisher's Acknowledgments

Acquisitions Editor: Stacy Kennedy

**Project Manager/Development Editor/
Copy Editor:** Chad R. Sievers

Technical Editor: William B. Donato

Art Coordinator: Alicia B. South

Production Editor: Antony Sami

Illustrator: 24 Slides

Cover Photos: © Rawpixel Ltd/
iStockphoto.com